EMOTIONS ONLINE

*Feelings and Affordances
of Digital Media*

Alan Petersen

 Routledge
Taylor & Francis Group

LONDON AND NEW YORK

Designed cover image: Getty Images

First published 2023
by Routledge
4 Park Square, Milton Park, Abingdon, Oxon OX14 4RN

and by Routledge
605 Third Avenue, New York, NY 10158

Routledge is an imprint of the Taylor & Francis Group, an informa business

British Library Cataloguing-in-Publication Data
A catalogue record for this book is available from the British Library

Library of Congress Cataloging-in-Publication Data
Names: Petersen, Alan R., 1953- author.
Title: Emotions online: feelings and affordances of digital media/
Alan Petersen.
Description: New Yok, NY: Routledge, 2023. |
Includes bibliographical references and index.
Identifiers: LCCN 2022031659 (print) | LCCN 2022031660 (ebook) |
ISBN 9780367706678 (hardback) | ISBN 9780367706654 (paperback) |
ISBN 9781003147435 (ebook)
Subjects: LCSH: Social media. | Emotions–Social aspects.
Classification: LCC HM742 .P484 2023 (print) |
LCC HM742 (ebook) | DDC 302.23/1–dc23/eng/20220829
LC record available at https://lccn.loc.gov/2022031659
LC ebook record available at https://lccn.loc.gov/2022031660

ISBN: 978-0-367-70667-8 (hbk)
ISBN: 978-0-367-70665-4 (pbk)
ISBN: 978-1-003-14743-5 (ebk)

DOI: 10.4324/9781003147435

Typeset in Bembo
by Deanta Global Publishing Services, Chennai, India

CONTENTS

ACKNOWLEDGEMENTS

I would like to thank the many people who directly or indirectly contributed their ideas that inspired me to write this book and/or who have offered other forms of support or guidance. This includes those with whom I have worked on various projects, including Megan Munsie, Claire Tanner, Casimir MacGregor, Jane Brophy, Allegra Schermuly, Alison Anderson, Kiran Pienaar, Barbara Barbosa Neves, Gill Bendelow, Iain Wilkinson, Ivan Krisjansen, and Tim Caulfield. Much of this work has also been undertaken in collaboration with patient organisations, including Chronic Illness Alliance, Multiple Sclerosis Australia, Cerebral Palsy Alliance, and Chronic Pain Australia, and I would like to acknowledge their support. I am grateful to Monash University which provided a period of Outside Studies in 2021 which enabled me to give concentrated attention to the project. I would also like to acknowledge the support of my colleagues at Monash University who have helped provide a highly congenial environment in which to write. I would also like to thank Chris Parry and colleagues at Taylor and Francis, and Vijay Bose and colleagues at Deanta Global for their assistance. My research has also been supported by awards from the Australian Research Council, which has provided invaluable time and research assistance. Chapter 4 draws on material from two of these projects (DP120100921 and DP170100402), which I should acknowledge. Finally, I wish to thank Ros Porter, with whom I have discussed many of the ideas and who has offered her love and support.

1

DIGITAL MEDIA AND THE EMOTIONS

From the early days of television, concerns have been raised about the emotional manipulations and de-humanising effects of electronic technologies of communications. In recent years, however, these concerns have intensified as digital media have intruded ever-more deeply into people's lives and awareness of their deceptions and harms grows. Yet, assessments of digital media as they affect emotional life remain mixed. While some writers celebrate digital media for the options they offer, including reducing social isolation and providing instant access to a vast array of products and services, others portray them as producing psycho-social or emotional harms, including social disengagement, the fragmentation of experience, restricted affective repertoires, or the generation of polarised views. Assessments tend to bifurcate along lines of claimed media 'effects'—reflecting different visions of technologies and their power. Hopeful or utopian visions vie with fearful or dystopian visions, with the balance shifting between the two positions over time as technologies evolve or—as is often the case—fail. On the one hand, digital media are seen as *tools of empowerment and/or sociality*, providing the means for users to gain increased control over their lives, to enable them to do things they may otherwise be unable to do or to do them more easily. On the other hand, digital media are deemed to be *tools of distraction and/or of abuse*, adversely impacting users' attention spans, empathetic capacities and 'emotional intelligence', and disconnecting them from 'meaningful' conversations and experiences (Turkle, 2015). According to some writers, digital media are 'addictive' technologies that rule users' lives, being designed to keep them 'hooked' (Alter, 2017). The term 'addiction' is widely employed to describe the perceived compulsions associated with digital media engagements which, like alcoholism or drug addiction, suggests users' *absence* of control over their technology use. This addiction, it has been argued, makes it difficult for users

DOI: 10.4324/9781003147435-1

to 'switch off' by blurring the lines between work and non-work and the public and the private (see Chapter 5).

In this book, I question these common representations of the role of digital media in contemporary emotional life, which reflect either determinism (the belief that technologies *determine* social structures, cultures, actions, and/or outcomes in a relatively straightforward manner) or voluntarism (the belief that individuals freely *choose* their goals without social constraint). As I argue, these representations are simplistic in overlooking the complexities of the digital ecosystem that is supported by an emotional economy comprising diverse actors and powerful interests who often pursue very different goals. In this chapter, I introduce my guiding concepts and assumptions with reference to some relevant seminal contributions to the social study of electronic/digital media. To begin, however, I should first clarify what I take to be 'digital media' and 'users', since writers who use these terms often seem to be referring to quite different phenomena.

Digital media and users

As Bowker and Star (2000) note, classifications have consequences, for what we see or do not see and what is valued and what is silenced. The written or spoken language used to classify objects, events, or identities shapes how people respond to them. This language, then, is performative in that it produces or enacts that that is named. By 'digital media', I mean the dissemination of digitised content via internet-based or computer technologies, which may include software, mobile apps, audio, video, and photographic images captured in electronic format, webpages and websites, social media, electronic documents, virtual and augmented reality and books, holograms (three-dimensional images generated by a computer), and newspapers and magazines that are distributed in an electronic format. 'Digital media' is sometimes used synonymously with 'information and communication technology' and to designate access to its devices (e.g. mobile phones), connections, and applications (Van Dijk, 2020: 1). This definition includes wearables that may be worn as accessories or be embedded in clothing or implanted in the user's body and have the capacity to send and receive data via the internet (Hayes, 2020). Digital media can be distinguished from 'old media', or so-called legacy media, such as newspapers, books and non-digitised audio or video tapes, and photographic film, and as distinctive enough to warrant a separate classificatory label. As digital media evolves, and potentially becomes more 'immersive'—as predicted by Mark Zuckerberg, CEO of Facebook during his announcement in 2021 that his company would rebrand as Meta—virtual and augmented reality *may* become mainstream in the future. In this vision, virtual public spaces and customised 'home spaces', to which other people can be 'invited', for example, may profoundly disrupt notions of digital mediation and the distinction between the public and the private as time, space, and reality take on new meanings (Velazco, 2021). Digital technologies are being developed at rapid speed as different forms of media develop and converge, giv-ing rise to new concerns and resistance, making it difficult to foresee how media may evolve in the future.

An element that tends to be missed in definitions of digital media—which largely focus on the nature of the communications and the form and/or func-tion of technologies—is that they are largely governed by *algorithms* that provide instructions for the automated systems or artificial intelligence (AI) that enable these media to operate as they do. These algorithms are increasingly designed to facilitate 'machine learning' whereby computers in effect learn on their own how to 'mine data' and recognise patterns ('pattern recognition'). The distinc-tion between 'machine learning' and AI is not always clear—the terms often being used synonymously. Machine learning is best conceived as a part of AI. However, while machine learning uses structured data (which is quantitative, highly organised, and easily analysed) to automatically complete a task, AI can be fed unstructured data (which has no organisation and does not fit into a defined framework, such as audio, video, images, social media posts) and still function. This data mining and automated pattern recognition frees up people's time and allows computers to undertake mundane tasks and may be used to cre-ate models for predicting the future and creating advertising (so-called program-matic advertising), but also for purposes of surveillance and control (Chapter 2). It is now well known that algorithm-driven processes reinforce discrimination—notably that based on differences of gender, race/ethnicity, socio-economic sta-tus, age and sexual preference—because algorithms are programmed by humans who introduce their biases and often-faulty assumptions into their programs (e.g. Eubanks, 2018; Noble, 2018). The operations of algorithms have been shown to encourage the expression of *extreme* emotions, as I discuss later in this chapter and in Chapter 3. However, despite the ubiquity of algorithm-driven processes, the 'rule books' that instruct algorithms are generally opaque, or 'black-boxed', and so their impacts on behaviours are little understood (Pasquale, 2015). I dis-cuss the significance of algorithm-driven processes at various points in the book, emphasising their centrality in what I call the *online emotional economy*.

The term 'user' is also employed in somewhat different ways in the litera-ture, according to where writers focus their attention, and on the nature of the transaction that is seen to occur between an actor and the media or technology of interest. From the perspective of the software industry, it is applied to various parties who may engage with the media or technology in different ways, which may include advertisers, ordinary people, and organisations (Shestakofsky and Kalkar, 2020: 865). These 'users' (sometimes called 'clients' or 'customers') may pay directly for the use of services (e.g. advertisers) on a one-off, occasional or ongoing basis, or indirectly via the generally opaque process of exchanging one's personal data for the seemingly 'free' use of services or via a 'user-pay' contract (ordinary citizens) (the conditions of service generally being in small print or communicated via an obscure language). With ride-hailing platforms like Uber, 'users' may be drivers and passengers, while with food delivery platforms like

Deliveroo, they may be restaurants, drivers, and diners (Shestakofsky and Kalkar, 2020: 865). These different interpretations of the term 'user' is significant since they shape how one assesses the personal consequences of digital media and the regulatory responses that are or should be made; for example, who is deemed to be responsible for a certain problematic communication, technology, or process, and who is judged to suffer or potentially suffer harm as a consequence (Chapter 6). 'Users' of digital media technologies, regardless of their type, are different from users of other technologies such as medical treatments, household implements, and cars and trains, in that they are also 'factors of production', or contributors to the resources employed to produce goods and services. In using digital media, individuals contribute their personal data (to varying degrees, depending on the platforms used and their level of usage), which is harvested by search engines and platforms to create value via 'personalised', algorithm-driven advertising—the ultimate objective being to sell them goods or services. Users' contributions of personal data are crucial to acknowledge in assessing the implications of digital media for the online emotional economy—as I will explain. Before moving on though I should also mention another, less visible category, namely the 'non-user', that cannot or will not engage with digital media for various reasons, including holding concerns about certain functions or features of technologies, or not wishing to submit themselves to their demands and associated fears about data theft, loss of privacy, online abuse, scamming, and the multitude of the risks one faces when online. 'Non-users' are a difficult group to identify and study in an age of digital media, when researchers rely on these very media to undertake their studies, but it is important to acknowledge their exclusion, which may be self-imposed and a response to the demands and intrusions of technologies.

In making their evaluations of the personal impacts of digital media, commentators focus on the level of emotional engagement and/or sociality that these media enable or call for. Digital media are seen to offer users options for action that did and do not exist with older or so-called legacy media, such as newspapers, books, and magazines, namely continually accessible, seemingly inexhaustible *multisensorial* experiences. These options include 'personalised' experiences enabled by data-driven algorithms, the potential to connect with others from virtually anywhere at any time (that is, 24/7) to form relationships, the ability to forge communities that would otherwise not exist or exist only to a limited extent offline, and the capacity to create and share content with other media users. It is these functions and features of digital media that are seen to make them highly appealing and empowering tools, enabling their users to assume command of their lives, to do things they may not otherwise be able to do, and to determine when, with whom, and on what terms they engage with others. As such, they represent the *epitome of neoliberal responsibilisation*, the philosophy that ascribes accountability to individuals for decisions affecting many areas of their lives. In so-called digital health, for example, it is claimed that related technologies will enable patients to receive a kind of personalised or 'tailored' treatment and care that was previously unattainable with other technologies (e.g. paper-based) and to gain seamless access to information via 'interoperable' ('joined-up') systems that will enable them to better manage their own health (Petersen, 2019). The promissory discourse of digital media underpins huge investment in a host of new health technologies, including self-tracking and monitoring devices, genomic and facial recognition-based diagnosis, and the recent movement of Big Tech companies such as Google, Apple, and Amazon into the healthcare marketplace.

In this book, I hope to make clear that the common, dualistic depiction of digital media—as either tools of empowerment and/or sociality or means of distraction and/or abuse—is simplistic, misleading, and an impediment to developing policies for governing the use of digital media so as to reduce their harms and exploit their benefits. Most portrayals of digital media 'influence', 'effect', or 'impact' convey a reductionist conception of human agency and reflect ideas about and visions of technologies and their assumed impacts that are long standing in modern Western societies. Many studies and debates are technologically determinist, in that they suggest that technologies shape social structures, cultural values, or behaviours or minds in a relatively direct way. These conceptions and visions have also underpinned anxieties about other media technologies in the past, such as television and print news media. The so-called 'media effects' model, or hypodermic needle model, which assumes that readers or audiences passively receive and are directly influenced by intended messages, has long dominated studies of media and communications—and continues to do so. This book has its origins in questions arising from my own research on the socio-cultural and politico-economic processes underpinning the development of and responses to new and emerging technologies, much involving analyses of users' perspectives and experiences. The questions I have explored over a period of more than 20 years concern how technologies are represented in science, policy, and wider public discourse including news and other media, and by those who develop or use them, for example as researchers, clinicians, patients, and carers, or communicate their significance (typically, scientists, journalists, editors), and how this representation in turn shapes responses to and engagements with those technologies.

Digital media affordances and the emotions

My approach is sociological and draws on insights from various related fields, namely science and technology studies, media studies, the history of emotions, and gender studies, that offer their own theories and approaches to analysing the emotions and the affective impacts of technologies. As yet, we do not have an adequate conceptual framework for making sense of the contributions of digital media to emotional life; for example, in encouraging, discouraging, or reinforcing certain emotional experiences or modes of expression. However, growing debate on the personal and social implications of digital media—especially in the wake of COVID-19 and enforced lockdowns and other restrictions when these media quickly assumed a central role in many people's lives and debates about their impacts increased significantly—makes it imperative that we do. My approach pays cognisance to the *complex interactions between digital technologies and the affordances they offer, their users, and the social contexts of media use*—and thereby aims to move beyond the simplistic, dualistic, and essentialist approaches that dominate studies of digital media and the emotions. The concept of affordance has a long history and has been used in many different ways, but I use it here to refer to the way in which it is generally used in science and technology studies, design studies, media studies, and studies of human–computer interaction, namely, the design of objects that guides users' perceptions and actions, which includes the perceived and actual properties that determine how they are used (Davis, 2020: 29–31).

As Davis (2020) notes, in her review of the extensive literature on the subject, 'affordance' has taken on new meanings as the concept has been adopted by different disciplines; however, studies using the concept have become more 'relational' in their approach, in that they pay cognisance to the relationships between technical, social, and material aspects of the environment, and the co-creation of objects (in this case, material technologies and systems, digital platforms) and subjects (diverse users) (2020: 32–33). Thus, the affordances of technologies refer to the relationship between artefacts, users, and environments broadly understood that, I suggest, includes the *emotional communities* (Rosenwein's [2006] term) or cultures to which users of digital media belong that shape members' values, outlooks, and dispositions, and the *attention economy* that involves the harvesting and monetizing of citizens' personal data in real time (Webster, 2014; Vaidhyanthan, 2018). Emotional communities comprise those who share emotional experiences and modes of emotional expression, for example, patients living with different diseases or conditions, or individuals with impairments or disabilities, people who feel lonely, or those who hold specific grievances or hopes (Chapter 4).

Contemporary Western understandings of the emotions are dominated by psychological, psychoanalytic, and psychotherapeutic approaches that tend to ignore socio-cultural and politico-economic contexts, thereby restricting our understanding of the many dimensions of emotional life. Sociologists and other social scientists and historians have emphasised the social construction of the categories of emotion and the great variability of emotional experiences and expressions (performances or enactments) within and between groups and communities (e.g. Ahmed, 2014; Hochschild, 1983; Rosenwein and Cristiani, 2018). While the emotions find diverse *public* expressions—for example, in rituals of suffering or grief or enactments of hope—they are also 'felt' and are an aspect of self-identity. Emotions, such as pain and loneliness, for example, are often described as private feelings that cannot be shared with others, but the pain and loneliness of others may be invoked in public discourse demanding a collective and individual response (Ahmed, 2014). The sociologist Arlie Russell Hochschild (1983) introduced the idea that emotions may be—and in contemporary, service-based economies, frequently are—commodified and that their enactment (in undertaking one's job) involves 'work' in the presentation of the self. The concepts of 'emotional work', 'emotional labour', and 'emotional management' introduced by Hochschild have been highly influential in sociology, feminist studies, and other fields and have inspired new programs of research. This work provides the foundation for *a political economy of the emotions* that pays cognisance to the inextricable links between culturally and economically valued expressions and experiences of emotions, the material aspects of the environment that encourage or enable their articulation, and the workings of politics and power. The concepts, I suggest, are highly relevant to understanding emotional life in an age of ubiquitous digital media whose use calls for certain kinds of affective engagement and emotional labour—often invisible, unacknowledged, highly exploited, and demanding labour, as I will argue (see especially Chapter 2).

The chapters will discuss the operations and implications of the *emotional regimes* that frame and shape online interactions, including the techniques that Big Tech and advertising companies use and are developing in their efforts to shape users' emotional responses and the psychological theories that inform them. I employed the concept of emotional regime in my book, *Engendering Emotions* (2004) drawing on the work of William Reddy (2001). This refers to the normative order for the expression of emotions which varies according to the latitude allowed for emotional liberty—or the scope to express one's feelings in certain ways—the strategies of emotional management and the forms of self-control that are suggested, encouraged, or imposed and the penalties incurred for the violation of norms. *Engendering Emotions* was published in the same year as Facebook (now Facebook/Meta) was launched, the first and now most widely used social media platform, which was soon followed by other popular digital platforms including YouTube (2005), Reddit (2005), Twitter (2006), Instagram (2010), and TikTok (2012). Over this period, AI technology has advanced dramatically with applications in virtually all spheres of life, including business operations, health and social services, and personal relationships (dating apps) and recreation (for example, online gaming). Hence, it is important to examine the role of AI-driven processes in the shaping of emotional life. I consider the consequences of the way digital media operate *in practice* including the options they offer for sociality, new forms of emotional harm and abuse (in Chapter 3), and the generation of the positive emotion of hope (in Chapter 4). Sociologists and media scholars have employed the concept of 'affective labour'—that is, 'the labour that produces or manipulates emotions such as a feeling of ease, well-being, satisfaction, excitement or passion' (Hardt and Negri, 2004: 108) to explore, for example, the affective practices of those offering peer support online to people with mental health issues (McKosker, 2018) and with cancer (McKosker and Darcy, 2013). In Hardt and Negri's conception, 'affective labour' (or what Hochschild calls 'emotional labour') can be distinguished from other forms of immaterial labour—that is, labour that creates immaterial products such as knowledge, information, and communication (broadly understood as service work, intellectual labour, or 'cognitive labour')—in referring equally to body *and* mind (Hardt and Negri, 2004: 108). This form of labour the authors suggest can be found in the work of legal assistants, flight attendants, and fast-food workers, who are expected to provide a 'service with a smile'. This kind of labour is highly valued in modern economies, where employers value workers with a 'good attitude' and social skills along with the qualifications gained via formal education. It is the kind of labour that is exploited to enable the internet and digital platforms to operate as they do. It comprises the 'frontstage' labour of diverse groups of users including so-called influencers who perform self-presentation work, and the much less visible 'backstage' labour of those who moderate and curate information (e.g. offensive posts) and those who research 'user experience' and design the 'user interface' to make the internet seem 'smart' and easy to navigate (see especially Chapters 2 and 5).

While recent debate about the impacts of digital media on emotional and social life has focused on the manipulations of social media, one should not overlook the significance of search engines, which profit from the sale of advertisements and by tracking users by selling information via real-time bidding, using techniques of search engine optimisation designed to attract attention, and reinforce particular responses. The operations of algorithms that 'instruct' the search engines (a form of AI) are crucial in making the internet seem 'smart': aggregating and correlating diverse kinds of data in real time at great speed and enabling the predictive text that saves users' time. Because search engines provide the gateway to the internet, it is important to assess their potential role in the online emotional economy, that is the kind of affective exchanges that are enabled, encouraged, and exploited online to create value for Big Tech companies and advertisers and the media organisations that rely on advertising and various state and non-state actors that stand to benefit in one way or other from these exchanges. I focus on emotions that are commonly encountered and shared online, particularly hope, fear, and hate, and on widely used digital technologies (for example, smartphones, apps) and platforms (for example, Facebook, Twitter, Instagram [owned by Facebook's parent company Meta], Reddit, and TikTok), addressing questions such as: what 'feeling rules' guide citizens' online interactions? Are these interactions different from those that occur offline? If so, to what extent and how, and what are the personal and social, and politico-economic implications? What kinds of emotional expression do digital media promote, amplify, tolerate, or discourage—and why do they have these effects? Do media restrict certain kinds of emotional experience or expression?

To help lay the groundwork for my analysis, I offer a wide lens on digital media and the emotions, examining the politico-economic and socio-cultural context shaping responses to technologies in general. It is important to offer this perspective since researchers and media commentators often assume that digital technologies are somehow unique in terms of their personal and social impacts, which is far from the case. Indeed, as I will argue, there are many commonalities in the representations of technologies and user responses to and engagements with them that are important to consider in any analysis of digital media and the emotions. Writings on digital media exhibit a strong inclination to *presentism*: to view ideas and events as timeliness, without a history and future, and unaffected by the workings of politics and power and commercial influence. This presentism can lead one to overlook the interests and issues at stake in a particular framing of technologies and their significance, and to neglect the significance of shifting emotional regimes in shaping views on and expectations of technologies, especially their role in enabling or encouraging, or discouraging, certain types of emotional expression and experience. Different periods present different options for action or degrees of constraint on individuals' freedom to express themselves, which are shaped by educational and workplace institutions, religion, law, apparatuses of state security, and diverse media. This is where a historical perspective on the emotions, such as that offered by Barbara Rosenwein (2020), is useful.

Historical and socio-cultural studies unsettle the idea that the emotions are 'hard-wired', biological phenomena, and thus fixed. There is ample evidence showing that emotional categories and experiences—what is acceptable to express or suppress, and when and how they may be expressed or suppressed, and by whom—vary between societies and communities and across time. As Reddy observes, emotions are subject to profound social influence and hence are of 'the highest political significance' (2001:124). For a political regime to endure it must establish a normative order for the expression of emotions that is enforced by strategies of emotional management. Schools, the military, workplaces, and other institutions produce and uphold emotional regimes and offer varying degrees of constraint on emotional expression and different opportunities for 'emotional navigation' (2001: 125–126). When digital media users log on, they do so not as emotional blank slates but as sentient beings with affective dispositions that have been formed in their communities and cultures, and these will shape their interactions with others and with the information they encounter online. The media that they use also constitute emotional regimes: they shape the expression of emotion through providing certain options for action and interaction, but this will vary according to the features and functions of the media employed, the actors involved in the communications, and the context of media use. Media offer considerable scope for the performative self to express one's agency using one or more of the digital platforms available: for self-promotional purposes to enhance one's online profile and build cultural capital, and to create economic capital by selling one's services to the many companies that value such emotional labour.

Drawing on work such as the above on the emotions and a wide range of other literature from the social sciences and media and communication studies, including the contributions of seminal social theorists and media scholars such as Erich Fromm, Marshall McLuhan, and Neil Postman, I critically appraise some enduring assumptions about media technologies, their operations, and their consequences. It will ask, can anything be learnt from the history of technological developments in regard to the formation of public views on the impact of digital media on emotional life? In this chapter, I offer some observations on some recurring representations of technologies and how they shape views on and responses to digital media technologies, albeit in ways that are generally not widely understood. In science and the wider culture, technologies tend to be portrayed as being unaffected by social contexts and the workings of politics and power, and as exerting an independent influence on the development of societies. Their own development is conceived as linear, mostly progressive, and the inevitable culmination of the workings of invisible market forces. This is evident in government communications about the economy, where investment in specific technologies, such as genetics, stem cell therapies, and AI is often seen as 'market-driven'. I suggest that technologies are most fruitfully conceived as material *and* social artefacts whose meanings and applications vary across time and context and subject to the influence of politics and power. Science and technology studies, histories of technology, feminist history and philosophy of science, and organisation studies in their different ways highlight that 'technology' is inescapably a socio-historical product. The inelegant term 'socio-technical system' is frequently used to capture this intertwining of the social and technical that is often disregarded in conventional accounts of technological development. However, this term is interpreted in somewhat different ways, sometimes (as in organisation studies) to refer to the 'interaction' of people and technology in work organisations and other contexts, which suggests that 'technology' is pre-social. The term has its origin in organisation studies and psychology in work carried out by the Tavistock Institute in the 1950s and 1960s and then closely associated with management science in the UK; however, it is now used in different fields with scholars offering their own interpretation, which has led to confusion (Baxter and Summerville, 2011).

In what follows, I take 'socio-technical' to mean that the material aspects of technologies, including their form and function, are entangled with socio-cultural and politico-economic processes. The meanings that individuals, groups, and communities ascribe to a technology shape how they respond to it, including whether they embrace, adapt, or resist it, and consequently how the technology evolves. As Patrice Flichy (2004) has argued, technical design processes incorporate implicit assumptions about the uses to which technologies will be put. I would add that they also reflect assumptions about the *users*, including their identities, backgrounds, and modes of thinking, acting, and feeling. Considerable research has revealed that racial, gender, class, and other biases are 'baked' into the design of algorithms (Benjamin, 2019; Noble, 2018; Pérez, 2019). These assumptions shape how technologies are viewed and whether they are adopted and used in ways envisaged. Many technologies fail to fulfil their promise because those who design them either fail to take account of or inadequately grasp the complexities of the contexts, including communities, in which innovations will be used. Whole communities may share 'socio-technical imaginaries', or shared visions of how technologies might be used and how this will impact their lives. For example, many racial or ethnic minorities have suffered from medical experimentation and genetic discrimination in the past, which has influenced their views on and responses to technologies such as genetics and genomics or biomedical research in general. Both large datasets and small datasets have been used to classify, identify, stigmatise, and persecute entire communities such as the Jewish population especially in the years preceding and during the Second World War. 'Data-driven' technologies, which enable the internet to function as it does and underpin many modern healthcare systems, present a particular challenge in this regard since they rely on the harvesting, sharing, and analysing of personal data using automated systems that may be used for purposes of advertising, identity theft, surveillance, control, and abuse. Actual and potential surveillance and control is most evident in authoritarian societies, such as China, where facial recognition is now used to monitor citizens, especially minorities such as the Uyghurs who present a threat to the Chinese Communist Party; however, it is evident in virtually all societies to varying degrees. Understanding the histories of technologies is critical to understanding contemporary responses to digital media.

Digital technologies in socio-historical perspective

Many of the questions raised by digital media technologies, including AI, I suggest, are similar to those posed by other technologies. These concern their applications, benefits, and impacts and reveal the ambivalence that tends to surround technologies, especially those that offer functions or features that are unfamiliar to users. I discuss sociological work on ambivalence later in this chapter. This ambivalence is manifest in the emotion-laden language and imagery used to depict technologies circulating in media and the wider culture. Discourses of hope or optimism tend to co-exist with discourses of fear or pessimism. On the one hand, technologies are seen to offer the promise of improving people's lives and 'empowering' their users; on the other, as having the potential to inflict harm and 'disempower' users. These hopes and fears have long played out in news and popular media, including influential science fiction books and films such as Mary Shelley's *Frankenstein* (1818), Aldous Huxley's *Brave New World* (1932), Andrew Nicoll's *Gattaca* (1997), Michael Crichton's *Prey* (2002), and Brad Peyton's *Rampage* (2018). Recently, AI imaginary has played out in books and films, such as David Egger's *The Circle* (2013), Spike Jonze's *Her* (2013), Ian McEwan's *Machines Like Me* (2019), and Kazuo Ishiguro's *Klara and the Sun* (2021). From a natural science perspective, humanities and social science research on popular cultural portrayals of science and technology in productions such as these may be seen as trivial and not relevant to how 'real' science is practised. But I would argue that this research is of critical importance since, as my own work has revealed, these portrayals shape public responses to technologies—often in ways that significantly affect how science is practised and regulated.

The metaphors and imagery that are used to convey the hopes and fears of technology are used strategically by different actors to pursue certain objectives.

In science, metaphors are crucial in research, in sparking the imagination and in allowing scientists to communicate the significance of their work to the community. Proponents and opponents of technologies emphasise or downplay the novelty and implications of a technology in a strategic game that plays out over time with the dynamics of representation shifting according to the technology, the context, and the period (Shelly-Egan, 2010: 185). The scientists who undertake research on technologies and the businesses that hope to profit from their sale frequently over-emphasise, or hype, the potential benefits of technology, using analogies drawn from the wider culture to highlight the 'breakthrough' nature of their work, whereas those who are closer to the practices of the technology, such as clinicians, tend to be more modest or qualified in their claims. Scientists and pro-science communities generally think of science as devoid of metaphors and of social values, and as being apolitical. However, research is inherently value-laden and inescapably political, and researchers rely on metaphors to attract attention to their research, to inspire creativity and to convey complex ideas to 'lay' audiences. The use of war and military metaphors are common in popular science journals, most evidently with references to 'the war on cancer' and 'fighting' disease.

During the COVID-19 pandemic, scientists, along with public health authorities and governments, have made extensive use of metaphors; for example, when referring to the virus as 'the enemy' and calling for governments to make a 'military-like response' to the pandemic. In this case, the metaphors have been used to underline the gravity of 'the crisis', to assist audiences to grasp the issues at stake, and to accept the need for urgent action, for example, on containment measures and the rollout of vaccinations. Many scientists contribute to research programs dedicated to making machines more 'human-like' as in the field of artificial intelligence (AI). The question of whether machines will ever be able to 'think', 'reason', and 'feel' like humans is hotly debated among scholars. Nevertheless, many research efforts are founded on the vision of 'intelligent' or 'feeling' machines, most evident in the area of *affective* computing that was founded more than two decades ago (Picard, 2000). Affective computing has grown significantly since then and research in the field is predicted to expand rapidly in future years. The affecting computing market was $US26 billion in 2020 and is anticipated to grow at an annual growth rate of 33 percent to $US192 billion in 2027 (Grand View Research, 2020). I will discuss the rise, operations, and implications of affective computing in detail in Chapter 2. The important point to note here is the use of the human attribute of affect to describe computers that shapes responses to technologies regardless of whether or not there could be feeling machines of the type envisaged. Other metaphors also widely circulate in science and science-based communities that convey biases that are often sexist, racist, classist, ageist, heteronormative, and ableist—a point that I will return to at various points in the chapters.

While they routinely use metaphors to describe their work and communicate its significance, scientists and authorities often struggle to control them once they gain wide acceptance and shape public responses in unexpected ways. Consequently, they may modify their claims and step back from their earlier, more optimistic assessments and alter their language in their public communications. Metaphors serve to simplify complexity regarding the nature and operations of objects, processes, or systems, and their use may raise hopes and expectations to a level that is higher than warranted by the evidence, for example, through the use of references to 'breakthroughs' or, alternatively, heighten fears, through the use of terms such as 'viral' or 'contagion' or 'designer babies'. In my own research, I found the latter term to be widely used in news reports on the potential of stem cell technologies for medical treatments (Petersen et al., 2005). The language employed to describe science is of utmost *political* significance and much is at stake for science in the ability to frame issues. Scientists and pro-science communities (for example, public health professionals) routinely use news media and other forums, such as news releases, to establish the control of public discourse and draw and, if necessary, re-draw the boundary between science-based and non-science-based representations in order to bolster their epistemic authority (Gieryn, 1999). All large research programs make news releases, which are often timed (with embargos on access) to have maximum impact in terms of attracting the attention of journalists and the wider public. In making these news releases, it is common for scientists and their PR staff to use popular analogies that are assumed to resonate with non-science audiences. In fact, this is one of the most common sources for science news, although the exact proportion is difficult to quantify (Mcnamara, 2009). (For an analysis of the role of public relations in science, especially regarding the generation of expectations of developments, see Petersen, 2011: 42–46.)

One of the recurring themes in popular culture (and to some extent science), which reflects broader societal anxieties, is creators' *loss of control* of technologies, which may then 'bite back' (as in Frankenstein's monster) or wreak havoc on the world (via the experiment that goes awry), for example, via environmental destruction or total surveillance. Science offers the promise of the capacity to control the natural and social world, which is equated with 'progress' and 'improvement'. Writings about technology tend to represent technologies as becoming ever-more powerful in terms of their capacity to alter the natural and social world. This is clearly evident with biotechnologies that alter the biology of the body, presenting the danger of developments progressing 'too far' and creating technologies that 'take on a life of their own', figuratively or literally. These hopes and fears were evident with news media reports of many genetic 'breakthroughs' during the 1990s and early 2000s, perhaps most evidently with publicity surrounding the cloning of Dolly the sheep, which was seen as providing the potential for the development of cloned humans, who were sometimes depicted in news and other media as malevolent characters, such as 'carbon-copy' Hitlers (Petersen, 2002).

Digital technologies likewise have also been the focus of a mixture of hopes and fears which have heightened as technologies find newer applications. David

Egger's *The Circle* is a notable recent example and seems prescient in many respects, given the subsequent development of Apple Park in Cupertino City, California, a circular building, the kind of total institution including a wellness centre, care clinics, and campus transportation depicted in the book and film. This film is also interesting in its depiction of the routine use of holograms which have now become a 'reality' via Microsoft's Mesh which, according to marketing blurb 'uses 3D capture technology to beam a lifelike image of a person into a virtual scene' (Langston, 2021). Kazuo Ishiguro's depiction of the 'Artificial Friend' in his *Klara and the Sun* (2021) who possesses sentience and is able to express hopes and fears, portends a future of the affective computer which has been long-imagined and is currently in development (MIT Media Lab, 2021). The British drama series, *Years and Years*, produced in 2019 on the cusp of the COVID-19 pandemic but released in 2020 as it unfolded, captures the visions and fears surrounding technologically mediated futures, along with anxieties about the groupthink associated with political populism and economic instability that seems prescient in many respects. In short, the hopes and fears of digital technologies can be seen to be part of a much longer history of socio-technical imaginaries and technological ambivalence. However, their ubiquity and the widely perceived potential for companies and third parties to intrude deeper into our lives by controlling our minds and emotions—especially through the harvesting and commercial exploitation of personal information—would seem to have taken expectations and fears to a new level.

Fears about the dangers of digital media have evidently heightened in the wake of the Cambridge Analytica scandal, which revealed that the personal details of 87 million people were harvested from Facebook to influence the 2016 US elections, and growing reports on cyber hacking, cyberwarfare, cyberespionage, ransomware attacks, trolling, revenge porn, identity theft, deepfakes, and other online manipulative and abusive conduct perpetrated by state or non-state actors. The COVID-19 pandemic served to exacerbate anxieties about the intrusive and potentially manipulative power of digital media with the World Health Organization warning of a social media-driven 'infodemic' of misinformation and rumours causing confusion and contagion of public health messages, and then concerns about misinformation about vaccinations spreading online and fuelling 'vaccine hesitancy' or resistance. The use of 'infodemic' is highly revealing in the context of COVID-19, implying an information 'contagion', equivalent to that of the virus itself; it also bears similarities with the description of an earlier model of communication, namely the now largely discredited hypodermic needle model, which posits that information is directly received and largely accepted by passive audiences. In this case, the epidemic effect is assumed, or rather feared, rather than empirically demonstrated. Many of the anxieties that attach to the 'infodemic' during COVID-19 concern the potential for malicious actors to exploit the uncertainties and turmoil of the pandemic to advance their goals, including influencing the outcomes of the 2020 US elections.

As this brief discussion should make clear, technologies are socially produced and their representations change over time—with hopes and fears rising and falling to varying degrees—which then shapes people's engagements with them. Although designers and producers of digital technologies may not view their products in socio-historical perspective or as 'socio-technical assemblages', they are evidently cognisant that, if they are to find application, they need to identify a market and generate profit. For digital technologies, this is the *marketplace of attention* that has become increasingly competitive and subject to measurement and ratings—for example, how many visited a website, viewed a page, or downloaded a video? (Webster, 2014: 82–86). In this marketplace, designers aim to cultivate and sustain certain practices of personal digital media use.

Technologies designed to appeal

Digital media technologies offer features and functions *designed* to appeal to assumed users so as to attract and sustain their attention. The designers and marketers of technologies are known to monitor and experiment on users to make technologies ever-more attractive, by incorporating aesthetically appealing and claimed 'user-friendly' features, 'free' pricing, and use of default settings (Berthon et al., 2019). Google has been found to employ deceptive design practices, so-called 'dark patterns', to 'nudge' users towards making choices that favour the service providers and against their own interests (Forbrukerrådet, 2018). Nudge theory is underpinned by a distinct conception of human motivation and action that has been influential among those who design technologies, buildings, public spaces, and public policies. This includes the premise that people, in making their decisions, will pursue the path of least resistance and that their behaviours will respond to external rewards and punishments, including feedback on performance (Thaler and Sunstein, 2008: 93–100). The theory includes a mix of behavioural psychology that focuses on the factors that shape human behaviours and rational actor theory that is premised on the assumption that individuals will 'weigh up' the 'pros' and 'cons' of different options in order to advance their own best interests.

Nudge philosophy has been widely adopted by governments and experts in their efforts to guide actions in desired directions or 'steer people's choices' (Thaler and Sunstein, 2008: 5). Indeed, the goal of nudge is to 'help people make better choices'—the assumption being that, left to their own devices, individuals will make decisions that may be 'bad', namely contrary to their 'best' interests. According to two of its influential proponents, Richard Thaler and Cass Sunstein, nudge is a 'new movement', namely libertarian paternalism, that involves designing policies that 'increase freedom of choice'—the goal being to 'improve people's lives' (2008: 5). As the term suggests, the aim is not to constrain the liberty ('free choice') of individuals but rather to guide or shepherd their conduct so as to advance their best interests. Proponents of nudge claim that while the choice architecture will alter people's behaviour in predictable ways, this will not foreclose any options or alter their economic incentives. As Thaler and Sunstein explain, nudges are not 'mandates' but rather positive or negative incentives that encourage or discourage certain behaviours, meaning that the intervention must be easy and cheap to avoid (2008: 6). The architecture and operations of digital media technologies incorporate the key elements of nudge philosophy. In making online encounters relatively cheap, easy, and engaging—assisted by numerous default options—technology designers aim to provide users with emotionally rewarding experiences to keep them engaged so that they may reveal private, intimate aspects of their selves through the data trails that they leave behind—which may be exploited by advertisers and others seeking to monetise users' data.

Nudge philosophy is underpinned by a behavioural model of reward-punishment that assumes that people seek rewards and avoid pain and will respond to appropriate signals or messages communicated overtly or covertly. Attempts to manipulate individuals' emotions and actions, however, predate the popularity of nudge theory in research and policy as can be clearly seen in the history of advertising—a topic to which I turn later in this chapter and Chapter 2. Emotional manipulation is also at the very core of the design of digital technologies, and is likely to endure in the next iteration of the internet. The aim of Google and many other Big Tech companies is to harvest users' attentions for purposes of advertising and, ultimately, to sell consumers products and services. Google has been reported to be already planning for 'Web3 innovations'—that is, 'a decentralised online ecosystem built on a blockchain' whereby users own and control their data which they can then monetise—which is envisaged as the internet's next phase whereby users 'take back control from the Big Tech giants' (Redrup, 2022). I explore the concept of Web 3.0 in some detail in Chapter 6. However, it is worth noting at this point Redrup's comment that the 'the topic of web3 is a vexed one for Google as many proponents view it as a movement against the tech giant and other Big Tech gate keepers, who have cornered the market in the web2 era, deriving huge profits off the data accumulated from people using free online services' (Redrup, 2022). Yet, while digital media users may not fully control their data, they may use various platforms to curate themselves and advance their own and/or their communities' interests.

Extreme emotions and 'emotional contagion'

Since the beginnings of the internet, digital technologies have provided a powerful means for individuals and groups to express their emotional selves. This may include expressions of hope, love, and respect, as well as despair, hate, and disrespect. An area of particular concern to policymakers and researchers in recent years has been the potential for digital platforms to serve as vehicles for inflicting harm and abuse directed at individuals or particular groups or communities via the posting and circulation of hurtful messages and images, including image-based abuse and revenge porn, humiliating comments, bullying, and gossip and rumours (Chapter 3). The question of what constitutes 'harm' or abuse' online and whether it is different from that occurring offline is discussed in Chapter 3. However, it is now widely recognised that the algorithm-driven systems of the internet both encourage and reinforce the articulation of *extreme emotions*, especially expressions of outrage and abuse. I examine some of the evidence that has come to light on this effect later in this chapter and other chapters, especially Chapters 3 and 4. Big Tech companies and smaller technology-based businesses indeed profit from inciting and reinforcing these emotions. This is clearly evident with video games, that are increasingly popular, which some research suggest heighten emotional states to the extent that they become 'addictive' and 'distort perceptions' of players which then leads to them to confuse pleasure with happiness (Gros et al., 2020). In 2020, revenue from the worldwide PC gaming market, in which Big Tech companies such as Apple, Tencent, and Sony have a stake was estimated to be $US37 billion while the mobile gaming market generated about $US77 billion. The market is oriented to not just children but also adults who comprise a large proportion of the players. Video games use photorealistic graphics and simulated reality which are designed to make them appealing to players. And, the evidence suggests that these designs do appeal to many users with almost 18 percent of players spending six hours per week online (Statista, 2021). The short-term and longer-term effects of gaming on media users are difficult to evaluate. However, it is noteworthy that, in 2018, the World Health Organization included 'gaming disorders' in its list of mental conditions, which reflects growing concerns about this phenomenon (WHO, 2018).

A new generation of games, such as *Splash*, a music-making video game that has 3 million active monthly users on the Roblox platform, include features that have the potential to detrimentally affect mental health especially of the mostly young users. According to *Splash*'s developers, the game 'intersects the increasing use of artificial intelligence in new media generation with a next-gen game that enables people to express themselves beyond the constraints of social media' (Bailey, 2021). When released in May 2020 on the Roblox platform, the game was reported to have evoked a huge response. As it is described in a news report, '*Splash* allows players—overwhelmingly tweens and teenagers—to create their own musical compositions from "sound packs", which contain loops, vocals and other effects synthesised by Mr Phillips [the founder of the business] and his AI engineers'. As the article explains, 'Although the packs are free, players can trade Roblox—which is the Roblox platform's currency—for "splash coins" that enable them to jazz up public performances of their songs within the game' (Bailey, 2021). The report notes that '*Splash* has its own star-making machine, with about 1000 players spending over five hours a day honing their compositions and performances'. Phillips believes that the Roblox platform portends what Meta will become, in that 'The idea of having a persistent avatar moving seamlessly between games is already there—it's breaking down the barriers between gaming and social media' (Bailey, 2021).

The development and application of facial recognition technology, which scans faces using data points, which are then matched with multiple photographs taken from various sources, provides another potential new means for emotional manipulation and abuse. Facial recognition technology is finding growing application in many areas of daily life, including for security systems (e.g. check-ins at airports) and medical diagnosis of neurological conditions such as Parkinson's disease (Jin et al., 2020). This technology is now freely available online, for example via PimEyes, a face-searching tool that can reportedly scan 900 million images across the internet to find matches with, it is claimed, 'startling accuracy' (Harwell, 2021). PimEyes website presents the technology as a tool to 'protect your privacy' and 'to audit copyright infringement' (PimEyes, 2021). The website invites users to 'upload your photo and search for images containing your face'. However, facial recognition technologies, although not necessarily this one, may also be used by stalkers and abusers to create images that may be used for abuse. An example where this has occurred is so-called deepfakes. Deepfakes are realistic AI-generated videos, images, and audio recordings which are manipulated to create a synthetic representation of people to make them appear to say and do things they never did (Chapter 3).

Facebook, Instagram, TikTok, and other social media and video games enable individuals to enact their expressive or emotional selves in ways unimaginable until relatively recently. Emotion-laden messages, including of love, anger, and hope, can be readily crafted by users who may then share them within their communities and beyond. However, there have been different assessments of the manner and extent to which emotional experiences and expressions are shared online. Research undertaken to date has relied largely on large-scale studies that examine single dimensions of human behaviour at a fixed point in time. A frequently cited source of reference is the controversial large-scale experiment on Facebook undertaken in 2012 involving 689,003 people (Kramer et al., 2014). The findings of the study, published in an article 'Experimental evidence of massive-scale emotional contagion through social networks', sought to test 'whether exposure to emotions led people to change their own posting behaviours, in particular whether exposure to emotional content led people to post content that was consistent with the exposure'. The study was controversial because it sought to manipulate users' emotions without first gaining their consent (Hallinan et al., 2019; Hunter and Evans, 2016). Since the study focused only on 'verbal affective expressions' and on Facebook users' posts, it provides only limited insight into individuals' online emotional experiences. The study is widely cited as providing evidence that emotional states may be transferred to others via 'emotional contagion', which may lead others to experience the same emotions without them being aware of this and without direct interaction between people. The experiment, which the researchers argued provided some of the first experimental evidence to support claims that emotions can spread through networks, found that exposure to positive and negative emotional content in users' news feed led people to post content that was consistent with the exposure. However, while the claimed effect was statistically significant, it was small: altered news feeds revealed a *slight* 'emotional contagion' effect.

While the mechanisms that account for observed shared emotional experiences online continue to be hotly debated among media scholars, recent attention has centred on the operations of platforms' content-recommendation algorithms that are designed to boost content that engages users regardless of what the content entails (Chapter 3). Many scholars argue that extreme views and emotions are amplified via 'filter bubbles' and 'echo-chambers' whereby algorithmic personalisation reinforces certain views. These two concepts are often invoked in debates about the contributions of digital media to the polarisation of political views. The term 'filter bubble', introduced by Eli Pariser (2011) to describe the way an increasingly personalised internet 'traps' people in self-reinforcing information silos, is now widely used in studies of digital media. Although not widely discussed in public discourse, some policymakers have raised concerns about the implications of filter bubbles. At the time of writing (in early 2022), Australia's former privacy commissioner, Malcolm Crompton, said, he has 'warned of the issue over a decade ago'. Referring to debate about the national broadcaster Australian Broadcasting Commission's (ABC) decision to proceed with its plan to personalise digital media offerings and mandating the logins for 1.7 million ABC viewers of its iview streaming service—in light of a loss of audience to large international streaming platforms—Crompton commented: 'there are risks to personalisation that we are not discussing as a society … .One of those has since become starkly clear: the attacks of democracy through personalisation of messaging and "filter bubbles"' (Burton, 2022). Another widely used concept 'echo chamber' tends to be ill-defined and sometimes used interchangeably with 'filter bubble', which has led to confusion and hampered its empirical investigation. As Bruns notes, analyses based on the concepts tend to be technologically determinist (Bruns, 2019a: 8). In Bruns's (2019b) view, concerns about the working of filter bubbles and echo chambers 'constitute an unfounded moral panic' that serves to divert attention from a more critical problem, namely, growing social and political polarisation.

I suggest that while the evidence of the sharing of online emotional states is compelling, one needs to exercise caution when generalising across user communities. Online communities are highly diverse in many respects and their members express their agency in different ways. Users from some communities, comprising people who live with chronic illness or have a disability or experience stigmatisation or marginalisation, for example, will have different needs and priorities to those in other communities (Chapter 4). The use of 'contagion' in the Facebook study—like the use of 'epidemic' in discussions of loneliness (see Chapter 4)—is problematic in implying an infection-like spread of emotional experiences via the internet and underplays the role of human agency and the diversity of users' experiences and engagements with digital media. Users may ignore or 'switch off' (literally) from watching or listening to certain messages (including advertising, as I will show) if these do not accord with their values and priorities (Chapter 2). Users engage with technologies in complex ways and may adapt them to suit their purposes and resist their demands and intrusions. For example, as I have found from my own research on patients' use of digital media, those from stigmatised communities tend to prioritise privacy in their online engagements to avoid discriminatory practices and especially value the affordances offered by Facebook's privacy settings (Chapter 4).

Sociological research shows that users' engagements with digital technologies are not just diverse but also often *ambivalent*: they may simultaneously hold two opposing affective orientations to technologies (Marent, et al., 2018). As Marent et al. argue, ambivalence can be understood as a phenomenon that exists on both the individual and collective level (2018: 134). For individuals, this can mean that they have contradictory experiences of technologies in that they may simultaneously feel 'empowered' by their use and 'disempowered' by the feeling of a lack of control of their operations and/or implications of their use. This may lead them to be sceptical users of technologies and to use them selectively or cautiously. Their responses to and engagements with technologies are likely to vary according to factors such as the technology in question—the functions and features they offer (e.g. connectivity, instantaneity)—and previous experiences of using digital media (2018: 135–136). Whole communities often exhibit ambivalence towards technologies, especially if they share backgrounds or characteristics that make them liable to online abuse; for example, HIV/AIDS communities, disabled groups, and other stigmatised groups. Research I have undertaken with colleagues, focusing on patients' use of digital media, highlights these variable responses to technologies, which are both embraced as valuable tools of connection and also feared for the risks that they are perceived to present (Petersen et al., 2020) (see Chapter 4). The risks feared are many but include, notably, trolling, the posting of abusive comments, the sharing of misleading information, and infringements on data privacy and the collecting of personal information for purposes of advertising and surveillance. The ambivalence expressed by users towards technology is hardly surprising when one considers the multiple communities that they inhabit, both online and offline, that shape views and actions to varying degrees. In much research and public debates about technology and its influences, however, 'online' and 'offline' are assumed to designate distinct rather than interacting and overlapping spheres of communication and expression.

Challenging the online–offline distinction

The online emotion economy is *inseparable* from the wider emotional economy and the mechanisms of power that sustain it. These employ technologies of surveillance and related control, which are diffuse and panoptic, in the sense described by Michel Foucault (1977). As Foucault argued, the panopticon is a metaphor for the modern disciplinary society, one governed not so much by an external authority but rather through mechanisms of power that are omniscient, silencing, and internalised by citizens. In the idealised surveillance society, rule does not require an external governor since subjects will conduct themselves in accordance with internalised norms. Foucault's articulation of the panopticon pertained to the modern penal system and he was interested in the architectural configuration that embodied and enabled this form of rule, namely, one designed to ensure that inmates never knew when they were being watched and would consequently engender compliance. The idea of the panopticon was promoted by the English social reformer Jeremy Bentham in the eighteenth century and subsequently applied in many prisons and other institutions such as factories, schools, asylums, and hospitals.

In recent decades, scholars have pointed to parallels in the operations of the internet—some using the concept of dataveillance, first introduced in 1986 by Roger Clarke (1988) to describe the rapidly evolving practices of data capture, storage, and processing in IT. Some writers argue that the user-generated content and dynamic communication flows of digital platforms like Facebook and Instagram enable 'a system of panoptic sorting, mass surveillance and personal mass dataveillance' (Fuchs, 2011). Siva Vaidhyanathan, on the other hand, argues that the allegory of modern power is best represented not by Bentham's panopticon—by which individuals are subjected to the gaze of a single, centralized authority—but by the cryptopticon: 'an inscrutable information ecosystem of massive corporate and state surveillance' (2018: 67). In this ecosystem, the lines between public and private and commercial and state surveillance blur or disappear, in that information is easily transferred between domain and individuals constantly surveil themselves and other users. Recently, Shoshana Zuboff (2019) has highlighted the surveillance trends in contemporary capitalism—what she terms 'surveillance capitalism'—which is powered by data, which is 'mined' (one can question the metaphor—see Petersen, 2019) or digitally extracted, to create surplus and used to predict behaviours for purposes of advertising and social control. In her analysis, Zuboff points to the role of affect in surveillance capitalism, with 'emotion analytics' and 'sentiment analysis' being employed to render citizens' emotions as *behavioural information* that can be measured and used to 'personalise' advertisements and other applications (2019: 282–290). In Chapter 2, I discuss how emotional life has become a focus for online advertising and explore the ramifications for personal online interactions and experiences.

As noted, responses to technology, including fears about its applications in surveillance, are shaped by visions of their potential to change people's lives that circulate in the wider culture. These fears often centre on technologies' potential effects on children's developing minds and on sociality more generally. An example of the former is various experts' and authorities' exhortations to parents and teachers to limit children's or students' online time. In recent years, there has been a growing trend to prohibit students from taking their phones into the classroom. In the latter case, some restaurants have encouraged guests to leave their devices in baskets near the front door before entering. The assumption in both cases is that technologies operate as devices of distraction that erode 'meaningful' conversations—which suggests that online-based conversations could be 'non-meaningful'—or at least offend established protocols regarding respectful and attentive in-person interactions. Spending time attending to one's emails or Facebook or Instagram postings when in the company of friends or business colleagues may be judged to be rude by some people according to norms of politeness, but the conversations are arguably no less 'meaningful' to the participants than those occurring in-person. However, the tendency to differentiate online and offline life implies discrete spheres of communicative action, namely, the mediated and the unmediated. All communications, whether they occur offline or online are mediated; there is no such thing as 'pure' unmediated communication. However, in some situations, digital technologies provide the preferred, only available or one of the few available means for communication; in short, the options for action are limited or non-existent (Chapter 4). This may be because public places or workspaces are designed in ways that prohibit non-digital interactions, or changes in work practices such as the move to hybrid working (for example, as occurred during the COVID-19 lockdowns) engender reliance on digital media communications, or individual circumstances (for example, chronic illness or disability or loneliness) make this the most convenient or only realistic option.

While the exercise of one's communicative options may be shaped by the availability and affordances of technologies, it is not limited to their use. When considering the implications of the embedding of digital media into people's lives, it is important to reflect on the *meanings* that attach to these communications and what people actually *do* with knowledge; how they produce meanings that 'work' for them in different contexts (Illouz, 2007: 19). As Eva Illouz argues, 'communication' evolved in the field of business management and is strongly influenced by a therapeutic discourse that focuses on the emotional, linguistic, and personal attributes needed to be a good manager and competent member of a corporation (2007: 18). The language of psychology has been highly influential in developing what Illouz calls 'a new emotional style' that was suited to the unique demands posed by the large-scale transformations of the workplace (2007: 17–18). 'Communication' was the assumed means of fostering cooperation, of preventing and resolving conflict and cultivating one's sense of self and identity. The objective of communication was to, as Illuoz expresses it, 'buttress "social recognition" by creating norms and techniques to accept, validate and recognize the feelings of others' (2007: 21). This focus on 'communicative competence' attends to how actors coordinate relations among themselves as presumed equals entitled to the same rights and can be viewed as a technology of self-management relying extensively on the language and correct management of the emotions with the ultimate purpose of 'engineering inter- and intra-emotional coordination' (Illuoz, 2007: 19). As Illouz explains, the dominant emotional style called for one to be a good communicator, to show a high level of self-awareness, and to listen to and empathise with others with whom one is interacting (2007: 19–21). Moreover, as Illouz argues, the concept and practice of communication, although initially presented as a technique and ideal attribute of the self, became a quality of an ideal corporation. That is, companies began to market themselves on their capacity to recruit staff with requisite communication skills, including the ability to work with others, and to nurture these skills on the basis of their contributions to business success. Thus, while modern capitalist enterprises tend to be portrayed as devoid of emotions, they are suffused with emotions and psychology has played a central role in nurturing their expression (2007: 24–39).

As economies become ever-more digitally based, online platforms present a new terrain for the production and enactment of new emotional selves. With growing access to the internet, and the advent of social networking platforms, beginning with Facebook in 2004, a growing number of citizens began to spend much of their lives online, which presented new opportunities for the monetisation of emotions. The growing use of Facebook for both personal and business communications and presentations both reflects and contributes to processes of neoliberalisation and globalisation that have advanced over more than four decades. Many people now spend much of their time online and Facebook and other social media have become their default platforms for sociality. In 2021, a quarter of the world's population (over 2 billion people) were active users of Facebook. Many other citizens are regular users of Instagram, Snapchat, and TikTok (SocialMediaNews.com.au, 2020). For many, it is clear, the line between 'online' and 'offline' life is blurred as a large part of their waking lives is spent 'connected'.

Social identity online

The potential implications of growing digitally mediated communications for users' self-conceptions were explored as early as 1994 by Philip Agre and contributors to a special issue of a journal he edited that focused on the 'emergent phenomenon of the digital individual' (Agre, 1994). The digital individual, Agre argued, 'is a form of social identity that individuals acquire as their activities become influenced by—and often mediated through—digital representations of themselves' (1994: 73). One of the contributors, Max Kilger (1994), discussed the concept of the virtual self, exploring how employing digital technology altered users' identities and personal privacy. Kilger was interested in how face-to-face interaction with other humans—which enabled one to garner verbal cues, such as speech rates, verbal latency, and tone of voice, and non-verbal cues, such as gestures, posture, and 'line of regard'—differed from interaction via digital media. Drawing on George Herbert Mead's work on how individuals conjured an image of themselves based on the attitudes and behaviours of other individuals and institutions towards them, Kilger was interested in how digital media changed individuals' reflected concepts of the self, or what Mead called the 'Me'. Kilger posed the question: 'does the transmission of verbal and non-verbal cues by digital channels

affect how individuals perceive others and therefore the construction of the Me?'
(1994: 94). He argued that 'the digital individual can function as an approximate
representation of a human being—a "digital shadow"' (a term borrowed from
Philip Agre), which raised major issues of privacy, especially given the growing
widespread use of social security numbers to identify an individual's medical, education, and tax records (1994: 98). The 'dataprints' that individuals created when
using digital media, Kilger argued, could then be used as a means of identifying
individuals. In his own contribution to the special issue, Agre observed the development of a new model of privacy, which he called the 'capture model', which
'focuses on the deliberate and systematic rearrangement of human activities to
permit computers to track them' (1994: 74). This model, he argued, was different
from the 'big brother' surveillance model whereby 'human activities are relatively
unaffected by computerized monitoring' (1994: 74). In the article, he outlined
the process as 'a five-stage cycle, beginning with the analysis of existing activities
and ending with the intensive processing of the data that results from the newly
established tracking mechanisms' (1994: 74–75). It should be noted that Agre and
his contributors were writing before widespread access to the internet and even
personal computers, making this work seem prescient today (Albergotti, 2021). As
Albergotti notes in reference to Agre's contribution, Agre saw the threat of this
'mass collection of data on everything in society' as originating not with a 'big
brother' government but rather with different entities collecting data for different
purposes which meant that 'people would willingly part with massive amounts of
information about their most personal fears and desires' (Albergotti, 2021).

That the growing turn to 'online life' has been the source of growing social
anxiety is revealed by the burgeoning commentary and scholarly research on digital media's psychological and social impacts, referred to earlier. Davis (2012), for
example, observed some years ago the difficulty for many people to 'opt-out',
even if one 'logs off' (deletes their social media account) in a social system that
is premised on operating via social technologies. The question of whether it is
possible to completely 'log off', given the centrality of digital technologies in
many people's lives, is far from clear—as many users of Facebook have found
when trying to delete their accounts. But Davis's point about the difficulty for
many people of 'opting out' would seem to be supported by evidence. Drawing
on findings from a qualitative study with Facebook participants, she notes (like
others), the ambivalence—or 'the simultaneous presence of utopic hopes and dys-
topic fears'—that characterises participants' experiences of digital media. Davis
has commented,

> Technology is so deeply intertwined with our social reality that, even
> when we are logged off, we remain a part of the social media ecosystem.
> We can't opt out of social media, without opting out of society altogether
> (and even then, we'll inevitably carry traces).
>
> *(2012: 967)*

Davis may be reflecting on her own personal experience, but this feeling of being denied sociality is likely the case for many who have established their main networks via Facebook and other social media. Yet, for the many others who do not use social media and have most or all of their social networks offline, this may not ring true at all. In a similar vein to Davis and writing around the same time, Gregg (2011) described the ways in which online technology is changing conceptions of and relationships to work and blurring the lines between the public and the private. As Gregg notes, the distinction between labour and leisure is less distinct that was once the case and how, for many people, it has become increasingly difficult to draw a line between intimate and public life and between 'work' and 'non-work'. Focusing on workers in the so-called knowledge economy, namely employees in information, communication, and education professions, Gregg argues that the impact of online technology on personal life has been profound, shaping how people plan and conduct their domestic activities, construct their workspaces (for example, creating spaces at home for work) and articulate and enact their personal passions and commitments.

While it is important to acknowledge the profound impacts of digital media on many people's lives, especially those who work in the business, education, and service sectors, it is crucial that one acknowledges the digital inequalities that exist between and within nations and regions. In 2021, 36 percent of the world's population were either not digitally connected or only connected to a limited extent (Miniwatts Marketing Group, 2021). Globally, internet penetration rates vary considerably between countries and regions. While in Africa around 43 percent of the population were connected to the internet in 2021, in North America and Europe, it was close to 90 percent (Miniwatts Marketing Group, 2021). In absolute figures, the overwhelming majority of internet users are from Asia: about 2.7 billion versus 728,000 in Europe and 478,000 in Latin America and the Caribbean, and 333,000 in North America (Miniwatts, 2021). Other, US-based research shows that those who have greatest difficulty accessing online health information come from socially disadvantaged groups, which include racial and ethnic minority groups, older adults, those living in rural areas and those with lower incomes; moreover, these groups are likely to report negative perceptions and experiences of healthcare (Rutten et al., 2019). These statistics underline patterns of social inclusion and exclusion, and inequality, that scholars have dubbed the 'digital divide'—a term which some writers see as oversimplifying what is in reality a highly complex phenomenon (Van Dijk, 2020: 2–3). As Van Dijk rightly argues, the term 'digital divide' has been used since 1995 and suggests a neat division between the 'haves' and 'have nots', which obscures the vast variations in access to and use of digital technologies within and between countries and suggests that digital-based inequalities are fixed and unfixable (Van Dijk, 2020: 3). Further, it suggests that the division is at core a technical issue, the solution generally turning to more or better technologies rather than the politico-economic conditions that underpin inequalities. The focus on 'technology' or 'media' also serves to detract from the fact that 'digital' also includes data which, increasingly, is viewed (misleadingly, in my view) as the 'new oil' that is expected to 'power' economies in the future (Petersen, 2019). This framing of 'the problem' diverts attention from the conditions that give rise to and reinforce economic and social inequalities at global and national levels, the multiple risks that citizens in all countries confront as a consequence of growing digital connections, and the inherent and potentially unsolvable flaws of the digital architecture that has been created by the most powerful companies in the world. However, while many people in the richer nations may believe that their online or offline lives do not affect and are unaffected by those who live in poorer parts of the world, as COVID-19 has made patently clear, the modern world is highly interconnected, and information, like viruses, may travel quickly even if not strictly in ways implied by the term 'pandemic'. In the chapters that follow, I explore the mechanisms by which emotions are formed, expressed, and conveyed online showing how the seemingly mundane interactions of individual digital media users may help reinforce and, in some cases, challenge processes and practices at the societal level.

A methodological note

Before proceeding further, however, I should first explain my methods. Digital media are rapidly evolving, which makes it challenging for any researcher to keep up with developments. Academic research takes time, and the publication process can be slow, meaning that the findings of research can quickly date. Moreover, the format of peer-reviewed journal articles, where much research is published, is generally narrow in focus. The seminal work (mostly books) on electronic/digital media, on the other hand, offers a broad perspective on trends and issues and much can be learnt from (re-)reading them. In developing my argument, I draw extensively on this work, my own empirical research funded by the Australian Research Council, and other sources: journal articles, webpages, and reports published by governments, the World Health Organization, the UN, digital rights/activist groups, research institutes, think tanks, and companies with a stake in digital media, as well as news reports appearing in various outlets, but especially *The Guardian*, *New York Times*, *Washington Post*, and *The Australian Financial Review* (all of which I subscribe to). Most of the material I draw on was located through databases, such as Scopus, news alerts, and online searches. News articles provide insights into many current and emergent issues and concerns, and often lead to other sources. In using news articles, I have sought, where possible, to trace the original cited sources; where I have been unable to, I have made this clear.

Outline of remaining chapters

In Chapter 2, I explore the operations and implications of the online emotional economy and its affective regimes. I identify the diverse groups of actors and the techniques used to attract and monetise users' attention, highlighting the role of algorithm-driven advertising in creating personalised, 'emotionally resonant' messages. Advertising has, from its beginnings, exploited consumers' emotions. However, affective computing that uses software to create an 'emotion database' looks set to provide advertisers with the unprecedented ability to elicit emotional responses. The chapter also examines the kinds of emotional labour exploited online including that undertaken by social media influencers—a diverse category comprising ordinary citizens and celebrities who market themselves—and the highly exploited 'ghost workers' whose contributions help make the internet seem 'smart'. I argue that while the operations of the internet suggest a kind of intelligence at work, it is a human creation—a technological system that is subject to resistance and prone to failure. As the chapter concludes, various developments threaten the longer-term viability of the internet in its current form, including growing public outrage about various forms of online harm and abuse.

In Chapter 3, I assess arguments and evidence regarding the role of digital media in shaping conceptions and experiences of harm and abuse, as well as the responses that have been made. Children and young people are the focus of many anxieties about online abuse which reached new heights during the COVID-19 pandemic-induced lockdowns and citizens' increased reliance on digital media. The chapter examines the early, seminal contributions of Marshall McLuhan, Erich Fromm, and Neil Postman, to the study of electronic media which are useful in placing current debates on online harms in a wider context. It discusses the phenomenon of 'image-based abuse', including 'deepfakes' and 'self-generated abuse', that is facilitated by new technologies, and some of the difficulties faced by regulators in grappling with these behaviours. The chapter also explores the growing incidence of online harms including misogynistic and racist abuse during the pandemic lockdowns. In conclusion, it is suggested that the use of technological solutions and behavioural changes to tackle online harms and abuse is limited and serves to deflect attention from the operation of the platforms that facilitate or reinforce these practices.

In Chapter 4, I examine the hopes that have shaped the development of digital media and their current operations and use. The chapter assesses the influence of the libertarian philosophies and visions that have underpinned the development of the World Wide Web since its inception and remain influential. It is argued that the COVID-19 pandemic restrictions served both to highlight the affordances of digital media and intensify concerns about their impacts and the power of Big Tech. The chapter sheds light on the dynamics of hope in the online emotional economy, with reference to two case studies: loneliness and the pursuit of stem cell treatments. To help cast light on the former, the influential work of Robert Putnam, who wrote about social capital and the internet in 2000, is examined; for the latter, the chapter draws on the findings from a major research project on stem cell tourism that I led. In conclusion, it is argued that, while media technologies are widely portrayed as 'technologies of hope', the internet and digital platforms operate in ways that are bound to frustrate hopes and sometimes produce harm.

In Chapter 5, I investigate the phenomenon of digital well-being, highlighting its largely unacknowledged implications. In recent years, a growing market of 'digital well-being' (or 'digital wellness') products and services has emerged oriented to addressing 'digital addiction' and other technology-related compulsions and distractions. The chapter critically examines these concepts, pointing to their shortcomings and ramifications. As I explain, the language of addiction to describe certain patterns of digital media use, especially among children, is problematic for various reasons. The chapter traces the dimensions of the digital well-being/wellness industry—one that offers many opportunities for start-ups and Big Tech, especially given reported cases of technology-related 'burnout' during COVID-19. The chapter concludes by arguing that the digital well-being/wellness phenomenon is largely oriented to and benefits the relatively rich, privileged professionals who can afford to pay for the advertised products and services and that the interventions do little to counter the intrusions of media created by the 'attention merchants'.

In Chapter 6, I conclude by summarising the main points of my argument and discuss some trends in the development of digital media as they potentially impact emotional life. The chapter considers the implications of growing challenges to Big Tech's control of the digital ecosystem, as trust in companies plummets in the wake of various highly publicised cases involving the companies' data harvesting practices, intrusions on privacy, and the use of deceptive designs. It discusses projected changes in the future of the internet, which promise decentralised media and 'open governance'. It is argued that one should be sceptical about these proposals, given the visions and interests involved. The libertarianism promoted by techno-enthusiasts is idealistic, naïve, and dangerous. A change agenda should focus on exposing Big Tech's deceptive designs and practices and the techniques used to attract and retain users. The chapter concludes by proposing a multifaceted approach to change that involves scholars from different disciplines, and state and non-state actors who are concerned about the implications of digital media.

References

Agre, P. E. (1994) 'Understanding the digital individual', *The Information Society*, 10, 2: 73–76.

Ahmed, S. (2014) *The Cultural Politics of Emotion*. Edinburgh University Press, Edinburgh.

Albergotti, R. (2021) 'He predicted the dark side of the internet 30 years ago. Why did no one listen?', *The Washington Post*, 12 August, https://www.washingtonpost.com/technology/2021/08/12/philip-agre-ai-disappeared/?utm_campaign=runway-2021&utm_medium=email&utm_source=newsletter&wpisrc=nl_most&utm_content=philip-agre-ai-disappeared-runway&carta-url=https%3A%2F%2Fs2.washingtonpost.com%2Fcar-ln-tr%2F35389ed%2F618802649d2fda9d413b0ae0

%2F5e86729bade4e21f59b210ef%2F55%2F70%2F618802649d2fda9d413b0ae0 (Accessed 9 November 2021).

Alter, A. (2017) *Irresistible: The Rise of Addictive Technology and the Business of Keeping Us Hooked.* Penguin Press, New York.

Bailey, M. (2021) 'Game gets a $27m splash for the metaverse', *The Australian Financial Review*, 3 November: 17.

Baxter, G. and Summerville, I. (2011) 'Socio-technical systems: from design methods to systems engineering', *Interacting with Computers*, 23, 1: 4–17.

Benjamin, R. (2019) *Race After Technology: Abolitionist Tools for the New Jim Code.* Polity Press, Cambridge, MA.

Berthon, P., Pitt, L. and Campbell, C. (2019) 'Addictive de-vices: a public policy analysis of sources and solutions to digital addiction', *Journal of Public Policy & Marketing*, 38, 4: 451–468.

Bowker, G. C. and Star, S. L. (2000) *Sorting Things Out: Classification and Its Consequences.* MIT Press, Cambridge, MA.

Bruns, A. (2019a) 'Filter bubble', *Internet Policy Review*, 8, 4: 1–14.

Bruns, A. (2019b) 'It's not the technology, stupid: how the "echo chamber" and "filter bubble" metaphors have failed us', Presented paper at the IAMCR 2019 conference in Madrid, Spain, 7–11 July. Submission No. 19771. Mediated communication, public opinion and society section.

Burton, T. (2022) 'ABCs login plan to stem viewer exodus fuels privacy fears', *Financial Review*, 22 February. https://www.afr.com/companies/media-and-marketing/personalisation-needed-to-stem-exodus-from-broadcast-tv-says-abc-20220222-p59yk5 (Accessed 26 August 2022).

Clarke, R. (1988) 'Information technology and dataveillance', http://www.rogerclarke.com/DV/CACM88.html (Accessed 19 May 2021).

Davis, J. L. (2012) 'Social media and experiential ambivalence', *Future Internet*, 4: 955–970.

Davis, J. L. (2020) *How Artifacts Afford: The Power and Politics of Everyday Things.* The MIT Press, Cambridge, MA.

Egre, P. E. (1994) 'Understanding the digital individual', *The Information Society*, 10, 2: 73–76.

Eubanks, V. (2018) *Automating Inequality: How High-Tech Tools Profile, Police, and Punish the Poor.* Picador, New York.

Flichy, P. (2004) 'Connected individualism between digital technology and society', *Réseaux*, 124, 2: 17–51.

Forbrukerrådet (2018) 'Every step you take: how deceptive design lets google track users 24/7', 27 November, https://fil.forbrukerradet.no/wp-content/uploads/2018/11/27-11-18-every-step-you-take.pdf (Accessed 11 April 2022).

Foucault, M. (1977) *Discipline and Punish: The Birth of the Prison.* Translated by Alan Sheridan. Vintage Books, New York.

Fuchs, C. (2011) 'New media, Web 2.0 and surveillance', *Sociology Compass*, 5, 2: 134–147.

Gieryn, T. F. (1999) *Cultural Boundaries of Science: Credibility on the Line.* The University of Chicago Press, Chicago, IL.

Grand View Research (2020) 'Affective computing market size, share and trends analysis report by technology (touch based, touchless), by software, by hardware, by end-user (healthcare automotive), and segment forecasts, 2020–2027', https://www.grandviewresearch.com/industry-analysis/affective-computing-market#:~:text=The%20global%20affective%20computing%20market%20size%20was%20estimated%20at%20USD,USD%2026.17%20billion%20in%202020.&text=The

%20global%20affective%20computing%20market%20is%20expected%20to%20grow%20at,USD%20192.45%20billion%20by%202027. (Accessed 16 May 2021).

Gregg, M. (2011) *Work's Intimacy*. Polity Press, Cambridge, MA.

Gros, L., Debue, N., Lete, J. and van de Leemput, C. (2020) 'Video game addiction and emotional states: possible confusion between pleasure and happiness', *Frontiers in Psychology*, 27 January, https://doi.org/10.3389/fpsyg.2019.02894, https://www.frontiersin.org/articles/10.3389/fpsyg.2019.02894/full (Accessed 5 May 2021).

Hallinan, B., Brubaker, J. R. and Fiesler, C. (2019) 'Unexpected expectations: public reaction to the facebook emotional contagion study', *New Media and Society*, 22, 6: 1076–1094.

Hardt, M. and Negri, A. (2004) *Multitude: War and Democracy in the Age of Empire*. The Penguin Press, New York.

Harwell, D. (2021) 'This facial recognition website can turn anyone into a cop—or a stalker', *The Washington Post*, 14 May.

Hayes, A. (2020) 'What is wearable technology?', *Investopedia*, 11 May, https://www.investopedia.com/terms/w/wearable-technology.asp (Accessed 30 March 2020).

Hochschild, A. R. (1983) *The Managed Heart: The Commercialization of Human Feeling*. University of California Press, Berkeley, CA.

Hunter, D. and Evans, N. (2016) 'Facebook emotional contagion experiment controversy', *Research Ethics*, 12, 1: 2–3.

Illuoz, E. (2007) *Cold Intimacies: The Making of Emotional Capitalism*. Polity Press, Cambridge, MA.

Jin, B., Qu, Y., Zhang, L. and Gao, Z. (2020) 'Diagnosing Parkinson disease through facial expression recognition: video analysis', *Journal of Medical Internet Research*, 22, 7: e18697.

Kilger, M. (1994) 'The digital individual', *The Information Society*, 10: 93–99.

Kramer, A. D. I., Guillory, J. E. and Hancock, J. T. (2014) 'Experimental evidence of massive-scale emotional contagion through social networks', Proceedings of the National Academy of Sciences, June. DOI: 10.1073/pnas.1320040111

Langston, J. (2021) '"You can actually feel like you are in the same place": Microsoft Mesh powers shared experiences in mixed reality', *Microsoft Innovation Stories*, 2 March, https://news.microsoft.com/innovation-stories/microsoft-mesh/ (Accessed 17 March 2021).

Macnamara, J. (2009) 'Journalism and PR: beyond myths and stereotypes to transparency and management in the public interest', Unpublished manuscript, https://www.academia.edu/830291/Journalism_and_PR_Beyond_Myths_and_Stereotypes_to_Transparency_and_Management_in_the_Public_Interest (Accessed 5 May 2021).

Marent, B., Henwood, F., Darking, M., on behalf of the EmERGE Consortium (2018) 'Ambivalence in digital health: co-designing an mHealth platform for HIV care', *Social Science & Medicine*, 215: 133–141.

McKosker, A. (2018) 'Engaging mental health online: insights from *beyondblue*'s forum influencers', *New Media & Society*, 20, 12: 4748–4764.

McKosker, A. and Darcy, R. (2013) 'Living with cancer: affective labour, self-expression and the utility of blogs', *Information, Communication & Society*, 16, 8: 1266–1285.

Miniwatts Marking Group (2021) 'Internet world stats', https://www.internetworldstats.com/stats.htm (Accessed 29 March 2021).

MIT Media Lab (2021) 'Affective computing', https://www.media.mit.edu/groups/affective-computing/overview/ (Accessed 15 April 2021).

Noble, S. U. (2018) *Algorithms of Oppression: How Search Engines Reinforce Racism*. New York University Press, New York.

Pariser, E. (2011) *The Filter Bubble: What the Internet Is Hiding from You*. Penguin, London.

Pasquale, F. (2015) *The Black Box Society: The Secret Algorithms That Control Money and Information*. Harvard University Press, Harvard, MA.

Pérez, C. C. (2019) *Invisible Women: Data Bias in a World Designed for Men*. Abrams Press, New York.

Petersen, A. (2002) 'Replicating our bodies, losing ourselves: news media portrayals of human cloning in the wake of Dolly', *Body & Society*, 8, 4: 71–90.

Petersen, A. (2004) *Engendering Emotions*. Palgrave, Houndmills.

Petersen, A. (2011) *The Politics of Bioethics*. Routledge, New York and London.

Petersen, A. (2019) *Digital Health and Technological Promise*. Routledge, London and New York.

Petersen, A., Anderson, A. and Allan, S. (2005) 'Science fiction/science fact: medical genetics in news stories', *New Genetics and Society*, 24, 3: 337–353.

Petersen, A., Schermuly, A. and Anderson, A. (2020) 'Feeling less alone online: patients' ambivalent engagements with digital media', *Sociology of Health and Illness*, 42, 6: 1441–1455.

Picard, R. W. (2000; orig.1997) *Affective Computing*. The MIT Press, Cambridge, MA.

PimEyes (2021) 'Face search engine reverse image search', https://pimeyes.com/en (Accessed 12 July 2021).

Reddy, W. M. (2001) *The Navigation of Human Feeling: A Framework for the History of Emotions*. Cambridge University Press, Cambridge.

Redrup, Y. (2022) 'Google lays groundwork to be ready for internet's next phase' (Technology section), *The Australian Financial Review*, 10 May: 22.

Rosenwein, B. (2020) *Anger: The Conflicted History of an Emotion*. Yale University Press, New Haven, CT.

Rosenwein, B. H. (2006) *Emotional Communities in the Early Middle Ages*. Cornell University Press, Ithaca, NY and London.

Rosenwein, B. H. and Cristiani, R. (2018) *What is the History of Emotions?* Polity Press, Cambridge, MA.

Rutten, L. J. F., Blake, K. D., Greenberg-Worisek, A. J. (2019) 'Online health information seeking among US adults: measuring progress toward a healthy people 2020 objective', *Public Health Reports*, 134, 6, https://doi.org/10.1177/0033354919874074

Shelly-Egan, C. (2010) 'The ambivalence of promising technology', *Nanoethics*, 4: 183–189.

Shestakofsky, B. and Kalkar, S. (2020) 'Making platforms work: relationship labor and the management of publics', *Theory and Society*, 49: 863–896.

SocialMediaNews.com.au (2020) 'Social media statistics Australia—September 2020', https://www.socialmedianews.com.au/social-media-statistics-australia-september-2020/ (Accessed 9 October 2020).

Statista (2021) 'Video game industry—statistics and facts', 29 April, https://www.statista.com/topics/868/video-games/#dossierSummary (Accessed 5 May 2021).

Thaler, R. H. and Sustein, C. R. (2008) *Nudge: Improving Decisions About Health, Wealth and Happiness*. Penguin Books, London.

Turkle, S. (2015) *Reclaiming Conversation: The Power of Talk in a Digital Age*. Penguin Press, New York.

Vaidhyanathan, S. (2018) *Anti-Social Media: How Facebook Disconnects Us and Undermines Democracy*. Oxford University Press, Oxford.

Van Dijk (2020) *The Digital Divide*. Polity Press, Cambridge.

Velazco, C. (2021) 'Mark Zuckerberg just laid out his vision for the metaverse. These are the five things you should know', *The Washington Post*, 28 October.

Webster, J. G. (2014) *The Marketplace of Attention: How Audiences Take Shape in a Digital Age*. The MIT Press, Cambridge, MA.

World Health Organization (2018) 'Addictive behaviours: gaming disorder', 14 September, https://www.who.int/news-room/q-a-detail/addictive-behaviours -gaming-disorder (Accessed 5 May 2021).

Zuboff, S. (2019) *The Age of Surveillance Capitalism: The Fight for a Human Future at the New Frontier of Power*. Profile Books, London.

2

THE ONLINE EMOTIONAL ECONOMY

In January 2020, Netflix released a documentary, *The Social Dilemma*, that sparked much media and public commentary. The film offered a critique of social media platforms, including 'insiders'' confessions regarding algorithm-driven messaging intertwined with a fictional account of an archetypal American family whose children are manipulated and harmed by their 'addiction' to social media. The all-male cast of insiders comprised those who have worked for Big Tech companies, including Tristan Harris, president and co-founder of Center for Humane Technology and previously design ethicist at Google. The film addressed themes that are of growing community interest, namely social media's use of algorithm-driven 'personalised' messaging, the harvesting of private data and the intrusions on privacy. The presentation of 'insiders'' perspectives on the largely hidden secrets of Big Tech seemed especially damaging. Yet, while critics acknowledged that the film made some valid and significant points, it missed the mark in a number of respects. Some commentators argued that the key messages were diluted by sensationalism (e.g. Hutchinson, 2020). One journalist commented that it failed to identify the fundamental causes of social media's corrupting influences and that the 'insiders'' suggestions for addressing the damage were 'incoherent' (Naughton, 2020). Indeed, their comments were limited to vague references to social media 'not going in the right direction', 'a failure of leadership', the need for 'public pressure', and for people to be 'free of manipulation systems'. Facebook's official two-page rebuke, published in October 2020, perhaps not surprisingly, claimed that the film 'buries the substance in the sensationalism' and that it sought to 'correct what the film gets wrong' (Facebook, 2020). It argued that many of the issues raised had been addressed and that the film's creators had not included *current* employees working at the companies or included the perspectives of experts offering a different point of view to those put forward in the film. Meanwhile, some wondered why the companies should even bother responding, especially when it was unlikely

DOI: 10.4324/9781003147435-2

that the film would have any impact on their operations, as its response would 'only add fuel to the fire' (Hutchinson, 2020). As one commentator argued, despite the increasing scrutiny of social media companies by regulators and users, and the 'Delete Facebook' movement, users of Facebook and other platforms continue to grow (Shead, 2020).

The responses to *The Social Dilemma*, especially regarding its claims about social media's manipulations and harms, and the general sense of the futility of effecting change conveyed in the comments of some reviewers of the film, reflect long-standing concerns about the effects of electronic communications on how people think and feel. As I discussed in the last chapter, beginning with television in the 1950s and then later the internet, mobile phones, and social media, fears about electronic media's 'addictions', its diversions via 'entertainment' and corrupting influences on people's (particularly children's) lives, have been recurring themes. Anxieties about the impact of electronic communications and technology in general found early expression in the influential contributions of Marshall McLuhan and Quentin Fiore (1967), Erich Fromm (2010; orig. 1968), and Neil Postman (2005; orig. 1985). These writers documented how new electronic technologies of communication shaped minds in manipulative, albeit subtle, ways, through exploiting people's psychological vulnerabilities and particularly their assumed instinctive seeking of pleasure and avoidance of pain, or the so-called 'pleasure principle'. As I have argued in my previous book, these writings focus on the de-humanising impacts of electronic media and reveal technological determinism. The prognoses suggest little scope for human agency, including creative engagement with and resistance to technologies and offer little guidance for effecting change (Petersen, 2019). Both scholarly writings and popular productions such as *The Social Dilemma*, likewise, tend to focus on social media's de-humanising impacts and imply that technologies shape views and actions in a straightforward manner. What these critiques generally overlook is the central role that *agency and affect* play in the contemporary online economy.

This chapter explores the operations and implications of the online emotional economy, focusing on the emotional regimes (Reddy, 2001) that are integral to its workings. It discusses the influential actors in this economy and the techniques used to attract and monetise users' attention, which rely heavily on harnessing the emotions and exploiting emotional labour. In digitally mediated societies, many interests compete in the marketplace of attention, and digital platforms and the advertisers whom they employ to attract users have had to adapt. The chapter begins by examining the central role that advertising plays in the economy and society and how its meanings and practices are being transformed in the digital age. Before the internet, advertising denoted a relatively bounded array of practices involving PR men located in specialised ad agencies producing products for businesses who would then pay media companies to display them—in the case of television, at times judged to be most favourable for engaging with the target audience. While these agencies endure, Big Tech companies now play a central role in advertising through their deployment of automated, algorithm-driven systems that operate in real time, exploiting the skills and attributes of diverse actors, including celebrities who work in a paid or unpaid capacity, paid employees who are able to 'connect' with their audiences, and 'ordinary' citizens who play a crucial part in the online economy as social media influencers, who monetise their labours, or who work as voluntary moderators. Social media influencers are paid to endorse products and promote them to their followers and often post self-generated content about their lives, experiences and opinions (see, e.g. Campbell and Grimm, 2019; Sands et al., 2022). Both the use of algorithm-driven AI technologies and techniques of advertising and the use of these influencers reflects the individualisation and responsibilisation of neoliberalism. On the one hand, the technologies aim to 'tailor' or 'personalise' messages to meet the assumed unique needs and desires of the consumer; on the other, individuals are encouraged to capitalise on this supposed uniqueness, using their personal skills and attributes to 'curate' and promote themselves. Digital media enable these technologies, and personal skills and attributes to be combined and utilised in novel ways that serve the extraction of value. The use of AI influencers used in synthetic advertising illustrates how technologies have evolved to develop more 'human-like' qualities, with recent research suggesting that consumers may be equally open to following an AI or human influencer (Sands et al., 2022). In the following paragraphs, I discuss the nature and significance of these developments and then elaborate on the personal and socio-political implications.

Advertising and the emotions

The history of advertising can be traced back to premodern times. However, advertising rapidly expanded with the advance of new technologies of communication that evolved with the ascendance of industrial capitalism in the nineteenth century, namely, first newspapers and mail delivery, then later radio, television, the internet, and smartphones and other mobile devices. Over this period, advertising developed in lockstep with the maturation of psychology and psychoanalysis whose ideas about the emotions and emotional 'drivers'—especially fear, love, and hate—were applied to sell goods and services in the rapidly expanding consumer markets of capitalist societies. In the early decades of the twentieth century, it was widely believed that human instincts could be harnessed into the desire to purchase goods, and psychologists and psychoanalysts were recruited to lend their research insights to develop creative marketing practices. An influential figure in the history of advertising was the PR consultant Edward Bernays, a nephew of Sigmund Freud, who developed innovative advertising techniques that were initially applied with cigarette advertising but then expanded to white goods, automobiles, and other consumer goods. Adam Curtis's 2002 British television documentary *The Century of the Self* provides fascinating insights into how the ideas of the psychoanalysts Sigmund Freud and Anna Freud on the role of unconscious desires and base emotions in shaping behaviours were used by Bernays to develop techniques of mass consumer persuasion. These ideas were applied in *subliminal* advertising, which employs subtle messages and images to manipulate individuals' subconscious, especially through linking the product or service to sex and power, without the user being aware of this.

The US journalist and social critic Vance Packard was an especially influential figure in early debates about the role of psychoanalysis in advertising. In 1957, Packard published his best-selling book *The Hidden Persuaders*, which discussed the power of ad men and their use of psychoanalysis and research from the social sciences to manipulate consumers, especially through 'hidden' or subliminal messages. As Packard explained (and is now well understood), advertising is about building images and associations for the phenomenon that is being advertised—whether a product, service, identity, lifestyle, or state of being—that consumers can identify with and that they 'consume' in order to project a particular image of themselves. The consumed item provides a symbol of the consumer's personality and position. In the introduction to his book, Packard outlined the ways that citizens were 'being influenced and manipulated' to a far greater extent than was generally realised. He wrote that 'large-scale efforts were being made, often with impressive success, to channel our unthinking habits, our purchasing decisions, and our thought processes by the use of insights gleaned from psychiatry and the social sciences' (1957: 3). He indicated that these were occurring 'beneath our level of awareness; so that the appeals which move us are often, in a sense, "hidden"'. Moreover, he observed, 'the use of mass psychoanalysis to guide campaigns of persuasion has become the basis for a multimillion-dollar industry' that comprised 'professional persuaders' trying to sell not just products but also 'ideas, attitudes, candidates, goals, or states of mind' (1957: 3). Although Packard did not use the term 'subliminal', in his book he referred to advertisers' experiments with 'subthreshold effects' that sought to 'insinuate sales messages to people past their conscious guard', citing the case of a cinema in New Jersey that flashed ice-cream ads onto the screen during regular showings of film that was claimed to boost ice-cream sales (1957: 42). Subliminal messages have been used extensively in television, although prohibited in Britain, Australia, and some other countries (although not the United States); however, research on its effects, except in highly artificial settings, has been questioned (Broyles, 2006). From its very first applications, subliminal advertising caused a public outcry concerning the psychological manipulation of consumers, and the marketing researcher who first used it—in a purported 1957 study that involved showing movies while projecting the words 'eat popcorn' and 'drink Coca-Cola' on the screen in a split second—admitting he had faked his experiments' results to help revive his failing research company (Broyles, 2006: 392). It is important to acknowledge this early public response to subliminal advertising, since it is often assumed that such efforts of consumer persuasion are introduced without resistance and have certain claimed effects—assumptions which, as I will explain, are questionable, especially in the age of the internet.

The applications of psychoanalysis and psychology in advertising continue in the contemporary era, but advertisers have developed new techniques to capture and retain media audiences' attention. Print media, including newspapers, maga-zines, billboards, and banner ads have relied on static forms of advertising to attract readers' attention which can be easily ignored by simply turning the page or shifting one's attention away from the advertisement. Electronic media, such as television, radio, and movies also enable viewers and listeners to avoid adver-tising, by switching channels or stations, or 'switching off' during their airing. These pre-digital forms of advertising are targeted to particular 'niche markets' (age groups, genders, and so on), but use a 'broad brush' or so-called 'spray and pray' approach that advertisers have come to acknowledge is of questionable effectiveness in terms of changing behaviours. There is a long history of efforts to assess the impacts of advertising, with a variety of methods used, including recall tests, laboratory tests that measure people's physical reactions to an ad, statistical approaches that correlate past sales to advertising, and 'portfolio tests' where con-sumers listen to or watch a portfolio of advertisements and recall the ads and their contents. However, findings are often contradictory and inconclusive and there remain many unknowns. One of these unknowns is whether those who purchase or consume the advertised product or service would have done this regardless of seeing or hearing the advertisement.

Some critics of advertising, such as Michael Schudson, argue that the focus on the *direct psychological impact* of advertisements is misguided. Schudson notes that while advertisements may affect the goods available to individuals, there is no evidence that they *directly* influence their purchasing decisions. Nevertheless, he says, 'advertising may be powerful even when it has no direct psychological impact on consumers' which is explained by its symbolic significance in the commercial world. The *belief* that advertising 'works', he says, has been shown to shape businesses', retailers', and investors' decisions (Schudson, 1993; orig. 1984). Schudson describes the 'self-fulfilling prophecy' that reinforces retailers' decisions to advertise:

> Retailers generally prefer to stock well-advertised goods than nonad-vertised or poorly advertised goods because they think that advertising directly influences consumers and that consumers will ask for or look for widely advertised brands. The result, of course, is that widely advertised brands become the brands most widely available; consumers pick up what they find on the shelves whether ads influenced them or not, and the retail-ers are thus 'confirmed' in their conviction that advertised products sell.

> (Schudson, 1993: xv)

Schudson does acknowledge that advertising *may* shape purchasing decisions in some circumstances—especially the selection of the *brand*. However, as he notes, consumers have access to many sources of knowledge besides advertising when making purchasing decisions, including that derived from schools, govern-ment, and news media, although these sources are unequally distributed. The consequence is that different groups suffer different degrees of vulnerability to advertising and that this vulnerability has less to do with the quality or character of the advertisement than with 'the information resources they can claim by age, education, station in life, and government guarantees of consumer protection' (1993: xvi). In Schudson's view, an advertisement communicates just *one* message, namely 'consumer choice', and 'glorifies the pleasures and freedom' from exercising this choice—a simple message, he says, which is both pervasive and constantly repeated, which makes it different from other forms of communication, such as serious works of fiction which call for a higher level of time and emotional investment and involvement (1993: xix).

Digital advertising, its proponents claim, is superior to traditional 'spray and pray' or 'scattergun' forms of advertising in their use of algorithm-driven systems that 'micro-target' individuals ('targeted ads'). This AI-driven 'programmatic' advertising employs techniques of 'data mining' involving the harvesting of individuals' data, namely information on search histories and collected in real-time data to 'tailor' or 'personalise' messages. The *belief* that programmatic advertising is more effective than traditional forms of advertising has powered a huge online advertising industry. Spending on digital advertising, especially via mobile devices, has grown exponentially and spending was expected to exceed all other media combined (TV, radio, and print) in 2021 (Jarvis, 2020). This move to digital advertising is hardly surprising given that consumers—at least those in the richer parts of the world with access to the internet—are spending more time online. This trend accelerated with the COVID-19 pandemic and national lockdowns of varying duration when people were homebound and advertisers had little reason to advertise in public spaces, such as bus shelters, digital billboards, train stations, airports, and subways (Influencer Marketing Hub, 2020). I discuss various implications of the pandemic on the online emotional economy, including consumption patterns, later in the chapter.

As noted, digital media presents new options for advertising, allowing, *in theory*, a depth of emotional engagement with audiences unavailable with older media. Since the beginning of advertising, marketers have known that the provision of information about a product or service is insufficient to change behaviours and that 'emotional connection' is crucial. The emotionalisation of online advertising has precedence in television commercials. Writing in the mid-1980s, Neil Postman wrote about the social control exerted by television as a medium through its anaesthetising effects of its visual entertainment. He described the role of 'vivid visual symbols' of television commercials and the visual politics at work in connecting with audiences. His concern was with the effects of the 'habituation' of visual entertainment on politics and public discourse, including on education, journalism, and religion when they become forms of show business. As Postman emphasised, emotional connection is critical in television commercials and this is provided through a slogan, 'a symbol or a focus that creates for viewers a comprehensive and compelling image of themselves' (2005; orig. 1985: 135). The television commercial, he observed, was less about selling the product than communicating a message about 'how one ought to live one's life' (2005: 131). Postman described how ads may use actors, musicians, novelists, scientists, and other socially prominent figures to 'speak for the virtues of a product in no way within their domain of expertise' and how political figures had 'become assimilated into the general television culture as celebrities' ('as sources of amusement') (2005: 132).

The rise of automated (programmatic) advertising

The automated, algorithm-driven systems that dominate the online ecosystem today are seen to offer new opportunities for exploiting the emotions and monetising emotional responses. As mentioned, they enable advertisers—now mostly Big Tech companies—to measure digital media users' responses, such as the amount of time spent reading an advertisement, return visits to sites, purchasing decisions, search for similar products, and so on, and aggregating that data in *real time* to target ads. These algorithms are 'black-boxed' in that the mechanisms that dictate how they operate (how they are programmed) are not transparent which makes them difficult to regulate (Pasquale, 2015). However, since they are subject to human decisions, it is inevitable that they have discriminatory effects, as has now been well documented (e.g. Eubanks, 2018; O'Neil, 2016). As explained in Chapter 1, they may also elicit or reinforce extreme emotional responses and polarise views, which has been demonstrated by various studies, including a large-scale study on emotional contagion that I described.

An important observation to make about AI-driven programmatic advertising, or 'micro-targeting', is its use of content that aims to be *emotionally resonant*. A study undertaken by Affectiva, an MIT Media Lab spin-off co-founded by Rana el Kaliouby and Rosland Picard (the purported founders of affective computing) that claims to be on 'a mission to humanise technology', explored 'consumers' emotional engagement with ad content over the last eight years … show[ing] that advertisers are increasingly pulling on people's heartstrings to generate a response' (Affectiva, 2021a). The study, reported in October 2020, used the company's Media Analytics software, to create the 'first-of-its-kind emotion database' consisting of 'data on 10 million consumer responses to more than 53,000 ads in 90 countries over eight years'. A summary of the study appearing on the company's website notes that 'The analysis reveals that advertisers are becoming more effective at eliciting emotional responses—both positive and negative—from consumers, *with a trend towards invoking more sadness and polarised emotions*. Many ads referencing the COVID-19 pandemic this year have shown this pattern' (Affectiva, 2021a; my emphasis). The summary of the company's research findings posted on its webpage notes that 'There is an overall increase in emotional responses to ads, indicating that advertisers have become better at telling emotionally powerful stories'. Elsewhere on its website, it claims that 'Today, 70 percent of the world's largest advertisers, 28 percent of the Fortune Global 500 companies and leading research firms such as Kantar, are using Affectiva's technology to test the unbiased and unfiltered emotional responses that consumers have with brand content such as TV programming' (Affectiva, 2021a). A link to 'Affective Media Analytics Ad Testing' reveals that the software 'measures' viewers' 'moment-by-moment facial expressions of emotion' to the stimulus, and then 'the results are aggregated and displayed in an easy to use dashboard'. This information is then used to create 'norms that tie directly to outcomes such as brand recall, sales lift, purchase intent and virality', which then provide a benchmark for how the client's ad performs relative to those of its competitors in terms of 'geography, product category, media length and on repeat view'. The company claims that the construction of these norms is 'unparalleled in the industry' being built on 'the world's largest emotion database' (Affectiva, 2021b). This approach to 'reading' and 'measuring' the emotions, aggregating data on facial expressions and then constructing norms which are correlated with outcomes, such as recall and purchasing decisions, is highly reductive, and its effectiveness in online advertising can be questioned. Yet, it provides the basis for a massively expanding economy which, as I will explain, is fragile and prone to failure.

The attention economy

Digital technologies are part of an ecosystem or digital infrastructure that has been designed and is controlled by powerful (white male-dominated) Big Tech companies, whose profits *derive* largely from advertising: Google, Apple, Microsoft, Facebook, Amazon, Netflix, Instagram (owned by Meta), and YouTube (owned by Google). Meta, the parent company of Facebook, generates 99 percent of its revenue from targeted advertisements, and Google 80 percent (Jarvis, 2020). Despite their frequent claims to be concerned with 'empowering' media users through enhancing 'choice', these companies' business models are premised on *exploiting* users by harvesting their attention and personal data (Halavais, 2018; Srinivasan and Fish, 2017; Vaidhyanathan, 2018). The more time users spend online, the greater the opportunities for Big Tech companies to gain personal information which can then be sold to advertisers for profit. This information includes users' search histories, purchasing decisions, and movements through space and time. This data is collected in real time and provides the raw material for so-called programmatic advertising. This AI-driven advertising has grown dramatically in recent years, with a 2019 report by UK-based Juniper Research which, it claims 'specialises in identifying and appraising high growth market sectors within the digital ecosystem', noting that digital advertising was expected to reach \$US520 billion by 2023, rising from \$US294 billion in 2019, an average annual growth of 15 percent over this period (Juniper, 2019). An online summary of a research report notes that Amazon is expected to gain an increasing share of the 'global digital ad spend'—from 3 percent in 2018 to 8 percent in 2023 (Juniper Research, 2019).

For companies, attracting consumers and keeping their attention long enough for them to complete tasks and transactions is challenging, and cannot be taken for granted. Consequently, they employ specialist web and app designers to undertake research on 'user experience' ('UX') and the 'user interface' to determine what design features are needed to keep users engaged. User experience has been described as 'one of the most critical factors for Electronic Commerce (e-commerce) success and as such, it has become a competitive requirement' (Bonastre and Granollers, 2014). According to the Baymard Institute, which undertakes large-scale research on online user experience, about 70 percent of users abandon online shopping carts—a figure it says is based on 46 different studies (Baymard Institute, 2021). The question of how to improve conversion rates for different products, and categories of product, and how rates vary across devices (desktop versus mobile) and regions, and by month and day of the month, is of major concern to companies and the subject of much research. Surveys garner considerable data on users' behaviours. One report, undertaken during 2020, noted that abandonment surveys had found that 'some users are just browsing (34%), and not ready to buy, some have issues with shipping prices (23%), some users abandon checkouts because they are forced to create an account (34%) and there are many more' (SaleCyle, 2021: 48). The report also noted that during 2020 when various lockdowns were in place, online transactions increased by about 40 percent and the global conversion rate by the same amount (2021: 4). Interestingly, during this period 'Retailers focused heavily on omnichannel marketing and intensified features and actions to maximise the opportunity of the increased demand and volume of online traffic' (2021: 4).

There are now many so-called UX consultancies who help their customers design those parts of websites that users see and interact with to 'optimise their experience'. This includes attention to the layout, content, and any interactive elements. The aim is to enhance the 'useability' or ease or use of sites and platforms. As one such company describes the UX consultancy role, 'Consultants will focus on making a site easy to use, or an application work in the way users would expect and find logical' (DevToolsGuy, 2013). The expertise offered by these companies is diverse, but typically includes those with skills in graphic design and human–computer interactions. Many UX consultancies emphasise their 'consumer-centric' design. One Sydney-based start-up, Particular Audience, uses a software commonly known as API (application programming interface) which it claims is 'used by some of the largest retailers in the world … allow[ing] retailers to create a personalization experience synonymous with Netflix, Amazon and Spotify'. It explains: 'Powered by billions of data points and the latest in AI and Big Data technology, the PA API supercharges the user experience on a retailer's website' (Particular Audience, 2022). A news article examining the company's success in raising venture capital to open new offices in London, Amsterdam, Delaware, and New York, cites the founder James Taylor as saying that 'his company was unique in that it does not use any personal customer data in making its recommendations' but rather 'serves up its predictions based on item-to-item data'. That is, it 'shows you items that you're actually interested in purchasing that day. And the technology behind that is understanding item–to–item relationships' (Gillezeau, 2021a). The author of the article rightly notes that the use of the technology raises the question about 'the legitimacy of using artificial intelligence to shape and narrow preferences' and that 'these types of algorithms are also common on Spotify, Netflix, Facebook, TikTok, YouTube as well as dating apps Bumble and Hinge' (Gillezeau, 2021a).

One Australian company, Bapple, which says it offers services for SaaS (Software as a Service) application providers (e.g. Google Workspace, Dropbox, Cisco), e-commerce, NGOs and non-profits, IT and technology companies, government, medical education, law firms or finance, claims to 'have been helping businesses to thrive online since 2006!' (Bapple, 2021). The company's website provides a summary of what it offers:

> Get to know how your customers think with our user experience design process. Supercharge your existing web application performance or ecommerce website with CRO [conversion rate optimization] … strategy or digital transformation. Keep your customers engaged with crafty content and copywriting. Then delight them with insight led custom website design, powered by meticulous code and website development.
>
> *(Bapple, 2021)*

The acronym CRO is short for 'conversion rate optimisation', a term that may not be familiar to those outside the UX consultancy field. As explained on a website of hotjar, a web developer that claims to 'serve customers in 180+ countries', 'CRO' refers to 'the practice of keeping the percentage of users who perform a desired action on a website', which 'can include purchasing a product, clicking "add to cart", signing up for a service, filling out a form, or clicking on a link' (Hotjar, 2021). This conversion tends to be measured by percentages, averages, and benchmarks. The CRO is of concern to advertisers since many consumers often fail to complete tasks and abandon sites.

Increasingly, it is recognised by various industry actors that the use of such metrics to measure CRO provide limited insight into the factors impeding conversion, and that to improve outcomes they need to first understand how users think and feel. This is where the insights of psychology, and especially the study of heuristics, or the short-cut methods or 'rules-of-thumb' routinely used by people when making judgements and decisions, find application. Heuristics (or heuristic analysis) is a well-established field of research, and the findings are applied to many areas of social life, including law, medicine, education, economics, advertising, business, design, insurance, planning, disaster management, policy design, risk management, and technology development (e.g. Blumenthal-Barby and Krieger, 2015; Green, 2019; Mousavi and Gigerenzer, 2014; Wenzel and Stjerne, 2021). Heuristic analysis also finds extensive application in digital media, in the design of the user interface. For example, the principal of UX consultancy, Nielson Norman Group, Jakob Nielson has identified '10 usability heuristics for user interface design', which include: keeping users informed about the outcomes of prior interactions through providing 'appropriate feed-back'; using words, phrases, and concepts familiar to users rather than jargon; allowing 'exists' for users who 'perform actions by mistake'; be consistent in the use of words, situations, or actions; provide users with a 'confirmation option before they commit to the action'; incorporate 'aesthetic and minimalist design'; and 'minimize the user's memory load by making elements, actions, and options visible' (Nielson Norman Group, 2021a). The aim of applying these heuristics is to make the interface appealing, familiar, easy to navigate, and provide users with a sense that *they* are in control and have options. On the webpage, examples are provided of ten usability heuristics applied to complex and domain-specific software applications, virtual reality, video games, and 'everyday life'. There also appear links to UX guidelines and principles for interface design, along with a list of Nielson's publications on the subject and downloads of 'heuristics posters'. A separate link will take users to a page 'Intranet Design Annual: 2021' where one can purchase a '629-page' report which, it is claimed, 'is the only place to find this information, with 235 full-color screenshots of before-and-after designs, which are usually protected behind the organisation's firewall' (Nielson Norman Group, 2021b; bold in original). In a note towards the bottom of the company's 'Articles' page, it is explained that Jakob Nielson originally developed the concept of heuristic in relation to 'usability problems' in 1990 and then 'refined the heuristics based on a factor analysis of 249 usability problems … to derive a set of heuristics with maximum explanatory power, resulting in this revised set of heuristics'. Then, in 2020, the material was updated with more explanations, examples, and related links and 'slightly refined' language. However, it is noted that 'the 10 heuristics themselves have remained relevant and unchanged since 1994', and that 'When something has remained true for 26 years, it will likely apply to future generations of user interfaces as well' (Nielson Norman Group, 2021a; bold in original).

Attracting and keeping users engaged through the application of techniques such as these is crucial for the operations of the attention economy, which involves the buying and selling of attention at split-second speed via real-time bidding among a pool of buyers. However, as Tim Hwang (2020) argues, the attention economy is vulnerable to implosion with catastrophic consequences for companies directly or indirectly reliant on its sustainability. As Hwang explains, the attention economy is sustained by a continuing belief that advertising 'works' in that it shapes behaviours in ways envisaged by advertisers. Yet, while advertisements can be targeted to specific audiences, and data can be collected on how long the ad is viewed, understanding the overall market and its workings remains obscure. According to Hwang, the public is largely indifferent to online advertising, and this is reflected in 'the surprisingly ambiguous empirical evidence that these ads do anything at all' (2020: 79). Hwang refers to research which indicates that this indifference is especially pronounced among younger internet users. A very large and growing proportion of digital media users employ ad blockers or simply ignore ads. Interestingly, in July

2021, an article reported that 'Facebook and its advertisers are "panicking" as the majority of iPhone users opt out of tracking' (Miller, 2021). The article noted that the software iOS14.5 released to the public earlier that year enabled iPhone and iPad users to 'easily opt out of cross-site and cross-app tracking and targeting' and that 'just 25% of users are opting in to tracking, which is causing panic in the advertising industry'. This ability to easily opt-out was reported to be of particular concern to Facebook as they were no longer able to provide certain metrics to advertisers that would let them know that their ads were working (Miller, 2021). Being ever inventive and cognisance of its bottom line, Facebook was reported as saying that it was working on new features to compensate for this lost data and was 'exploring ways to deliver ads based on data stored on the user's device' (Miller, 2021). In Hwang's view, the attention economy is also threatened by so-called click fraud which is a widespread practice of using 'automated scripts or armies of paid humans in "click farms" to deliver click-throughs on an ad' (2020: 84). As Hwang explains, this practice may deceive ad buyers into believing that they are purchasing attention and delivering their message to consumers when in fact the advertisements fail to capture the attention for the marketer (2020: 84). This opacity, Hwang contends, permits market bubbles to form in the same way that typified the mortgage crisis. As I argue, this has significant implications for the sustainability of the online emotional economy and for citizens' trust in digital media (Chapter 6).

While, on the face of it, these dynamics of the attention economy threaten to undermine the viability of the internet, it is important to keep in mind that internet users do not spend their lives entirely online. Indeed, for many if not most people, their lives are largely spent offline. The contemporary attention economy may be vast and pervasive, but its reach and influence is not absolute. Regardless of their level of internet use, 'offline life' and 'online life' are inextricably entwined, and people's investment in each varies over time in response to the changing demands of work, education, and leisure activities and developments in technology. Different groups have dissimilar levels of access to digital media and use technologies in different ways in line with their skills, values, and priorities. During the COVID-19 lockdowns, online life assumed greater importance for many people and new hybrid styles of work ('work-from-home') and education comprising a mixture of 'in-person' and online engagements quickly evolved, with media conferencing platforms such as Zoom rapidly finding applications, which some predict may become 'the new normal'—at least for some sections of the population. Demand for digital roles such as social media marketers, data scientists, app designers, and digital marketers was reported to have skyrocketed during national lockdowns (Bennett, 2021). The general shift to the internet for purposes of business transactions and sociable interactions over the last two decades, which has accelerated with the disruptions of the COVID-19 pandemic, has underpinned a thriving advertising economy and the emergence of a relatively new phenomenon: *the social media influencer*.

The role of social media influencer

The term 'influencer' as applied to digital media achieved widespread usage only relatively recently; indeed, it was only added to the English dictionary in 2019 (Brooks, 2019). In the definition provided in *Merriam-Webster*, an influencer is 'one who exerts influence: a person who inspires or guides the action of others', or, 'often specifically: a person who is able to generate interest in something (such as a consumer product) by posting about it on social media' (Merriam-Webster, 2021). However, it is important to acknowledge that definitions vary somewhat according to whether those using the term are emphasising personal attributes, the kind or level of influence they exert or the outcome of the influencing activity. While the term 'influencer' has gained currency as the term to describe a new distinct identity—sometimes a highly paid one, as I will explain—as Brooks (2019) rightly notes, there is a long history of individuals serving as role models to promote goods and services or sell a message. These include regal role models, fashion icons, sports and movie stars who endorse products and, more recently, bloggers (with 'blog' being named word of the year in 2004) and then 'micro-bloggers' used by Instagram from its launch in 2010. However, increasingly, ordinary people are seen to possess the personal skills and attributes that will attract an audience and are thus highly value in the emotional economy. They may possess what the sociologist Pierre Bourdieu (1984) referred to as cultural capital and/or symbolic capital, or accumulated material and symbolic resources, including a particular manner of speech, dress, deportment, certain knowledge, relational skills, and so on, which may be nurtured and exploited to accumulate economic capital. As one journalist recently commented in an article discussing the rise of the emotional economy in the age of AI, employees who possess 'soft-skills', or 'emotional intelligence', such as empathy, communication, adaptability, and problem solving are now an 'employer's most valuable asset' and 'the most sought-after attributes by HR departments and employers' (Belchamber, 2018). As this author notes, these soft skills are difficult to measure, but include qualities such as 'their general disposition and personality, their attitude and intuitions' (Belchamber, 2018). Another writer notes that as more work activities become automated, skills and qualities such as 'persuasion, social understanding and empathy are going to become differentiators as artificial intelligence and machine learning take over our other tasks' (Beck and Libert, 2017).

Influencers may use these skills and attributes to build a profile and make themselves attractive to companies or other third parties, including governments, who are all too willing to exploit their labour to 'sell' messages. Advertisers recognise that these individuals are valuable 'assets' in terms of their potential to 'connect' with 'niche' audiences in ways that were not possible or possible only to a limited extent with older, print and electronic (radio, television) media. Many individuals recognise that in becoming an influencer they, too, can profit—sometime handsomely—in the online economy, by monetising their personal skills and attributes and can become entrepreneurs in their own right. The rise of the influencer phenomenon would seem to represent a step change in the techniques used to attract attention: one centred on 'emotional connection'; on engaging consumers in ways that make them *feel* valued as active participants in a community defined by shared aspirations, lifestyles, and tastes.

According to a publication of Influencer Marketing Hub, 'What is influencer marketing: A beginner's guide',

> An influencer is someone who has: [firstly] the power to affect the purchasing decisions of others because of his or her authority, knowledge, position, or relationship with his or her audience; [and secondly] a following in a distinct niche, with whom he or she actively engages. The size of the following depends on the size of his/her topic of the niche.

It goes on to say, 'It is important to note these individuals are not merely marketing tools, but rather *social relationship assets* with which brands can collaborate to achieve their marketing objectives' (InfluencerMarketingHub, 2021; my emphasis). This description is revealing, conveying the commodification of the attributes these individuals are seen to possess. A critical 'asset' is their ability to facilitate consumers' decision-making in the now-substantial online marketplace. The attention marketplace is crowded and highly competitive and, as mentioned, advertisers have had to adapt to survive. As the InfluencerMarkingHub website notes, social media use has grown rapidly, with one report finding that 3.484 billion people actively using social media or about 45 percent of the world's population. And, it is argued, social media users 'look up to influencers … to guide them with their decision making'. As it is explained, these influencers have established a reputation through their knowledge and expertise on a specific topic and their regular posts on topics on their preferred social media channels and thereby have built large followings of 'enthusiastic, engaged people who pay close attention to their views'. Finally, it notes that social media influencers are popular with brands because they can 'create trends and encourage their followers to buy products they promote' (InfluencerMarketingHub, 2021).

It is difficult to accurately assess the dimensions, reach and impact of the influencer market, which is fast growing and ever-changing. Assessing the market is complicated by the fact that, according to the 2019 Influencer Survey, many influencers on Instagram do not identify with the term, which appears to have a negative connotation (Yallop, 2021: 36). However, the available evidence suggests that the influencer phenomenon is significant. It has been suggested that there may be 50 million influencers around the world, with 2 million being full-time professionals, with others being amateurs 'uploading in their spare time' (2021: 12). The vast majority though are considered to be minor players—what are called 'micro-influencers'—with an audience of tens of thousands who often hope to become major players. In the case of Instagram, only 2 percent of its influencers reach 'the top tier of social media stardom', which is achieving at least 1 million followers (2021:13). Despite these inequalities in influencer 'star-power', the influence effect appears to be sizeable: in 2020, Instagram reported that 87 percent of its users 'had been influenced into buying something by a creator' (2021: 11).

Being viewed as 'assets', influencers are assessed according to their potential to generate *value* for the companies or organisations for whom they work. In the above 'beginner's guide', influencers are broken down by 'types', according to criteria such as the number of followers, types of content, the level of influence, and the niche market within which the influencer operates. Thus, an influencer's value may be 'measured' as 'low' in one category but 'high' or 'more influential' in another. For example, many 'mega-influencers are also celebrities' but may have less influence on their audience than other types of influencers because they lack expertise in a particular niche, whereas 'micro-' or 'nano-influencers' may have 'tremendous impact on followers in their specialist niche' and consequently be of significant benefit to the firm selling a product to that sector. In the typology presented, influencer categories are broken down according to 'follower numbers', 'types of content', and 'level of influence'. Under the first category are: 'nano-influencers, who have a small number of followers (often less than 1,000) but are experts in obscure or highly specialist areas; 'micro-influencers', who are ordinary people who are known for their knowledge about a niche area (1,000–40,000 followers); 'macro-influencers' (40,000–1 million followers), comprising either 'B-grade celebrities' who have yet to make it to 'the big time' and 'successful online experts' who have established a more significant following than that of a 'micro-influencer'; and 'mega-influencer', who have 'a vast number of followers on their social networks' (1 million plus followers on at least one social platform). The 'beginner's guide' warns readers that mega-influencers, who are typically celebrities who have gained their fame offline (e.g. movie stars, musicians, sportspeople), should only be approached by 'major brands', since their services will be costly, 'up to $1 million per post, and they will most likely be extremely fussy about with whom they choose to partner'. It also notes that while macro-influencers 'can be excellent in raising awareness', this category is 'most likely to engage in influencer fraud—some have only reached their position thanks to the followers they have purchased' (InfluencerMarketingHub, 2021).

When classified according to the 'types of content', influencers may be 'bloggers' (who 'have the most authentic and active relationships with their fans'), 'YouTubers', 'podcasters' ('a relatively recent form of online content that is growing in popularity'), or producers of 'Social Posts Only' (where influencers may 'craft their posts around a stunning image', typically via Instagram). Finally, in terms of 'level of influence', 'celebrities' are the main and 'original influencers', although 'their importance is waning'. However, as the guide observes, the problem is that there are few celebrities willing to participate in an influencer campaign and they are expensive and they 'may lack credibility with the product's target audience'. The example cited is Justin Bieber (the Canadian singer) who 'may be highly influential if he recommended a type of acne cream, but would have little chance of influencing the buying patterns of those looking for a retirement village' (InfluencerMarketing Hub, 2021). Marketing companies highlight that an influencer's 'authenticity' and 'relatability' is an important consideration for a business to consider when deciding to use them for advertising. Later, the marketing platform for Instagram, Facebook, Twitter, and Pinterest, in its 'The Ultimate Guide to Instagram Influencer Marketing', explains the virtues of these influencers. It notes that, while they may charge 'a lot of money' (as much as $5,000–$10,000 per sponsored post), they are generally 'value for money', with 93 percent charging less than $1,000 per post, and that 'While Instagram influencers have attained a sort of "celebrity status", micro- and nano-influencers are more like everyday consumers, so they tend to be more **relatable**' (Warren, 2020; bold in original).

Influencers who have attained prominence or respectability in a certain field, for example, as a movie or sports star, possess the symbolic and cultural capital required to create *distinction* (Bourdieu, 1984; orig. 1979). Regardless of whether they have this prominence or are simply 'ordinary people' hoping to break into what is widely seen as a potentially lucrative field, they can hone their skills—to help them better 'relate' to audiences and maximise their potential—by undertaking courses offered by companies such as YouTube and Instagram (which is owned by Meta) paying cognisance of 'tips' offered by established influencers. YouTube's Creator Academy offers various courses that can be undertaken by individuals who wish to build their profile. This includes videos on topics such as 'Use comments to connect with your community', 'Express yourself with stories', and 'Interact with audiences with community posts'. The video, 'Use comments to connect with your community' for example, includes tips on 'building fan loyalty', on 'replying, filtering and moderating content', and showing one's audience that 'you are listening and interested in what they have to say' which may 'make them feel loved and may encourage others to write positive things' (YouTube Creator Academy, 2022). The marketing company, Later, includes '8 Tips for Becoming a Successful Instagram Influencer'. Contributed by Christina Galbato, who is described as a 'social media strategist' with more than 250,000 followers and claims on her Instagram site to 'help influencers build profitable businesses', notes, 'While massive growth on Instagram is more of an uphill battle in 2021, it isn't impossible' (christinagalbato, 2021). She comments that more brands are discovering the value of nano- and micro-influencers, and that, consequently, 'you don't need millions of followers to land big brand collaborations'; indeed, these influencers have 'the highest engagement rate on average'. Galbato explains in a post oriented to the new visitor ('since you're new, you probably won't know this') that she began her career in 2016 as a travel and lifestyle influencer and 'went full-time with it in 2017', and that 'I now use my experience building my 7-figure influencer business to help other women do the same', adding, 'I help women grow their audiences online by creating intentional content and monetize through brand collaborations' (christinagalbato, 2021). She offers various tips including: 'Identify your niche and content pillars' (noting that 'It's better to be an expert of a few things than a jack of all trades', and 'your content pillars could be personal wellness, entrepreneurship, and intentional living'); 'master short-form videos and post reels'; 'be consistent' ('pick a schedule and commit to it so your audience knows when to expect new content from you'); and 'write meaningful captions' ('a great opportunity to spark conversation, provide value, and form meaningful connections with your community'). The site includes examples of Instagram postings by other influencers, illustrating the techniques they use for attracting and connecting with audiences. Clearly, building and maintaining an online presence is hard work and requires dedication, commitment to the task and, beyond this, a level of personal and emotional investment that is likely to exceed that required for offline emotional work as demanded, for example, in customer management roles. Much is at stake in the ability to successfully hone a distinct, saleable image, to establish a niche in a crowded and evidently expanding marketplace, to establish and maintain connection with one's audience, and to ensure that one's expertise is kept current. For the influencer themselves, much is at stake: not just a potential loss of employment, but 'a loss of face'.

Influencers do not necessarily experience an attachment to the products or services that they promote. Many may promote whatever is seen as potentially saleable, seemingly regardless of its health, social, or environmental benefit. A new class of behind-the-scenes entrepreneurs serve as 'middle-men' taking ideas pitched by influencers and then designing, making, and sourcing products for them to sell. For example, an Australian company Atelier, founded by a former artist Nick Benson, raises funds from investors to launch and scale new products. In a news article on the start-up, it is noted that 'Atelier charges customers an upfront fee of $1500 to come up with product designs and manufacturing plans. It then takes a revenue cut of any products sold, which is where the real money is made' (Gillezeau, 2021b). The company's influencers may test out a small quantity of a product with followers to see whether it will sell before making large orders with suppliers. According to the article, instant feedback means that the popularity of products can rise and fall instantly, and it is expected that Atelier would grow as creators across Instagram, TikTok, and YouTube 'wanting to monetise their followers' grow (Gillezeau, 2021b). The idea underpinning this business model, it is explained is to make the 'customer experience' seamless. Rather than dealing with multiple manufacturers across many communication channels and using different payment gateways, Atelier employs one partner, one form of communication, one method of payment (Gillezeau, 2021b).

Experiences of emotional work and its exploitations

We know little about the lives and motivations of influencers themselves, apart from what they say about themselves online. Since they are in the business of marketing themselves, these descriptions provide little insight into their day-to-day experiences, including what it involves in terms of emotional labour and whether they feel exploited and/or develop a diminished sense of self-worth as a consequence of undertaking this work. An interview-based study of the impression management strategies used by 'Instagram Stories' users undertaken by psychology researchers revealed that users exerted a great deal of control over their online impressions and used the features of the platform to highlight their uniqueness and convey 'thematic consistency' in their storytelling (Sukmayadi and Yahya, 2019). This finding is hardly surprising given the strategies and the norms and expectations that pertain to influencers, outlined above. However, while 'impression management' has long been documented by sociologists as an aspect of the presentation of the self in everyday life, digital media provide new tools for curating the self, for hiding the 'backstage' work that goes into one's online performance—an affordance that I explore in chapters that follow. Another study, involving 11 interviews with travel influencers, combined with a visual and textual content analysis of their 12 most recent Instagram posts revealed the tensions involved in the effort to stay 'authentic' while approaching their followers in a strategic way in order to maintain their appeal to the advertisers, which ultimately leads to the standardisation of content shared by influencers (van Driel and Dumitrica, 2021). This finding is also not unexpected given the degree of emotional investment and management required of influencers. As Arlie Russel Hochschild (1983) noted in her classic study of (female) airline attendants, front-line service work demands a great deal of emotional work that may be exploited by others as labour to generate profit. As a requirement of the job, this emotional labour may exact a huge toll on the person undertaking such work. Hochschild distinguished between 'deep acting' and 'surface acting' to distinguish the different emotional investments that individuals may be called upon to make in different situations. While one may be able to step away from the demands of one's emotional work during 'down time' or after hours—to switch roles, so to speak—maintaining this distinction may not always be possible or feasible and the consequences may be profound for the individuals involved. Hochschild's study and many other studies that draw on her work pertain to employees in more conventional, typically ongoing paid employment. However, social media influencers, like Uber drivers and other gig workers are likely to live a more precarious existence and, as mentioned, while some do make a great deal of money, the majority do not and also lack the conditions that generally pertain to full-time ongoing employment, including sick pay, insurance, and holiday leave.

Relationship labour

The emotional labour of influencers can be considered a form of so-called relationship labour (Shestakofsky and Kalkar, 2020). As Shestakofsky and Kalkar explain, relationship labour refers to the interpersonal communications undertaken by agents of platform companies with their users to ensure that their activities and preferences align with the company's interests (2020: 486). Platform companies evidently recognise that their operations, which rely on algorithm-driven processes, can alienate and create tension among their many potential users, who may inhabit highly diverse communities and pursue different, sometimes conflicting objectives. The task of those undertaking relationship labour—which is largely undertaken by women who undertake the bulk of service and care roles in society—is to manage users' emotional states and cultivate long-term ties with their communities through building trust. This can be critical in a context where algorithm-driven systems (designed predominantly by white men) tend to depersonalise relationships, polarise opinion, and alienate users who may switch platforms, or abandon them altogether, or voice complaints about them via social media. For example, Apple, Amazon, Google, and other Big Tech companies provide a mix of online and offline services to build and improve their relationships with customers, and address their concerns and complaints, and provide a 'human face' to what would otherwise be an impersonal 'customer experience'. This may entail a mix of online forums, the use of chatbots or 'conversation agents' (with mostly female names and voices) to provide simulated conversations, and telephone connections with a 'real person' to ensure that platforms meet user needs and are accessible at all times. Designated 'relationship managers' play an important role in this regard. As one employment agency describes the role, relationship managers work for corporations 'to make sure business clients feel valued' and 'They work closely with the sales, marketing and customer service teams to develop new ways to attract clients and reduce client turnover ... [and] to understand their employer's values and the types of products they offer to best represent their employer during client meetings' (Indeed, 2021).

Amazon is but one company that is highly dependent on relationship labour. It employs 'relations managers' who work in various capacities to help nurture and sustain customer relations. In an advertisement for a 'channel relationship manager', for instance, the description for the position outlines how 'at Amazon, we're working to be the most consumer-centric company of earth' and that in order to serve its 'loyal customers' it is offering opportunities for 'a career as a leader in Operations Management' and that it will train candidates with 'great challenges in dealing with front-line management' (Amazon, 2021a). The 'Role summary' for the position states that 'He/she maintains relationships with the SPs [Service Delivery programs] and builds their capability' and that primary responsibilities include 'Develops and manages relationships with stakeholders (IHS [I Have Space] & SP)' (Amazon, 2021a). Amazon relies on an army of workers and businesses to sustain its operations and allow it to grow, and it is critical that the company establishes and maintains their loyalty and trust. These include those who work for its I Have Space program, launched in 2014, whereby store owners and businesses (for example, grocers, chemists, fast-food outlets) can provide delivery and pickup services for Amazon using their own vehicles and earn a part-time income if they have spare 'manpower' and make deliveries during their off-peak times. This program, which claims to offer 'an additional source of income with zero investment', is portrayed as being 'customer-focused'—the 'customers' being the store owners and businesses who work for them—but its overriding objective is to advance Amazon's goals. The program is not strictly speaking 'cost free' since those applying to participate need to spend time and effort undergoing a background check, undertake Amazon-approved training, and provide vehicles and staff. The I Have Space program has assumed a growing role in logistics in a developing world context. In early 2021, it was reported that Amazon was vastly expanding its I Have Space program across India 'by adding thousands of store owners for delivering its packages'. Whereas the company had 2,500 stores in 2015, this had grown to 12,500 stores in 180 cities in 2021. As one of Amazon's spokespersons was reported: 'Store partners delivered between 30 to 40 packages a day, earning a fixed amount per delivery and the program is open to all store owners who have the ability to service on foot or a two wheeler' (Editor, 2021). Those businesses working for Amazon are provided with incentives, such as receiving a 'badge' of approval as a Prime Seller, which 'guarantees a great customer experience—free, fast, and reliable delivery and world-class customer support' and 'lets customers in your locality discover you faster' (Amazon, 2021b). They are also offered 'Tools to help you grow', such as advice on creating limited time offers using 'lightening deals' and giving customers 'coupons for special offers on shipping, discounts, and future purchases' (Amazon, 2021b). Through the use of such incentives, sellers are, in effect, undertaking relationship labour on Amazon's behalf.

Behind-the-scenes 'ghost' workers

The emotional work undertaken by influencers and relationship managers is crucial for sustaining the public-facing, visible dimension of the online economy—although the underlying agenda, 'to keep customers happy' and to ensure they are not lost to competitors—will likely remain opaque to the former. What is much less well understood and appreciated is the emotional labour performed by those who work behind-the-scenes and hence are less visible. These workers, or so-called ghost workers, are employed either directly by Big Tech companies or, as is more often the case, work on a piecemeal, 'on-demand' basis. Their contributions are difficult to document because the companies that employ them do not wish to make their presence visible since they are highly exploited. They are also globally dispersed and mostly not organised into labour unions that can represent workers' collective interests. Stories from recent insiders at Big Tech companies, such as those told in *The Social Dilemma*, described at the beginning of this chapter, are mostly those of relatively privileged white men who occupied senior management positions, and provide little insight into the lives and conditions of the on-demand, precariously employed workers generally from poorer communities in developed and developing countries whose contributions to the online emotional economy are much less visible and hence remain largely unnoticed. It is valuable then to consider the research of Mary Gray and Siddharth

Suri (2019), authors of *Ghost Work*, who explored the experiences of the mostly lower socio-economic female workers who make the internet possible.

Gray and Suri are researchers at Microsoft Research (Gray is also described as an anthropologist), who observed and undertook interviews with hundreds of people in their homes and other makeshift workplaces, focusing on India and the United States, which are countries which have the largest on-demand labour pools. As they explore in their book, the rise of Big Tech companies like Amazon, Microsoft, Google, and Uber rely on an army of behind-the-scene workers who undertake content moderation, audio transcribing, identity confirmation, video captioning, and other critical tasks, yet whose presence is deliberately concealed. It is concealed, the authors argue, because they are exploited and highly vulnerable in that they are reliant on a process of competitive real-time bidding for work. These workers bring their own software tools to the job and are assigned to do tasks remotely with no training and bear the related costs. This work is algorithm-driven and -assessed, with the consequence that workers are constantly in fear of losing work or not gaining future work because they are judged to be under-performing. It is also a work relationship that lacks trust. As Gray and Suri observe,

> One of the first issues that comes up [during interviews] is establishing a relationship based on trust and accountability in this setting. It takes time to build trust between two people, but this is at odds with one of the major draws of using on-demand workers—to gain access to labor quickly. The rating and reputation systems that platforms implement … are an attempt to convey trust through an API [Application Program Interface], but these are incomplete solutions.
>
> *(Gray and Suri, 2019: 71–72).*

As the authors explain, trust issues 'can spill over into accountability issues' (2019: 72). In a traditional staffing-agency model, accountability for sub-standard work lies with the agency. But this is not the case in the on-demand setting. But this is not the case in the on-demand setting. The workers are, in effect, viewed as 'mere customers who are selling their labor' and denied all the protections and entitlements generally associated with undertaking paid work (2019: 75). The requesters build a trusted pool of workers off the platform, 'repeatedly hiring and trying out workers' and adding those who are judged to have performed well are added to the hiring firm's internal database of trusted workers (Gray and Suri, 2019: 74). Those who pass 'the vetting test' may be taken 'off the plat-form', thereby saving money which the platform charges the requester, which is a percentage of the fee paid to workers (2019: 74). Gray and Suri describe the 'algorithmic cruelties' that inflict pain on these on-demand workers, including hypervigilance, in being constantly alert to work opportunities and wading and sorting through spam and dubious offers of 'at-home work', social isolation and lack of guidance on navigating the complexities of a job, and not getting back due to technical issues of malfeasance (2019: 75–91). While such cruelty is not intentional, the authors explain, it is an unintended consequence of an economy increasingly based on precarious employment within a growing service sector and reliance on computational processes.

A major mechanism used to match these on-demand workers with tasks is Amazon Mechanical Turk (MTurk). MTurk is advertised as a means for individuals and companies to outsource their processes and work to 'a distributed workforce who can perform these tasks virtually'. According to its website, 'MTurk enables companies to harness the collective intelligence, skills, and insights from a global workforce to streamline business processes, augment data collection and analysis, and accelerate machine learning development' (MTurk, 2021). Presented as a 'crowdsourcing' platform for breaking down manual, time-consuming projects into smaller, more manageable tasks ('microtasks') undertaken by distributed workers, MTurk provides an ideal mechanism of both disciplining workers, who remain in constant fear of being judged to be unproductive and consequently denied further work, and ensuring the lack of a shared workplace that might encourage collective action by its labour. For potential customers who visit MTurk's website, the listed 'benefits' include 'optimise efficiency' by allowing the outsourcing of 'microtasks', thus 'freeing up staff time and resources for the company—so internal staff can focus on higher value activities'; 'increase flexibility' by 'enabl[ing] businesses and organizations to get work done easily and quickly when they need it—without the difficulty associated with dynamically scaling your in-house workforce'; and 'reduce cost', 'by leveraging the skills of distributed workers on a pay-per-task model … significantly lower costs while achieving results that might not have been possible with just a dedicated team' (MTurk, 2022). MTurk's business model employs a just-in-time production strategy allowing those who use the platform to increase efficiencies and save costs by employing labour when they need it. Workers, however, never gain the opportunity to learn about their individual contributions to the end product and have limited opportunities to be involved in collective efforts to gain some level over control over working conditions. Their experiences then are of alienation in the sense described by Marx with workers made to feel disconnected from the products of their labour.

Amazon, which owns MTurk and is the second largest private employer after Walmart in the United States, with 950,000 employees, is known to be hostile to labour unions and has made efforts to dissuade its workers from joining the company's first union (Sainato, 2021). In February 2021, the US National Labor Relations Board—an independent agency of the federal government responsible for enforcing US labour law pertaining to unfair labour practices and collective bargaining—claimed that Amazon tried to 'intimidate workers in Bessemer with anti-union messages related to the ongoing union vote' (Thornton, 2021). (If approved, the vote would have enabled workers in the warehouse at Bessemer [a suburb north of Birmingham] to be represented by the Retail, Wholesale and Department Store Union [RWDSU].) Amazon even created its own website doitwithoutdues.com (although apparently no longer active at the time of writing) to promote its anti-union message, claiming that members would be at the mercy of a union that could vote to strike and thereby endanger their jobs and benefits. Workers subsequently voted to reject the formation of the RWDSU in the warehouse at Bessemer, although the union announced it would launch a legal challenge to the outcome due to 'the high number of contested ballots and union allegations of unfair tactics during the campaign' (Sainato, 2021). It is worth noting that Amazon proved to be one of the most profitable businesses during the COVID-19 lockdown and helped confirm its founder Jeff Bezos as the world's richest man with a personal fortune of $US177 billion (Sainato, 2021).

The *emotional* experiences of the ghost workers who work for Big Tech, or the companies that provide content moderation services, have been little explored to date. However, recent news coverage of a series of lawsuits undertaken by these workers who have allegedly suffered emotional harm has shone a light on these experiences and resulted in increased scrutiny of companies' content moderation practices. One reported case involved a content moderator at Facebook (now Meta), employed to review child abuse, who claimed, 'She appealed to her manager to see a counselor to help her cope after reviewing a disturbing post, footage of a teenage girl being raped by a group of men' but received little support from her company (Dwoskin, 2020). This prompted her 'to join a lawsuit the following year charging that Facebook, as well as the companies it contracts with to hire tens of thousands of moderators, failed to protect its workers from the trauma associated with spending eight hours a day reviewing horrific images to keep them off social media platforms' (Dwoskin, 2020). The case resulted in a 'first-of-its-kind settlement', with Facebook agreeing 'to pay $52 million to thousands of U.S. workers who have suffered the psychological consequences of reviewing posts depicting acts of suicide, murder, child abuse and other disturbing content'. As the article noted, 'The settlement, in which Facebook did not admit or deny harms caused to these workers, applies to any U.S.-based content moderator who has ever worked for a third-party company providing services to Facebook and its subsidiaries WhatsApp and Instagram, a group that encompasses more than 10,000 people' (Dwoskin, 2020). The case, a report noted, may lead to other lawsuits from workers who provide services for social media companies who hire a large number of moderators, such as Twitter and YouTube. This report followed an earlier story regarding a Facebook moderator who sued the company alleging she had suffered post-traumatic stress disorder following the reviewing of 'thousands of extreme and graphic violence "from her cubicle in Facebook's Silicon Valley offices"'—a complaint that was joined by two other content moderators, who claimed that Facebook had 'failed to provide a safe workplace or compensate them for the psychological harm that they endured' (Dwoskin, 2018). As the reports on these US cases highlighted, the emotional costs incurred by content moderation may be severe for many of the tens of thousands of individuals who undertake this kind of work. However, as Dwoskin (2020) comments, US workers are generally in a better position than those in other countries, who are often 'not afforded the same legal protections and tend to work longer hours with more limited psychological support'.

Another reported case involved a content moderator for TikTok who was suing the company on the basis that it 'did not protect her from suffering psychological trauma after "constant" exposure to violent videos that showed sexual assault, beheadings, suicide and other graphic scenes' (Pietsch, 2021). According to the lawsuit, which was filed in California against TikTok and its parent company ByteDance, the videos included 'genocide in Myanmar, mass shootings, children being raped, and animals being mutilated' (Pietsch, 2021). The claimant argued that TikTok 'violated California labor law by failing to provide a "safe work environment" and it was also requested that the platform and ByteDance 'provide mental health support and treatment to former and current moderators' (Pietsch, 2021). Although the claimant was not an employee of TikTok, but rather worked for Telus International—a company that advertises itself as 'a leading digital customer experience (CX) innovator that designs, builds and delivers next-gen digital solutions for global and disruptive brands' (Telus International, 2022)—'the lawsuit alleges that "ByteDance and TikTok control the means and manner in which content moderation occurred"' (Pietsch, 2021). An article reporting on this case noted that evidence was tendered in the lawsuit claiming that 'Moderators are made to view as many as 10 videos simultaneously, while being pushed by TikTok software "to review videos faster and faster"'. It also noted that 'During the course of a 12-hour shift, workers are allowed two 15-minute breaks and an hour for lunch' (Pietsch, 2021).

The growing 'attention deficit'

While Big Tech companies, like Google, Amazon, and ByteDance, and smaller companies using their services have profited immensely from the emotional regimes designed to harvest people's attention and data, this may not be the case in the future. Like political regimes, online emotional regimes are unstable and subject to contestation and change. In one definition, a regime is 'a particular way of operating or organizing business' or 'a particular government or a system or method of government' (Cambridge Dictionary, 2021). Online emotional regimes may be viewed in both senses: they provide both a modus operandi of interacting online and a formalised system for governing those interactions. These regimes invite, facilitate, discourage, and restrict certain modes of expression—what can be expressed, how it should be expressed, and with what intensity and to whom (whether individuals, groups, or communities)—which makes them dynamic and unstable. Ultimately, they rely on the exploitation of users' personal data which needs to be harvested and then used by companies to create value. Yet, while data may have *potential* to create value, there are many activities and actors needed to realise it. Crucially, new data needs to be constantly generated. This creates vulnerabilities in Big Tech companies' business models, requiring them to develop ever-more intrusive techniques of emotional exploitation and manipulation to harvest people's attention. But attention is a finite resource and there exists an ever-growing array of interests seeking to extract value from it. While 'data pools' may be growing as more and more people go online or live a larger proportion of their lives online—especially with changes in economies and societies wrought by the COVID-19 pandemic—there is also growing questioning of and resistance to the intrusions of the internet, particularly the loss of privacy and relentless advertising. Another issue is the fierce competition in the market of attention. The decline of Facebook's user base, which has been attributed to the rapid rise in popularity of the video-sharing platform TikTok during the pandemic-induced lockdowns, highlights the vulnerability of Big Tech companies to competition (Chapter 6).

Conclusion

As I explained in this chapter, the online emotional economy is multifaceted and is sustained by the contributions of many actors, including app designers, data scientists, e-commerce specialists, user interface and user experience (UX) consultants, professional marketers, social media influencers, and relationship managers, and the less visible, precariously employed, and largely exploited 'ghost workers', discussed above, who are drawn from generally poor communities, who, as Gray and Suri (2019) express it, 'make the internet seem smart'. Yet, while the operations of the internet and various connected devices may suggest a kind of intelligence and sentience that has been long imagined in science fiction portrayals of computing, like other technology-based systems, it is prone to failure and to finding applications unimagined by its designers. Because the online economy relies on the contributions of many actors who have different values and interests and on 'black-boxed' automated processes that have unpredictable consequences, there is no certainty about how it will evolve in the future and whether it will survive in its current form. I discussed the vulnerability of digital advertising which underpins the online emotional economy and its risk of collapsing due to the misplaced faith in the power of advertising, which Hwang (2020) likens to subprime mortgages in being liable to implosion. Hwang's focus is mostly on the market effects of consumer indifference and resistance, such as consumers' use of ad blockers, and 'click fraud'. However, various other developments threaten the viability of the internet. This includes, notably, growing public outrage over online harm and abuse.

In the next chapter, I explore some of the diverse forms of online emotional abuse and the manner and extent to which the meanings of abuse are undergoing change in the age of digital media. I also explore some of the efforts to control online harms and abuse, especially that directed at children and young people, who are generally viewed as a vulnerable group. As I hope my analysis will make clear, online harm and abuse is a complicated matter in an age of algorithms, easy access to software that may be used to manipulate images, and rapidly circulating information that may endure online.

References

Affectiva (2021a) 'Research shows advertising is having a more emotional impact on consumers, but not all advertisers are using emotions effectively', https://www.affectiva.com/news-item/research-shows-advertising-is-having-a-more-emotional-impact-on-consumers-but-not-all-advertisers-are-using-emotions-effectively/ (Accessed 16 May 2021).

Affectiva (2021b) 'Affectiva media analytics for ad testing', https://www.affectiva.com/product/affectiva-media-analytics-for-ad-testing/ (Accessed 16 May 2021).

Amazon (2021a) 'Channel relationship manager', *Job description*, https://www.amazon.jobs/en/jobs/1534273/channel-relationship-manager (Accessed 17 June 2021).

Amazon (2021b) 'Become a prime seller', https://sell.amazon.in/grow-your-business.html?ref_=sdin_h_grow_prime#prime-seller (Accessed 18 June 2021).

Bapple (2021) 'Your business, your customers, our focus', https://bapple.com.au/?utm_source=visualobjects.com&utm_medium=referral&utm_campaign=directory (Accessed 24 November 2021).

Baymard Institute (2021) '46 cart abandonment rate statistics', https://baymard.com/lists/cart-abandonment-rate (Accessed 25 November 2021).

Beck, M. and Libert, B. (2017) 'The rise of AI makes emotional intelligence more important', *Harvard Business Review*, 15 February, https://hbr.org/2017/02/the-rise-of-ai-makes-emotional-intelligence-more-important (Accessed 3 June 2021).

Belchamber, J. (2018) 'The rise of the emotional economy in the world of AI', *hrmasia*, 15 October, https://hrmasia.com/the-rise-of-the-emotional-economy-in-the-world-of-ai/ (Accessed 3 June 2021).

Bennett, T. (2021) 'Key digital roles are attracting the biggest pay rises', *The Australian Financial Review*, 11 November: 4.

Blumenthal-Barby, J. S. and Krieger, H. (2015) 'Cognitive biases and heuristics in medical decision-making: a critical review using a systematic search strategy', *Medical Decision Making*, 35, 4: 539–557.

Bonastre, L. and Granollers, T. (2014) 'A set of heuristics for user experience evaluation of e-commerce websites', ACHI 2014: The Seventh International Conference on Advances in Computer-Human Interactions, https://citeseerx.ist.psu.edu/viewdoc/download?doi=10.1.1.672.2794&rep=rep1&type=pdf (Accessed 25 November 2021).

Bourdieu, P. (1984; orig. 1979) *Distinction: A Social Critique of the Judgement of Taste*. Routlege & Kegan Paul, London.

Brooks, A. (2019) '[Timeline] a brief history of influencers', *SocialMediaToday*, 9 May, https://www.socialmediatoday.com/news/timeline-a-brief-history-of-influencers/554377/ (Accessed 26 May 2021).

Broyles, S. J. (2006) 'Subliminal advertising and the perpetual popularity of playing to people's paranoia', *The Journal of Consumer Affairs*, 40, 2: 392–406.

Cambridge Dictionary (2021) 'Regime', https://dictionary.cambridge.org/dictionary/english/regime (Accessed 20 July 2021).

Campbell, C. and Grimm, P. E. (2019) 'The challenges native advertising poses: exploring potential federal trade commission responses and identifying research needs', *Journal of Public Policy and Marketing*, 38, 1: 110–123.

Christinagalbato (2021) 'Christina Galbato Instagram page', *christinagalbato*, 2021 (Accessed 28 May 2021).

DevToolsGuy (2013) 'What is a UX consultant?', *Infragistics blog*, https://www.infragistics.com/community/blogs/b/marketing/posts/what-is-a-ux-consultant (Accessed 24 November 2021).

Dwoskin, E. (2018) 'A content moderator says she got PTSD while reviewing images posted on facebook', *The Washington Post*, 24 September, https://www.washingtonpost .com/technology/2018/09/24/content-moderator-says-she-got-ptsd-while -reviewing-images-posted-facebook/ (Accessed 18 March 2022).

Dwoskin, E. (2020) 'Facebook content moderator details trauma that prompted fight for $52 million PTSD settlement', *The Washington Post*, 13 May, https://www .washingtonpost.com/technology/2020/05/12/facebook-content-moderator-ptsd/ (Accessed 18 March 2022).

Editor (2021) 'Amazon to expand "I Have Space" program across India', *Indian OnlineSeller.com*, https://indianonlineseller.com/2017/07/amazon-to-expand-i-have -space-program-across-india (Accessed 18 June 2021).

Eubanks, V. (2018) *Automating Inequality: How High Tech Tools Profile, Police and Punish the Poor*. Picador, New York.

Facebook (2020) 'What "The Social Dilemma" gets wrong'. https://about.fb.com/wp -content/uploads/2020/10/What-The-Social-Dilemma-Gets-Wrong.pdf (Accessed 14 October, 2020).

Fromm, E. (2010; orig. 1968) *The Revolution of Hope: Toward a Humanized Technology*. American Mental Health Foundation Inc, New York.

Gillezeau, N. (2021a) 'The Aussie start-up selling AI that makes you buy more online', *The Australian Financial Review*, 30 November: 23.

Gillezeau, N. (2021b) 'Atelier raises $3m catering to 'creator economy'', *The Australian Financial Review*, 2 November: 21.

Gray, M. L. and Siddharth, S. (2019) *Ghost Work: How to Stop Silicon Valley from Building a New Global Underclass*. Houghton Mifflin Harcourt, Boston, MA and New York.

Green, E. P. (2019) 'Refining heuristics for educators', *Medical Education*, 53, 4: 322–324.

Halavais, A. (2018) *Search Engine Society*. 2nd edition. Polity, Cambridge, MA.

Hochschild, A. R. (1983) *The Managed Heart: The Commercialization of Human Feeling*. University of California Press, Berkeley, CA.

Hotjar. (2021) 'CRO: the user-centric approach', https://www.hotjar.com/conversion -rate-optimization/ (Accessed 24 November 2021).

Hutchinson, A. (2020) 'Facebook issues official response to claims made in Netflix documentary "the social dilemma"', https://www.socialmediatoday.com/news /facebook-issues-official-response-to-claims-made-in-netflix-documentary-th /586351/ (Accessed 14 October 2020).

Hwang, T. (2020) *Subprime Attention Crisis*. FSG Originals x Logic, New York.

Indeed (2021) 'Relationship manager job description: top duties and qualifications', https://www.indeed.com/hire/job-description/relationship-manager?hl=en&co =US (Accessed 17 June 2021).

Influencer Marketing Hub (2020) 'Internet advertising statistics—the rise of mobile and ad blocking', https://influencermarketinghub.com/internet-advertising-statistics/ (Accessed 13 May 2021).

Influencer Marketing Hub (2021) 'What is an influencer?—social media influencers defined', [updated 2021], https://influencermarketinghub.com/what-is-an -influencer/ (Accessed 27 May 2021).

Jarvis, P. (2020) 'Does targeted digital advertising work?', *Fathom*, 12 October, https:// usefathom.com/blog/do-targeted-ads-work (Accessed 13 May 2021).

Juniper Research (2019) 'Digital ad spend to reach $520 billion by 2023, as Amazon disrupts Google and Facebook duopoly', 24 June, https://www.juniperresearch.com/ press/digital-ad-spend-reach-520-billion-by-2023 (Accessed 13 May 2021).

McLuhan, M. and Fiore, Q. (1967) *The Medium Is the Massage: An Inventory of Effects*. Gingko Press, Corte Madera, CA.

Merriam-Webster (2021) 'Definition of influencer', https://www.merriam-webster.com /dictionary/influencer (Accessed 26 May 2021).

Miller, C. (2021) 'Facebook and its advertisers are 'panicking' as the majority of iPhone users opt out of tracking', *9to5Mac*, 14 July, https://9to5mac.com/2021/07/14/ facebook-tracking-app-tracking-data/?utm_campaign=What%27s%20up%20with %20Tech%3F&utm_medium=email&utm_source=Revue%20newsletter (Accessed 16 July 2021).

Mousavi, S. and Gigerenzer, G. (2014) 'Risk, uncertainty, and heuristics', *Journal of Business Research*, 67, 8: 1671–1678.

MTurk (2022) 'Amazon Mechanical Turk', https://www.mturk.com/ (Accessed 26 August 2022)

Naughton, J. (2020) 'The Social Dilemma: a wakeup call for a world drunk on Dopamine?', *The Guardian*, 20 September. https://www.theguardian.com/commentisfree/2020 /sep/19/the-social-dilemma-a-wake-up-call-for-a-world-drunk-on-dopamine (Accessed 14 October 2020)

Nielson Norman Group (2021a) '10 usability heuristics for user design interface design', https://www.nngroup.com/articles/ten-usability-heuristics/ (Accessed 24 November 2021).

Nielson Norman Group (2021b) 'Intranet design annual: 2021', https://www.nngroup .com/reports/intranet-design-annual/ (Accessed 24 November 2021).

O'Neil, C. (2016) *Weapons of Math Destruction: How Big Data Increases Inequality and Threatens Democracy*. Allen Lane, London.

Packard, V. (1957) *The Hidden Persuaders*. D. McKay Co, New York.

Particular Audience (2022) 'What is particular audience?', https://docs.particularaudience .com/ (Accessed 26 August 2022).

Pasquale, F. (2015) *The Blackbox Society: The Secret Algorithms That Control Money and Information*. Harvard University Press, Cambridge, MA.

Petersen, A. (2019) *Digital Health and Technological Promise*. Routledge, London and New York.

Pietsch, B. (2021) 'TikTok content moderator sues company, alleging trauma from hours reviewing videos of rape and killings', *The Washington Post*, 28 December, https:// www.washingtonpost.com/technology/2021/12/28/tiktok-moderator-lawsuit -violent-content-ptsd/ (Accessed 18 March 2022).

Postman (2005; orig. 1985) *Amusing Ourselves To Death: Public Discourse in the Age of Show Business*. Penguin, New York.

Reddy, W. M. (2001) *The Navigation of Feeling: A Framework for the History of Emotions*. Cambridge University Press, Cambridge.

Sainato, M. (2021) 'Amazon workers in Alabama vote against forming company's first union', *The Guardian*, 10 April, https://amp.theguardian.com/technology/2021/ apr/09/amazon-union-vote-result-latest-news-bessemer-alabama-plant (Accessed 23 June 2021).

SaleCycle (2021) '2021: ecommerce stats and trends report', https://d34w0339mx0ifp .cloudfront.net/content/2021_Ecommerce_Stats_Trends_Report_EN.pdf (Accessed 25 November 2021).

Sands, S., Campbell, C. L., Plangger, K. and Ferraro, C. (2022) 'Unreal influence: leveraging AI in influence marketing', *European Journal of Marketing*, 18 February.

Schudson, M. (1993; orig.1984) *Advertising, the Uneasy Persuasion: Its Dubious Impact on American Society*, Volume 6. Routledge, London and New York.

Shead, S. (2020) 'Netflix documentary "the social dilemma" prompts social media users to rethink facebook, Instagram and others', *CNBC*, 18 September, https://www.cnbc.com/2020/09/18/netfixs-the-social-dilemma-restults-in-people-deleting-facebook-instagram.html (Accessed 14 October 2020).

Shestakofsky, B. and Kalkar, S. (2020) 'Making platforms work: relationship labor and the management of publics', *Theory and Society*, 49: 863–896.

Srinivasan, R. and Fish, A. (2017) *After the Internet*. Polity, Cambridge, MA.

Sukmayadi, V. and Yahya, V. (2019) 'Impression management within Instagram stories: a phenomenological study', *Open Psychology Journal*, 12, 1: 216–224.

Telus International (2022) 'Next-generation digitally-led customer experiences', *home page*, https://www.telusinternational.com/ (Accessed 18 March 2022).

Thornton, W. (2021) 'Amazon accused of anti-union activities through website', *AL.com*, https://www.al.com/business/2021/02/amazon-accused-of-anti-union-activities-through-website.html (Accessed 23 June 2021).

Vaidhyanathan, S. (2018) *Anti-Social Media: How Facebook Disconnects Us and Undermines Democracy*. Oxford University Press, Oxford.

van Driel, L. and Dumitrica, D. (2021) 'Selling brands while staying "authentic": the professionalization of Instagram influencers', *Convergence: The International Journal of Research into New Media Technologies*, 27, 1: 66–84.

Warren, J. (2020) 'The ultimate guide to Instagram influencer marketing', 8 November, https://later.com/blog/instagram-influencer-marketing/#micro (Accessed 28 May 2021).

Wenzel, M. and Stjerne, I. S. (2021) 'Heuristics-in-use: toward a practice theory of organizational heuristics', *Technological Forecasting and Social Change*, 164, 21 March, doi.org/10.1016/j.techfore.2020.120517.

Yallop, O. (2021) *Break the Internet: In Pursuit of Influence*. Scribe Publications, London.

YouTube Creator Academy (2022) 'Use comments to connect with your community', https://www.youtube.com/watch?v=5rvq_GhtS8Q (Accessed 26 August 2022).

3

EMOTIONAL ABUSE ONLINE

In June 2021, a news story reported that 13 students from diverse backgrounds around France were facing potential jail time for death and rape threats in what was claimed to be 'the first cyberbullying case tried in a new court set up to prosecute online crimes' (Vaux-Montagny, 2021). These crimes were said to include harassment and discrimination. The victim, a teenager (identified only by her first name, Mila), who 'harshly criticised Islam and the Koran' via videos on Instagram and later TikTok, was claimed to have received 'some 100,000 threatening messages, including death threats, rape threats, misogynist messages and hateful messages about her homosexuality'. The article noted that Mila, who was 18 years old, but 16 when she started posting the videos, felt as if she had been 'condemned to death' and was reported to be 'now monitored daily by the police for her safety'. One of the 13 individuals whom authorities had tracked and were facing trial, one wanted to become a police officer, while another said that 'he just wanted to rack up more followers by making people laugh'. Others denied any wrong-doing or had apologised. One of the latter had tweeted, 'you deserve to have your throat slit' and added a 'sexist epithet'. Most claimed to have tweeted or posted 'without thinking', with one who had commented, 'Have her skull crushed, please', saying that 'At the time, I was not aware that it was harassment'. Despite her bad experience, the article reported, 'Mila remains active on social networks'.

As the author of the article acknowledges, the case raises some interesting points, including in relation to freedom of expression and the freedom to criticise religion. The case also raises questions of a more *sociological* nature, namely, the role played by digital media in shaping conceptions and experiences of harm and abuse, and the character of official and community responses to the phenomenon. In this chapter, I examine various arguments and evidence on this claimed role, and then propose an alternative perspective that focuses on the operations of the online emotional

DOI: 10.4324/9781003147435-3

economy. As I argue, arguments are often confused by a lack of clarity in definitions used in research and policy and the influence of long-standing and questionable assumptions about technologies and their users. They tend to focus narrowly on the behaviours of the perpetrators and the victims, and sometimes the parents, and on the use of certain technologies, while neglecting the politico-economic and socio-cultural contexts within which harmful and abusive conduct arises. Many debates about online harm and abuse relate specifically to children and have precedent in concerns voiced many decades ago about children's vulnerability to the effects of television. Hence, I will also discuss arguments about children's use of digital media and exposure to related content, and authorities' responses. Children in general are assumed to be especially vulnerable and susceptible to media messages and images. I ask, to what extent have conceptions of agency, responsibility, and vulnerability changed with the advance of digital media? What would constitute effective governance of a system whose very *design* encourages and tolerates certain practices, including those that polarise views and contribute to harm and abuse? To what extent can Big Tech companies be held accountable for harm and abuse? Could digital media be *redesigned* to make them less harmful?

A history of concerns about electronic media and their impacts

As I argued in Chapter 1, contemporary anxieties about the personal and social impacts of digital media echo fears about the effects of new technologies, and specifically electronic technologies, articulated by scholars more than 50 years ago. While anxieties about online-based harms and abuse have heightened over the last few decades as more people have gone online, and as social media have evolved, there are clear parallels with fears about television and predictions of emerging computing technologies in the 1960s. These anxieties pertained especially to children, who were seen as especially vulnerable and manipulable. Writing in 1967, against a background of the Cold War and fears about growing technological domination and nuclear annihilation, Marshall McLuhan discussed the power of television—which he described as 'a totally new technology'—to shape minds, particularly children's minds (McLuhan and Fiore, 1967: 128). McLuhan saw television as exerting a more powerful influence on children than education.

> Today's television child is attuned to up-to-the-minute 'adult' news—inflation, rioting, war, taxes, crimes, bathing beauties—and is bewildered when he enters the nineteenth century environment that still characterizes the educational establishment where information is scarce but ordered and structured by fragmented, classified patterns, subjects and schedules. It is naturally an environment much like any factory set-up with its inventories and assembly lines.
>
> *(McLuhan and Fiore, 1967: 18)*

McLuhan argued that television was reflective of an emerging 'new form of "politics"', whereby participation in actions such as demonstrations on war, freedom marches, and activism on pollution occurred via this medium (1967: 22). In McLuhan's view, television profoundly shaped human sensory experience by demanding viewers' full attention by projecting images at them, and heightening awareness of events to an extreme level (1967: 125). Children, whom McLuhan referred to as 'the television generation', were becoming more serious and earnest than in the past when they were 'frivolous, more whimsical' (1967: 127). McLuhan was especially concerned about the influence of television commercials, which he saw as 'preconditioning' audiences to 'abrupt zooms, elliptical editing, no story lines, flash cuts' (1967: 128). In making these observations, however, McLuhan believed that people did not yet have the conceptual tools for understanding how their world had changed; how 'the new technology' had 'created the mass'. This was because people's perspectives derived from print technology which 'created the public' which 'consists of separate individuals walking around with separate, fixed points of view' (1967: 69).

Also in the 1960s, Erich Fromm described the 'de-humanizing' effects of technology which he linked to the advance of the 'second Industrial Revolution'. As Fromm observed, society had become 'a vast machine, of which man is a living particle' (Fromm, 2010: orig. 1968: 41). He presented a rather bleak picture of what he saw as an increasingly mechanized, consumer-oriented society, with many citizens experiencing truncated lives and seemingly resigned to their fates. His ideas, published long before the internet, now seem prescient, being part of contemporary discussions about digitalisation and AI, namely, his references to the 'unconscious values' programmed into the computer itself, the dangers of 'irrational reliance' on computers for decisions, 'emotion-free belief in the rationality (calculability) of the computer methods', the potential to create 'man-like' computers, belief that computers can 'replace man', and the loss of privacy (2010; orig. 1968: 53–70). He discussed the influences of the mass media and advertising, which he saw as part of a wider consumeristic, conformity-inducing industrial and governmental system (2010; orig. 1968: 47–49). In Fromm's view, in the emergent industrial society, humans were losing their individuality and capacity for independent thought, feeling, and aesthetic appreciation. He wrote: 'By the growth of literacy and of the mass media, the individual learns quickly which thoughts are "right", which behaviour is correct, which feeling is normal, which taste is "in"' (2010; orig. 1968: 61).

One of 'technological society's pathogenic effects', Fromm argued, was 'the disappearance of *privacy* and of *personal human contact*' (2010; orig. 1968: 55; emphasis in original)—concerns which pertain to digital media today. Fromm acknowledged that privacy was 'a complex concept' in that it was and still is the privilege of the middle and upper classes, yet he believed it was still important for personhood and 'free[ing] oneself from the constant "noise" of people's chatter and intrusion, which interferes with one's own mental processes' (2010; orig.1968: 55). He continued:

> If all private data are transformed into public data, experiences will tend to become more shallow and more alike. People will be afraid to feel 'the wrong thing'; they will become more accessible to psychological manipulation which, through psychological testing, tries to establish norms for 'desirable', 'normal', 'healthy' attitudes.
>
> *(Fromm, 2010; orig. 1968: 55)*

It is interesting to reflect on Fromm's views on private data now given the intrusions of digital media, especially the mass harvesting of data that is integral to the digital ecosystem and powers platforms such as Instagram that, critics argue, normalise certain bodily ideals that harm young female users.

In the mid-1980s, Neil Postman also articulated fears about television and its effects, especially on children, in a manner similar to that described by McLuhan many years before. Postman saw television as offering a fundamental challenge to the assumptions of education which are 'organized around the slow-moving printed word, and the equally rapid emergence of a new education based on the speed-of-light electronic age' (Postman, 2005; orig. 1985: 145). He called television 'a curriculum', which created new conceptions of knowledge and how it is acquired (2005; orig. 1985: 145). Postman believed television offered a shallow view of the world in that it involved the communication of slogans or symbols that create for viewers 'a comprehensive and compelling image of themselves'. In his view, television habituated citizens to constant entertainment with politicians becoming 'part of the world of show business' (2005; orig. 1985: 132). This 'image politics', he argued, operates as 'a form of therapy' which accounted for television's preoccupation with celebrities and personal disclosures (2005; orig. 1985: 135).

In summary, these early writings emphasised the ways in which electronic media, and especially television, contributed to the reshaping of social relations and subjectivities. This involved turning citizens into consumers, transforming education into entertainment, and narrowing worldviews by fragmenting experiences and diverting attention from the conditions that shape people's lives. Fromm seemed more optimistic than McLuhan or Postman in regard to the potential for humans to reshape their technological futures. For example, in his conclusion he states, 'We are in the midst of a crisis of modern man …. But there is hope— because there is the real possibility that man can reassert himself, and that he can make the technological society human' (2010; orig. 1968: 159). However, all three writers presented mostly gloomy portrayals of the sociocultural impacts of the then emerging technologies of communication. In light of this history, the question arises: are recent fears about the impacts of digital media simply a continuation of those expressed in regard to previous technologies? Do *digital* media technologies and/or communications shape views and actions in *distinct* ways?

Harm, abuse and digital media

In recent years, digital media have been front and centre of debates about inter-personal and group-based harm and abuse. The internet and social media are seen as having been weaponised or as constituting a dangerous space that calls for users to exercise constant vigilance and self-reflective practice, and demands more effective regulation. In some depictions, digital media present a radical disruption of conceptions of 'everyday life' and the habitual ways of thinking, acting, feeling, working, and sleeping by installing a 24/7 regime of control (Crary, 2014; Zuboff, 2019). In this view, the distinction between work and non-work time has effectively disappeared as technologies allow and demand constant attention and where every thought and feeling is constantly tracked, monitored, analysed, and then used to create personal profiles for purposes of algorithmic decision-making, surveillance, and marketing. According to Zuboff, a central feature of this so-called surveillance capitalism is the imperative to predict, to anticipate, and totally control behaviours, an objective that is assisted through technologies and techniques such as 'affective computing', 'emotion analytics', and 'sentiment analysis', that will 'mine' and 'extract' the most personal and private aspects of our data, to create surplus value. The longer-term vision shared by the captains of these Big Tech industries, Zuboff argues, is to create a world 'beyond the internet' where ubiquitous computing is woven into the very fabric of everyday life (2019: 199–204, 282–290).

Evidently reflecting this aspiration, in July 2021, Mark Zuckerberg, chief executive officer of Facebook, outlined his vision for the future of his company. He was quoted, 'In coming years, I expect people will transition from seeing us primarily as a social media company to seeing us as a metaverse company', adding, 'In many ways the metaverse is the ultimate expression of social technology' (Wagner, 2021). Then, in October 2021, in the wake of damning revelations by a Facebook/Meta employee-turned-whistleblower, Frances Haugen—which I discuss in detail later—and the release of the so-called Facebook Files that revealed that the company had been aware of but covered up evidence of how its platforms affected users, Mark Zuckerberg announced that Facebook (the company) would be rebranded as 'Meta'. In a news article announcing the name change, Zuckerberg was cited as saying that 'his company is rebranding itself as Meta in an effort to encompass its virtual-reality vision for the future, what he calls the "metaverse"' (AP/Reuters, 2021). Zuckerberg also said that through this new venture he expected 'to reach a billion people within the next decade'. In explaining the rebrand, he said that Meta 'would be a place where people would interact, work and create products and content in what he hoped would be a new ecosystem that created millions of jobs for creators'. His view was that Facebook no longer encompassed what the company did, which is building technology to 'connect people' (AP/Reuters, 2021). The article noted that 'Sceptics have suggested the rebrand appears to be an attempt to move attention away from the leaked documents' (AP/Reuters, 2021). Others in the technology community, including Google's co-founder Sergey Brin, and video game designers, have outlined similar visions using the term 'metaverse' in outlining their visions of a successor to the internet. The metaverse has been described as 'a parallel digital world' that is independent from the physical world and possessing its own economy and currency, where people can interact with one another simultaneously and in real time (Eisenbrand and Peterson, 2020). These visions of a post-internet world are inspired by science fiction portrayals particularly as conveyed in *Snow Crash*, published in 1992, where the author, Neal Stephenson, first coined the term 'metaverse' (Mathew Ball, 2020; Eisenbrand and Peterson, 2020). As I argued in Chapter 1, science fiction portrayals have provided inspiration for the scientific imaginary, and the hopes, expectations, and fears that they convey have powerfully shaped responses to technologies.

Many contemporary debates, however, focus not so much on longer-term impacts and societal harms but on more immediate, individual harms such as cyberbullying, stalking, trolling, sexting, harassment, impersonation, and the creation of deepfakes. Concerns focus particularly on the risks or harms to women and to children—which intensified during the COVID-19 pandemic. Attention has also focused on harmful conduct such as identity theft, fraud, hacking, and privacy intrusions, that are generally classified as 'criminal' and on harmful or abusive conduct perpetrated against entire groups or communities based on differences of appearance (e.g. skin colour, weight, age), identity (e.g. gender, sexuality), or belief (e.g. political or religious), which may or may not be criminal depending on the behaviour and context. These forms of harm and abuse are, of course, not mutually exclusive and in fact often co-exist, as I will later show. Studies, typically survey-based, offer a snapshot of views and experiences of harm and abuse but provide little insight into the underlying dynamics and long-term trends.

In 2021, the Pew Research Centre in the United States reported the findings from its survey finding that '41% of Americans have personally experienced some forms of online harassment in at least one of the six key ways that were measured' and that there was evidence that online harassment had intensified over the previous four years (Pew Research Centre, 2021a). This report also notes that those targeted by online abuse were more likely than four years earlier to 'report that their most recent experience involved more varied types and more severe forms of online abuse' (Pew Research Centre, 2021a). Another Pew Study, also published in 2021, found that 'three-quarters of U.S. adults who have recently faced some kind of online harassment say it happened on social media'; however, 'notable shares say their most recent such experience happened elsewhere, including on forum or discussion sites (25%), texting or messaging apps (24%), online gaming platforms (16%), their personal email account (11 %) or online dating sites or apps (10%)' (Pew, 2021b). A form of online abuse not mentioned in Pew's study, and generally overlooked in other studies, is that occurring via online financial transactions. In 2021, in Australia it was reported that a major bank, Westpac, 'has taken action against hundreds of customers, reporting some to law enforcement, who have tried to send abusive or threatening messages to victims alongside payments' (Bennett and Wooton, 2021). In the report, it was noted that payment transfers were being used as 'a messaging service to abuse or intimidate victims'. It was noted that, 'For example, an abuser might use the "reference" field in a bank transfer to send threats or offensive comments'. The bank's financial resilience officer commented: '"Since January, we've asked more than 22,000 customers to change transactions descriptions in real time and blocked inappropriate language" and that "using advanced data analytics to detect patterns of abuse, we've taken action against hundreds of customers—from warning letters, to suspension of online banking, to reporting to law enforcement and closing accounts"' (Bennett and Wootton, 2021).

Pew's study, above, showing increases in online harassment over recent years, raises the question of whether people's use of digital media has changed in ways that increase their *exposure* to such abuse—for example, through more time spent online and/or greater use of social media—or whether certain problematic conduct has increased. It may be that people's conception and awareness of 'harassment' or 'abuse' has changed over time, perhaps because of changing community values and/or greater publicity about the issue. Research indicates that reports of online abuse, including child sexual abuse increased following the onset of the COVID-19 pandemic, which may be due to people spending more time online creating more opportunities for abusers (UNICEF, 2020; Salter and Wong, 2021; World Wide Web Foundation, 2020). The Australian eSafety Commissioner, whose brief is to assist Australians to have 'safe and positive experiences online', found that the majority of online abuse reported is directed at women and girls, and 'tended to be more "violent, sexualized, [and] focused on appearance" than that received by men' (Wootton, 2021). The eSafety Commissioner's website refers to international research which 'has pointed to the stark findings that women and girls are subjected to very high levels of online abuse simply because they are women' (eSafety Commisioner, 2021a). Parents' fears about the dangers posed to children by the online environment have been emphasised in media and various policy statements.

While the phenomenon of online abuse and its dimensions is now widely acknowledged, we know little about the *communities* within which conduct deemed to be harmful or abusive arises and how these may be sustained or reinforced online. The dominant legalistic and psychological framing of issues serves to narrow understanding of the wider phenomenon, with attention being largely directed towards perpetrator actions, the victims, and the criminal processes to address harm and/or abuse rather than the online emotional economy that may predispose to such conduct. Recently, efforts have also focused on the Big Tech companies and their responsibilities to police online behaviours. In practice, this has largely involved the use of algorithm-driven mechanisms for detecting and 'blocking' objectionable content. I will discuss these efforts later in the chapter, pointing to limitations of current responses, especially in altering the conditions that predispose to conduct experienced as or judged to be harmful or abusive.

The difficulties in interpreting research on online harms and abuse are mani-
fold but contributed to by the lack of clarity in the use of definitions in academic
discussions and policies. In official statements, the terms used to describe harmful or abusive behaviour are often ill-defined, and the range of conduct labelled
'harm' or 'abuse' is often very broad. Further, descriptions often include a mixture of different criteria to classify phenomena. As I explain, discussions also fail
to clarify whether there is something *distinctive* about the *online environment* that
encourages or changes the character or experiences of harm or abuse, although
this is often implied. While some jurisdictions have specific laws governing
online harm and/or abuse, others do not or the laws are inadequate, although the
phenomenon may in theory be covered by standard laws against the conduct or
threatening conduct. Only a small proportion of complaints about online harm
or abuse result in prosecution (the proportion varying across jurisdictions) often
because the conduct is not judged to be criminal, or police do not act on complaints, or it is difficult to identify perpetrators and obtain evidence (Lyons et al.,
2016). In a report on national responses to online abuse reviewed by Lyons et al.
(2016), the police come under some criticism for often being 'blind' to the issue.
This blindness arguably reflects the limitations of current approaches to regulating online harm and abuse and the reliance on legislation that was largely created
in the pre-digital era. As with 'offline' forms of harms and abuse, approaches to
policing and community perceptions of the police shape citizens' propensity to
report behaviour experienced as harmful or abusive.

Categories and their consequences

The range of online harm and abuse appearing in the literature is extensive,
making it difficult to categorise conduct and hence attribute responsibility and
'blame'. Terminology used to describe harms and abuse varies across context
and time further complicating understanding and developing responses. Forms
of online abuse or harm or potential harm typically identified on eSafety sites
include cyberbullying and harassment; image-based abuse, including shared pornographic images including so-called deepfakes; grooming; and sexting. Other
forms of harm or abuse listed on such sites including trolling, impersonation,
harassment, threats, sextortion (a form of blackmail where someone threatens to
share sexual images of another person unless they give in to their demands), and
advertising in general, or specific types of advertising. These categories may not
be mutually exclusive. These categories may also be broken down according to
various criteria, such as the nature of the conduct, the potential recipient (e.g.
adult or child), and the nature and level of the harm or abuse. For example, the
Australian government's eSafety Commissioner website includes under 'cyber-
bulling' the following behaviours: 'abusive texts and emails; hurtful messages,
images or videos; imitating others online; excluding others online; humiliating
others online; spreading nasty online gossip and chat; creating fake accounts to
trick someone or humiliate them' (eSafety Commissioner, 2021b). Many of these

descriptions refer to subjective phenomena or behaviours that imply intent by an alleged perpetrator that may be difficult to prove.

One category of abuse that has received particular attention in recent years is 'image-based abuse' or 'image-based sexual abuse'. This form of abuse is sometimes called 'revenge pornography', which implies a narrower range of activity undertaken with a specific intent. Implicitly, this form of abuse is assumed to be male-to-female based and involving an intent to exploit and/or to control, hence, not surprisingly, much of the research has been undertaken by feminist scholars. In one recent definition, "imaged-based sexual abuse" refers to the *non-consensual* creating and/or sharing of nude or sexual images (or videos), including *threats* to share images and altered images' (Rackley et al., 2021: 1; emphases added). This reference to 'non-consensual' and the inclusion of 'threats' to share images also arguably adds to complexity, as it calls for determination of intention or being done deliberately with the conscious objective to cause harm. In relation to the type of abuse, legal descriptions place emphasis on gender-based abuse, while also acknowledging the reality of other forms of online abuse, for example, that targeted at those of a particular sexuality, religion, or culture. The eSafety Commissioner conceives image-based abuse as occurring when 'an intimate image or video is shared without the consent of the person pictured', adding that 'This includes images or videos that have been digitally altered (using Photoshop or specialized software)'. According to the description on the eSafety Commissioner's website, an 'intimate image is one that shows: a person's genital area or anal area (whether bare or covered by underwear); a person's breasts (if the person identifies as female, transgender or intersex); private activity (for example a person undressing, using the bathroom, showering, bathing or engaged in sexual activity); a person without attire of religious or cultural significance if they would normally wear such attire in public' (eSafety Commissioner, 2021c).

There are a number of points to note about the above descriptions. First, 'abuse' itself is mostly left undefined or defined in vague terms that are open to various interpretations. For example, on the eSafety website, 'adult cyber abuse' is described as 'behaviour that uses an online service or platform to menace, harass or offend someone' (eSafety Commissioner, 2021d). Nowhere is it specified what constitutes 'menace', 'harass', or 'offend someone'. There is no explanation of how 'adult cyber abuse' differs from cyber abuse that involves children— although one may assume that different standards of responsibility and vulnerability apply. I will return to this issue of children's assumed vulnerability later in the chapter. The categories of abuse listed are broad and include a mix of subjective criteria and actions, for example: 'being ridiculed, insulted or humiliated because of their physical appearance, religion, gender, race, disability, sexual orientation or political beliefs', having their personal contact details made public on social media or other online platforms, 'being threatened online or other people online being encouraged to harm them', and 'being stalked online'. This lack of definitional clarity makes it difficult to determine what is at issue: the range of conduct that is problematic and the manner and extent to which the harm or abuse varies across the population. Being on an official website, the descriptions are an important part of the public discourse on online harm and abuse. Their largely legalistic framing, focusing on risks and 'safety', restricts understanding of the *power relations* underpinning online harm and abuse and likely makes it difficult for those seeking to respond to incidences of such harm or abuse to know how best to respond. These power relations operate at the 'micro' level, between the individual perpetrator/s (very often male) and victim/s (generally female) and 'macro' level, within the society and culture that 'normalises' harmful and abusive conduct. It is important to acknowledge and address the power relations of online abuse to both counter the individualisation and psychologisation of the phenomenon of abuse and acknowledge the community-based and relational aspects of abuse. Those who are subject to abuse may tend to be viewed by others or themselves as 'victims', but it is important to recognise their agency, which widens the options for action beyond those implied by the ascription of a victimhood status.

Second, responsibility for documenting and responding to the harm or abuse lies with the targets of alleged harm or abuse, or their parents and/or guardians/carers. On the above eSafety website advice is provided for young people on 'what to do if you or someone you know is experiencing cyberbullying', advice for parents and carers, 'signs to watch for', and what schools can do. The webpage also includes some video resources including hypothetical scenarios and one on resilience ('The power to bounce back'), and on how to lodge a complaint about cyberbullying to eSafety (eSafety Commissioner, 2021c). Action on image-based abuse also places much of the responsibility for the response on those who are identified as or claim to be victims. The eSafety webpage provides details of a 'civil penalties scheme' explaining that, if one lodges a report, they may receive help in getting the material removed and potentially 'take action against the person who posted, or threatened to post, an intimate image without consent' (eSafety Commissioner, 2021c). The site includes links to how to get help to remove images and video, how to report to eSafety or a social media service or website, and how the police may help. This approach serves to responsibilise users and/or their carers or guardians by making them de facto governors of online decency—and by implication blameworthy in the event of them failing to report such harm or abuse—and shifts accountability from the companies that create the digital infrastructure and processes that predispose to harmful and abusive conduct. I will consider the implications of this responsibilisation later in the chapter.

Finally, information sources rarely make clear whether there is something *distinctive* about the harm or abuse that occurs online what warrants the use of 'online' (or 'cyber') in descriptions. The website stopbullying.gov, managed by the US Department of Health and Human Services, provides a level of detail about this category of abuse that is missing in many of the websites dedicated to eSafety that I reviewed. The definition includes reference to the technologies used to distribute messages or images, the conduct itself, the common settings where it occurs, and the particular concerns raised by the conduct. It describes cyberbullying as 'bullying that takes place over digital devices like cell phones, computers, and tablets … [and] can occur through SMS, Text, and apps, or online in social media, forums, or gaming where people can view, participate in, or share content' (Stopbullying.gov, 2021a). The entry also mentions that it 'includes sending, posting, or sharing negative, harmful, false, or mean content about someone' and 'can include sharing personal or private information about someone else causing embarrassment or humiliation'. It notes that some cyber-bullying 'crosses the line into unlawful or criminal behaviour' (Stopbullying .gov, 2021a). It also identifies 'the most common places where cyberbullying occurs', identifying social media, text messaging and messaging apps on mobile or tablet devices, instant messaging, direct messaging, and online chatting over the internet, online forums, chat rooms, message boards, Reddit, and email. Of particular significance, however, is the comment under 'Special Concerns' that digital content 'can often be viewed by strangers as well as acquaintances', that the content shared online 'creates a kind of permanent public record of their views, activities, and behaviour' and that this can become a kind of 'online repu-tation' accessible to others, including schools, employers, and clubs, 'now and in the future'. The site adds that cyberbullying 'can harm the online reputations of everyone involved—not just the person being bullied, but those doing the bul-lying or participating in it'. Finally, it points to the 'unique concerns' raised by cyberbullying: that it is '**Persistent**', given that 'digital devices offer an ability to immediately and consistently communicate 24 hours a day, so it can be dif-ficult for children experiencing cyberbullying to find relief'; '**Permanent**', with most information communicated online remaining public if not removed and reported, which may impact 'college admissions, employment, and other areas of life'; and '**Hard to Notice**' 'because teachers and parents may not overhear or see cyberbullying taking place' (Stopbullying.gov, 2021a; bold in original).

Is *online* harm and abuse distinctive?

These 'special' or 'unique concerns' in relation to reputational damage would seem to come closest to identifying the factors that make *online* harm and abuse *distinctive* and are worth close inspection. However, I suggest that some of the issues identified may have less to do with uniqueness or distinctiveness than with degree of opportunity for harm or abuse and potential for its concealment. If we unpack each of these concerns in turn, one can see that the distinction between 'online' and 'offline' is less clear than it may first seem. While digital devices do enable 24/7 communication, which for receivers may be relentless if they are unable to exert personal control over their use of media and/or do not have required filters on communications, it is important to acknowledge that 'offline' abuse can also be 'persistent'. This is the case with stalking and many forms of bullying and harassment. Removing oneself from potential harm by not using digital media or limiting one's use is an obvious option—but is it feasible and desirable? For some people, digital media may be the only way to establish connection with others outside their home, especially if they experience chronic illness or severe pain or are immobile. Even if pursuing the option of avoiding or limiting one's use of digital media is feasible, this shifts responsibility on to the individual user and diverts attention from other strategies that focus on the digital ecosystem and/or cultural values that predispose to harm or abuse.

The second concern, permanency, is one shared by many people, perhaps especially parents who worry about their children's future education and work prospects. Special efforts need to be made to remove online information with the onus falling squarely on individual users themselves. Specialist services have arisen to deal with this issue, or one can attempt to do this oneself. However, concealing one's digital footprint is far from straightforward (Ohlheiser, 2017). The concept 'right to be forgotten', whereby the private information of a person can be removed from internet searches, has been put into practice in various jurisdictions, such as the European Union. This is especially important in cases where there is the potential for individuals to suffer stigmatisation because of actions performed in the past, for example, inaccurate claims made by others about one's identity or behaviour. However, in practice, exercising this right is far from straightforward as objections have been voiced about the impacts. Concerns have also been expressed about the infringement on the right to freedom of expression and the devaluing of the internet through censorship and the revision of history (Mayes, 2011). In addition, individual users themselves are required to take the initiative and it is not always easy to delete one's digital footprint. One should acknowledge that non-digital media may also provide a 'permanent' record. Even in a digital age, paper-based records exist in many places and may be distributed in that form or be digitalised to facilitate distribution. However, digital content may be *more widely circulated* than paper records and consequently be *more difficult to locate* and destroy or make anonymous. This is a major concern in that the ability to control the flow of information and images across jurisdictions may be impossible or impractical. Perhaps most worrying is that digital information and images can be *manipulated and combined with other data and used for new purposes*—perhaps many years in the future.

Deepfakes

Permanency is a critical issue in an age of 'deepfakes', whereby videos, images, and audio recordings are manipulated via artificial intelligence to create synthetic representations. Although they are often applicable to faces, for example, the manipulation of facial expressions and speech, they may also involve transposing images, such as of faces and bodies, or face-swapping an individual into a video, to make it appear that a person is engaged in acts or activities in which they were not engaged. Deepfakes may be used for various purposes, including to influence elections and/or to inflict reputational damage, but are of particular concern given their use to abuse women particularly younger women and girls, via the manipulation of images of their bodies to create suggestive poses or to cast them in pornographic activities in which they were not actually involved. Deepfakes can be very realistic, at least on initial viewing or to viewers who are not aware of the telltale signs, such as distortion of facial features, unnatural blinking patterns, incongruities between speech and movements of the subject (Engler, 2021). The pace of development in the technologies that enable their production is rapid, and the tools that enable this manipulation to occur are now freely available online. As noted in Chapter 1, internet users can now access a facial recognition tool called PimEyes, which will allow them to search millions of images from across the internet and find matches with great accuracy, which can then be used to create synthetic representations. In October 2020, *Washington Post* reported that an AI service that was freely available on the web had been used to transform 100,000 images of women into nude photos without their consent, 'triggering fears of a new wave of damaging "deepfakes" that could be used for harassment or blackmail' (Harwell, 2020). According to the article, users of the service were able to anonymously submit a photo of a clothed woman and receive an altered version with their clothes removed. The technology is trained on a large database of nude photos, to create fakes with 'seemingly lifelike accuracy, matching skin tone and swapping breasts and genitalia where clothes once were'. Some of the images were of girls younger than 18. People were also able 'to place new orders through an automated "chatbot" on the encrypted messaging app Telegram' (Harwell, 2020). As noted by the chief executive of Sensity, the cybersecurity start-up that drew the *Washington Post*'s attention to the service, everyone who has an online persona is vulnerable to an attack of this kind. Just by having a social media account and posting photos of oneself and one's life publicly puts one at risk.

In a report on deepfakes, the US-based non-profit public policy organisation, the Brookings Institution (or Brookings), offers a pessimistic assessment of the potential to regulate the practice, given the rapid pace of the technological means to create deepfakes and the lack of societal awareness of the issue. While acknowledging that new algorithm-driven methods are being developed to detect deepfakes—for example, 'to discern if a specific image, audio clip or video has been substantially modified from an original'—the Brookings report concludes that 'these detection methods are likely to be short-lived' (Engler, 2021). The report noted that detection methods failed to keep pace with new means to correct imperfections and were 'difficult to scale' given that the materials could be 'mass-produced and mass-distributed by armies of bots and trolls, as is the case with most disinformation campaigns'. One problem is the AI used to detect the images was similar to that used to make deepfakes, and that 'research on detection inadvertently provides a roadmap for improving the fakes' or could even be used in the deepfake generation process to enhance their output. As the report observes, the rapid pace of AI development, supported by many systemic drivers, including considerable private investment, growing cloud-computing resources, proliferating datasets, and the open-source nature of the field makes 'deepfake supremacy' likely within the next decade. However, while Big Tech companies have made efforts to tackle the issue by developing better detection methods, which use deepfake detection algorithms, these are seen as short-term solutions (Engler, 2021).

Finally, the 'hard to notice' issue identified on the Stopbullying.gov webpage is undoubtedly of major concern to parents, teachers, and guardians such as carers who feel they are unable to exert control over children in their charge. It is noteworthy that the Stopbullying.gov website focuses on children as the vulnerable age group and emphasises the need to raise awareness among 'parents, teachers and other adults' about the apps that a child may be using and alerting them to 'warning signs a child is being cyberbullied or is cyberbullying others' (Stopbullying.gov, 2021b). I will shortly turn to the specific issue of how children are represented in research and policy on online harm and abuse. But I should note here that the issue of 'hard to notice' may apply to adults as well, who may or may not be under the care of guardians. Furthermore, bullying that occurs 'offline' may also be hard to notice, as it is often not seen or heard. Bullying is a complex phenomenon that invariably occurs in subtle ways, in non-public arenas and over time (it is formally defined as 'repeated demeaning behaviour') and is not always limited to two parties (the bully and the target) (Namie and Lutgen-Sandvick, 2010). As Namie and Lutgen-Sandvick argue, bullying may involve accomplices who may be publicly involved or privately participate behind the scenes and they may actively participate in abuse or support bullies by aligning against targets, making determinations in bullies' favour, ostracising the target, and so on (2010: 344). The authors note that when bullying occurs in organisations, managers' responses are also important and contribute to the collective character of the phenomenon, by setting the tone for others and symbolically conveying that the abuse is unimportant or trivial (2010: 344). Harm or abuse may also be contributed to by the wider community which trivialises or turns a 'blind eye' to such conduct or even reacts in a non-supportive manner—as was the case with the dominant conservative white community that reacted to the equity resolution to address online racial abuse, described earlier in this chapter.

This broader perspective on bullying helps shift the focus away from the dominant approach that focuses on behavioural interventions (e.g. 'mediation') that do little to change the cultural and organisational conditions and power relations that predispose to harmful and abusive conduct. In the online context, it also acknowledges that bullying rarely if ever involves just two parties. Indeed, it may be contributed to by *many others*, who may be both 'innocent' bystanders who fail to call out the conduct and those who actively contribute to the harms by offering comments and sharing information and/or images. Yet, there *is* a notable difference between bullying that occurs in physical places, such as organisations, and bullying that occurs online. As noted, in an organisational context, a manager may either intervene to stop abuse or contribute to the abuse by signalling that the behaviour is unimportant or within the bounds of acceptability, perhaps seen as part of the 'cost' of working in a highly competitive environment. But online, there are no 'managers' as such, but rather content moderators for particular media platforms—who often struggle to effectively police content—and the Big Tech companies that have created the technologies underpinning the emotional economy that facilitates harm and abuse.

Children and online abuse

As noted, debates about online harm and abuse often focus on the vulnerability of children. These debates reflect wider fears about the impacts of digital media on children's minds and lives, and efforts to limit children's screen time, for example, in schools. These fears, in turn, echo those of an earlier era in relation to television, as discussed earlier. Government health departments, parenting organisations, and other authorities often package information for parents or guardians pertaining to children of specific age groups, for example preschoolers, school age children, pre-teens, and teens, and sometimes part of a more general package of information on child health or health and well-being. These different ages are represented as presenting different degrees of vulnerability and susceptibility to harm and abuse. With children of school age, the anxieties about digital media are often of a broad character, including the amount of 'screen time', which are often linked to health concerns such as competing with off-screen activities, physical problems such as eye strain, repetitive strain and neck pain, and interruptions to sleep patterns. Much attention, however, is focused on 'online safety' which includes exposure to pornography, grooming, and sexting. The webpage of the Australian organisation raisingchildren.net.au, for example, includes detailed information and advice on these practices, including effects on children, recognising the warning signs of children having been exposed to such material, how to stop children 'accidently' coming across objectionable material online, and how to start conversations with children about the behaviour in question (raisingchildren.net.au, 2021). In this depiction, young children *in general* are portrayed as vulnerable to exposure to such information and in need of preventive and protective action. Adults, mostly parents and teachers, are ascribed responsibility for minimising risks. However, unlike in the pre-digital era when children were posited as mostly *passive* victims of television's manipulating and corrupting influences, in recent debates children are seen as vulnerable as a *consequence* of their *active* engagements with digital media. As I will explain, in some cases this results in children becoming participants in their *own* abuse and in the abuse of siblings and friends by producing and sharing material which may then be consumed by others.

COVID-19 and 'self-generated' abuse

While concerns about the online abuse of children have paralleled the rise of the internet and then social media, they heightened during the COVID-19 pandemic as many children in many countries began to spend more time online. In 2020, the Internet Watch Foundation, a UK-based charity dedicated to 'mak[ing] the internet a safer place, by identifying and removing global online child sexual abuse imagery', announced that it had processed a record number of reports on online child sexual abuse during 2020, up 50 percent on the previous year, corresponding with the lockdowns (IWF, 2020a). A report on the IWF website also notes that the increase occurred predominantly in March 2020, corresponding with the commencement of many lockdowns (IWF, 2021a). The IWF also observed 'a dramatic 77% increase in the amount of "self-generated" abuse material as more children, and more criminals, spend longer online in 2020' (IWF, 2021a). IWF's research showed that 'in the first six months of 2020, 44 percent of child sexual abuse content … involved *self-generated* material' (my emphasis). The website noted that 'In some cases, children are groomed, deceived or extorted into producing and sharing a sexual image or video of themselves', although no evidence is provided to support this particular claim. This self-generated content was up 15 percent on the year before, when almost a third of the 132,676 pages actioned, contained self-generated imagery' (IWF, 2020b). The website reported that this imagery 'can include child sexual abuse content, created using webcams, sometimes in the child's own room, and then shared online'. It was noted that some of this content was Category A material, meaning that it was the 'most severe level of abuse which includes penetrative sexual activity' (IWF, 2020b).

In response to these findings, in November 2020, it was announced that 'A national enquiry into "disturbing" increases of *self-generated* child sexual abuse images has been launched amid warnings of online communities "devoted" to contacting the grooming children' (UK Safer Internet Centre, 2021). In announcing this inquiry, which was claimed to be the first of its kind, it was noted that 'In some cases, children are coerced, deceived or extorted into producing and sharing a sexual image or video of themselves' and that 'In many cases this goes on without the victims' parents' or guardians' knowledge'. An internet content analyst at IWF warned about 'online communities' who were seeking to contact children via the internet so that they could coerce and groom them. These communities, he said, were not just looking for child sexual abuse content but were trying to find the victims themselves 'because they want to be ones to have them perform these sexual acts live'. As part of its investigations, the inquiry hoped to hear from teachers, parents, guardians, charities, and NGOs that work in the area, and also 'engage children and young people themselves to better understand the issues they face online'. It will then make recommendations to government and parliament about the action needed to regulate the online environment and improve education and awareness initiatives (UK Safer Internet Centre, 2021).

In March 2021, the IWF announced another study it had undertaken, which found that 'sex predators are manipulating children to record their own sexual abuse, and that of their friends and siblings' and that the '"disturbing" trend is eight times worse than the experts had feared' (IWF, 2021b). The study undertaken by the IWF involved an analysis of images and videos appearing online between 28 September and 23 December 2020. It found that 511 self-generated child sexual abuse images and videos assessed in this period involved siblings and that 'In 65 percent of cases, one or both children engaged in direct sexual conduct with the other'. The children were aged 3 years old to 16 years old, with the average age of the youngest sibling being 10 to 12 years old. While it was acknowledged that 'it is not easy to say with certainty whether the children are related', IWF's analysts assessed the content as '*likely* to involve siblings' (IWF, 2021b; emphasis in original). The material was then scrutinised by the quality assurance team to judge whether the children could be related, using criteria such as 'the similarity of their appearance, their environment, their behaviour towards each other, and where observed, and their conversation and the kind of language they used' (IWF, 2021b). The researchers reported that they saw evidence which led them to believe that some of the adults were posing as children. Children were observed reading comments, often getting close to the screen and reading aloud, and what were seen as probable instructions. The abuse sometimes took the form of a 'dare' game. The researchers observed that parents could sometimes be heard in the background behind closed doors talking or moving around 'just metres away from the children with no apparent knowledge of what was happening to the child' and that 'Some children even quickly stopped the live stream at the call of an adult or knock at the door' (IWF, 2021b).

These observations on online child abuse, and its increased incidence during COVID-19 lockdowns, raise important questions about digital technologies and their role in enabling or facilitating harm and abuse, and about conceptions of children's agency and vulnerability, especially during a period of increased reliance on digital media. Lockdowns have meant that children's lives (like adults') became or have become digital by default and thus considered more at risk of coming across sites, apps, and games used and controlled by online communities that aim to profit from their increased connections. Children's use of the internet—and hence their consequent risk of harm and abuse—is likely to vary according to their ages, interests, nationalities, and cultures. Research undertaken as part of the Global Kids Online project, which aims to develop cross-national evidence of children's use of the internet, indicates that while young people share many similarities in internet use (for information, entertainment, to connect with friends and community), there are also great variations *between* different groups of young people in different countries around the world. The research, a 'rapid evidence review', undertaken in 2020, revealed that what children do rather than how much time online is more important for their outcomes and that their risks increase with their participation in a wider range of activities (Stoilova et al., 2021: 7). As the research made clear, 'vulnerability' is a variable concept: those who have already been victims of one or more forms of harm or abuse are more likely to experience subsequent harm or abuse; older teenagers,

LGBTQI children, and those from lower socio-economic backgrounds are more likely to engage in 'sexting' and be victims of 'sextortion', and other forms of sexual-based violence (2021: 8–9).

Another project, #CovidUnder19, involving a survey of 26,258 children and young people aged 17–18 from 137 countries found (unsurprisingly) large regional differences in *access* to the internet (e.g. 20 percent in Africa versus 86 percent in Europe) and that children relied on social media to keep in contact with family and friends, using WhatsApp (75 percent), Facebook (41 percent), Instagram (33 percent), Snapchat (12 percent), and Text (10 percent). Interestingly, it was noted that 'most children reported feeling safer (14 percent) or as safe (70 percent) online during Coronavirus, 17 percent feeling less safe' (GlobalKidsOnline, 2021). However, as Stoilova et al. note, research on children's views and practices regarding digital media tends to focus on older children in the Global North, while evidence of the pre-teenage years and from countries of the Global South is sparse (2021: 9). As the authors indicate, many questions on children's engagements with digital technologies are yet to be explored. These include: the quality and context of their internet use, the longer-term consequences of children's internet use, children's 'digital ecology' (the nature of their devices, and online platforms, and their policies and services that may facilitate or protect against harm), and the 'cultures of childhood' and how they change online and are experienced by children. The latter includes the question of whether online sexual activities are tolerated or even encouraged because they bring benefits in terms of children's development, despite involving a level of risk (Stoilova et al., 2021). In identifying these gaps in understanding about children's online conduct, the authors show recognition that children do have *agency* and consequently may explore issues online which, in some cases, may be beneficial and use digital media in ways that are more creative and reflective than conveyed by many portrayals of children's digital media use. The issue that also needs to be acknowledged is that, as with harm and abuse involving adults, such as those discussed, Big Tech companies nurture and profit from this agency via their efforts to harvest their attention. Efforts have focused on encouraging Big Tech companies to remove offending material, identifying and punishing perpetrators of abuse, and making parents and teachers responsible for monitoring and restricting children's online behaviours by, for example, limiting their screen time. However, these measures reflect a particular framing of 'the problem' that diverts attention from the operations of the attention economy and how this is sustained and supports communities and cultures that contribute to harm and abuse. The attention economy is oriented to attracting children's attention, the ultimate goal being to generate profit from the harvesting of their data. And, while efforts may be made to limit their 'screen time', these do not address the workings of the online emotional economy that predisposes to abuse and harm. In these final paragraphs then I turn my attention to this economy and aspects of their operations that are generally overlooked in academic discussions and policies on online harm and abuse.

Online abuse, algorithms, and Big Tech

As noted in Chapter 1, the algorithm-driven processes that enable the internet to operate as it does invites or reinforces *extreme* emotions. Algorithms are *programmed* to have this effect by 'guessing' people's interests after tracking what they click on and watch and then using the result to feed them similar content. Ultimately, the aim is to attract and maintain the attention of users so that they can be sent highly targeted and lucrative ads. Algorithms enable images (often faces) to be matched, which may then be used for purposes such as image-based abuse. The instructions for the programs that drive algorithms, however, are 'black boxed' and there is little or no accountability in their use. Substantially altering the algorithms threatens the very viability of the internet and the business models of the Big Tech companies that govern its operations, as I explained in Chapter 2.

In recent years, national regulators have sought to hold Big Tech to account for the workings of their algorithms—or at least wish to be seen to be doing so—and to police and, if necessary, block postings on their social media platforms. Different countries have taken somewhat different approaches, but there have been moves in Europe to harmonise legislation. Germany enacted what has been described as 'one of the toughest laws against online hate speech', in 2017 (Satariano, 2021). Under this legislation, social media organisations such as Facebook/Meta, Twitter, and YouTube are required to remove illegal pictures, videos, and comments within 24 hours or risk heavy fines (Satariano, 2021). However, in 2021, the effectiveness of this legislation was called into question in the run-up to the German election, when far-right groups and others were able to intimidate female candidates. Some critics have argued that the laws lack effective enforcement and oversight, that many of the forms of abuse are not deemed legal by the platforms, which includes certain types of harassment of public officials and women, and that companies often do not alert authorities about posts, making it difficult to prosecute the perpetrators. Moreover, smaller platforms such as Telegram, popular with far-right groups, are not subject to the law (Satariano, 2021). A news article reporting this regulatory shortcoming notes that free-expression groups believe that the law should be abolished, not just because it fails to protect victims of online abuse and harassment, but because it establishes a dangerous precedent for government censorship of the internet (Satariano, 2021). In 2021, other countries in Europe were closely watching Germany's experience since officials from that country were playing a key role in drafting the Digital Services Act, which will require Facebook and other platforms to make greater efforts to address vitriol, misinformation, and illegal content on their sites. Facebook and Google, on the other hand, are reported to be resisting the new rules on the grounds that they provide the police with personal information that violates users' privacy (Satarino, 2021).

In Australia, in March 2022, a parliamentary Select Committee on Social Media and Online Safety released a report of an inquiry into 'the range of online harms that may be faced by Australians on social media and other online platforms, including harmful content or harmful conduct' (Commonwealth of Australia, 2022: xiii). The committee considered evidence on 'the potential impacts of online harms on mental health and wellbeing of Australians'; the role of algorithms in increasing or reducing online harms; platforms' age verification practices and their enforcement; 'the effectiveness and impact of industry measures, including safety features, controls, protections and settings, to keep Australians, particularly children, safe online'; 'the effectiveness and impact of industry measures to give parents the tools they need to make meaningful decisions to keep their children safe online', and other issues relating to the transparency and accountability of technology companies (2022: xiii). The inquiry resulted in 26 recommendations including: that 'the e-Safety Commissioner undertakes research focusing on how broader cultural change can be achieved in online settings'; the establishment of 'an educational and awareness campaign targeted at all Australians, focusing on digital citizenship, civics and respectful online interaction'; the extent to which social media companies prevent 'recidivism and bad actors, pile-ons or volumetric attacks, and harms across multiple platforms'; and better report mechanisms and support for victims ensuring that the latter pays cognisance to 'a variety of audiences such as children, parents/carers, women, people from culturally and linguistically diverse backgrounds, and other relevant vulnerable groups'. Most of the remaining recommendations concern matters such as the need for more research on and review of issues such as the operation of algorithms on different platforms and services and related harms and regulatory standards and reporting mechanisms for technology manufacturers and providers, for example, the setting of default privacy and safety settings (2022: xvii–xxiv). On the face of it, the recommendations seem comprehensive and reflect an acknowledgement of the scope of the problem of online harm. However, Australia's Digital Rights Watch heavily criticised the report arguing that 'cracking down on Big Tech is politically popular', but disrespected media users' rights to privacy, digital security, and democratic participation. In the organisation's view, the report does not grapple with the 'big, systemic issues wrapped up in online safety and social media'. In its submission to the inquiry, it said, it emphasised 'the need to address the underlying business models of the major social media platforms that create and exacerbate online harm, rather than merely focusing on surface level symptoms'. This included the creation of 'privacy regulation that restricts what companies can do with our personal information'. The organisation noted that the 'potent algorithms that amplify content and even manipulate our moods are only possible because these platforms extract vast amounts of personal information'. In its view, data privacy regulation is 'one of the key regulatory tools' required to protect citizens against 'algorithmic harms' (Digital Rights Watch, 2022).

Efforts to control online abuse and harm have intensified in the wake of the COVID-19 pandemic and the so-called infodemic of misinformation and rumours which, it is argued, enable malicious actors to exploit the uncertainties and turmoil of the pandemic to further their goals (Chapter 1). Non-government organisations have also contributed to efforts to curtail the harmful outcomes of algorithm-driven systems. Among these, the US- and UK-based Centre for Countering Digital Hate (CCDH), established in December 2017, is particularly active and well known. Describing itself as 'an international not-for-profit NGO that seeks to disrupt the architecture of online hate and misinformation', the centre has committed itself to disrupting what it describes as a 'digital counter Enlightenment' which through its 'trolling, disinformation and skilled advocacy of their causes has resocialised the offline world for the worse' (CCDH, 2021a). A study undertaken by the Centre in 2020 showed 'how the Instagram algorithm [owned by Facebook/Meta] has been actively pushing radicalizing, extremist misinformation to users' during the first year of the COVID-19 pandemic (CCDH, 2021b: 4).

The report of CCDH's study *Malgorithms: How Instagram's Algorithm Publishes Misinformation and Hate to Millions During a Pandemic* notes that Instagram's algorithms were adjusted in August 2020, to extend users' engagement, which included the feeding of unsolicited content to their streams. After users had exhausted the latest content, Instagram's machine-learning algorithms then identified users' potential interests based on their data and online behaviours and found content of the same variety which it injected into users' feeds. The report suggested that because of the way Instagram's algorithms work, which employ an 'Explore' feature to identify groups of users who share similar interests, as well as other mechanisms (for example, 'Suggested Post') to present recommended content, users were funnelled towards extreme content and towards a path of radicalisation. For the study, the researchers established new Instagram profiles based on the prescribed lists of accounts and recorded instances of misinformation. The findings found that the algorithms provided recommendations for extreme and anti-vaccination content, some of which were linked to 'wellness influencers' and 'leading anti-vaxxers who had been granted "verified" status by Instagram despite being flagged by experts' (CCDH, 2021b: 8). Based on the findings, the report's authors called for the suspension of the algorithm until the company had proven that it can prevent the promotion of harmful information (CCDH, 2021b: 8). They also suggested that spreaders of misinformation should be prevented from gaining 'verified' status, and that algorithmically published content should carry warnings to help 'inoculate' users about the misinformation they may encounter (2021b: 8).

In the face of growing regulatory demands and investigations by NGOs such as the CCDH, Big Tech companies have made *some* efforts—or at least presented themselves as making efforts—to alter the workings of their algorithms as they affect the spread of misinformation. However, the mostly *technologically focused response* has proved ineffective in limiting harmful and abusive content and has been resisted by some groups on the grounds that it restricts users' rights to freedom of expression (Dodds, 2021). In the event, for Facebook/Meta at least, the bulk of the company's budget to fight misinformation and hate speech has been skewed to the United States which, according to a news report published in the *Washington Post* in October 2021, comprises 'less than 10 percent of Facebook's daily users' (Zakrzewski et al., 2021). As the report noted, 84 percent of the company's [Meta's] 'global remit/language coverage' was allocated to America, whereas 'Just 16 percent was earmarked for the "Rest of the World", a cross-continent grouping that included India, France and Italy' (Zakrzewski et al., 2021). Big Tech companies have been called upon to address a problem that they have, in effect, enabled using the same technologies and applying them inequitably across the world—favouring those living in the rich Global North. The ineffectiveness of Big Tech companies' response to tackling the problems they have created was brought to light during the COVID-19 pandemic following resistance to vaccination in the United States, for which social media has been partly blamed. In an article, published in the *Washington Post*, in July 2021, the reporter commented, 'At the heart of the problem are the [social media] companies' content-recommendation algorithms, which are generally *designed* to boost content that engages the most people, regardless of what it is—even conspiracy theories' (De Vynck and Lerman, 2021; emphasis added). An ex-Facebook/Meta product manager, Frances Haugen, testified to a US Senate subcommittee in October 2021 that the crux of the problem is Facebook's and other social media's 'engagement-based ranking', whereby software gives priority to posts based on the number of likes, shares, and comments they generate—and this engagement is created through 'false, divisive and agitating content' (Kang, 2021). This ranking process, it was reported, promoted 'harmful, hyper-engaging content in the US'. Ms Haugen criticised 'Facebook's focus on technology tools to detect vaccine and other misinformation, saying it is "overly reliant on artificial intelligence they themselves say will likely never get more than 10 per cent to 20 per cent of the content"' (Kang, 2021).

There is mounting evidence that some Big Tech companies have been aware of but not acted on their own research showing their algorithms have played in producing harm and abuse. In September 2021, it was announced in the *Washington Post* that Facebook/Meta knew from its own research that teenage girls on Instagram 'reported in large numbers that the app was hurting their body image and mental health', and that its content moderation systems favoured celebrities over the average user, and that a 2018 change to its news newsfeed software 'intended to promote "meaningful interactions" ended up promoting outrageous and divisive political content', but 'didn't tell anyone' (Oremus, 2021). The report was in response to a series, published in *Wall Street Journal*, called Facebook Files, which drew on internal Facebook/Meta documents, whistleblowers who were seeking federal protection, and 'interviews with current and former employees, most of whom have remained anonymous' (Oremus, 2021). The reporter commented that while Facebook/Meta 'employs teams of people to study its own underbelly', it ignored, downplayed, or suppressed the results of their research when it proved awkward or troubling and that the reason for this lay at least partly in the company's organisational structure and culture. As the reporter explained, unlike some rivals, Facebook/Meta weighed decisions about 'impacts on users and society alongside business imperatives such as growth, profit and marketing', using some of the same executives tasked with government lobbying and public relations—which critics argued created a conflict of interest (Oremus, 2021). Facebook/Meta's own research on its 'Like' and 'Share' buttons, for example, revealed that people often used these features in ways that proved harmful, including amplifying toxic content and other effects. According to an August 2019 internal memo, 'several researchers said it was Facebook's "core product mechanics"—meaning the basics of how the product functioned—that had let misinformation and hate speech flourish on the site'. As the memo concluded, 'The mechanics of our platform are not neutral' (Issac, 2021).

In one of the articles in the *Wall Street Journal* series, it was reported that Facebook/Meta had conducted studies into its Instagram photo-sharing app, which is used by 'millions of young users' and repeatedly found that 'Instagram is harmful for a sizeable percentage of them, mostly notably teenage girls' (Wells et al., 2021). As the reporter of this article commented, 'Expanding its base of young users is vital to the company's more than $100 billion in annual revenue, and it doesn't want to jeopardize their engagement with the platform'. Despite Facebook/Meta recognising the dimensions of the problem and the fact that 40 percent of Instagram users were 22 years old and younger, its research showed that 'young users have been shrinking for a decade'. Consequently, efforts were being made to 'win' new young people and to emphasise the positive mental health benefits and to downplay the harms caused by social comparison (Wells et al., 2021). It should be acknowledged that Facebook/Meta subsequently disputed claims made by the *Wall Street Journal*, with the company's vice president of Global Affairs commenting on its website: 'The truth is that research into the impact social media has on people is still relatively nascent and evolving, and social media itself is rapidly changing' and that 'Each study has limitations and caveats, so no single study is going to be conclusive' (Clegg, 2021). However, perhaps more damning than these reports was the aforementioned testimony of Frances Haugen, before a US Senate subcommittee. Haugen said that Facebook had deliberately hidden research on how teenagers felt worse about themselves following the use of its products, and that the company was willing to use hateful content on its site to ensure that users returned (Kang, 2021). She was quoted in an article as saying: 'The company's leadership knows how to make Facebook and Instagram safer but won't make the necessary changes' (Kang, 2021). In a *60 Minutes* interview, Haugen commented, 'Facebook has realized that if they change the algorithm to be safer, people will spend less time on the site, they'll click on less ads, they'll make less money' (Sullivan, 2021).

In October 2021, the *Washington Post* reported that five years earlier, Facebook/Meta had provided its users with five new ways to react to a post in the news feed that added to the iconic 'like' thumbs-up, namely 'love', 'haha', 'wow', 'sad', and 'angry'. The article said that 'Facebook programmed the algorithm that decides what people see in their news feeds to use the reaction emoji as signals to push more emotional and provocative content—including content likely to make them angry' (Merrill and Oremus, 2021). Beginning in 2017, the company's ranking algorithms 'treated emoji reactions as five times more valuable than "likes"', according to internal documents. As the article continued, 'The theory was simple: Posts that prompted lots of reaction emoji tended to keep users more engaged, and keeping users engaged was the key to Facebook's business' (Merrill and Oremus, 2021). However, as the article noted, Facebook/Meta's own researchers noted a 'critical flaw': 'favoring "controversial" posts—including those that make us angry—could open "the door to more spam/abuse/clickbait inadvertently"'. In 2019, they confirmed that the posts that elicited angry reaction emoji were 'disproportionately likely to include misinformation, toxicity and low-quality news'. The article concluded that 'the algorithmic promotion undermined the efforts of Facebook's content moderators and integrity teams, who were fighting an uphill battle against toxic and harmful content' (Merrill and Oremus, 2021).

The case of incel

While some social media companies have sought to ban groups that circulate violent, harmful, or abusive messages, these efforts have been uneven across platforms and of limited effect. A clear example is that of efforts to tackle the activities of the online anti-women subculture, incel (involuntary celibates). Facebook/Meta has not stopped this group using its platform, despite its promulgation of hateful messages, including expressions of white supremacy and Nazism. While many groups are banned as designated 'hateful organisations', as one news report notes, this 'leaderless group' is subject to no such restriction although content that promotes violence or promotes hate based on someone's sex or gender is banned (Hern, 2021). Reddit, which has been home to one of the largest incel communities, has banned 'subreddits' such as r/incels and r/theblackpill for 'violating "sitewide rules regarding violent content"', and volunteer moderators seek to 'enforce a set of rules, which include "be polite, friendly and welcoming", and a strict ban on "any incel references, slang or inference"' (Hern, 2021). Reddit, it was noted, suspended the account of one of its members 'just hours before' undertaking a shooting spree in Plymouth, UK, in August 2021 (Hern, 2021). This led to the deaths of five people (BBC News, 2021). YouTube was one of a number of platforms that were reported to have been 'slower to act'. The shooter had an account with YouTube and 'regularly posted vlog-style videos', which was taken down soon after the shooting, on the basis that it was contrary to the platform's 'offline behaviour' policy (Hern, 2021). This policy is relatively new and it was noted in the article reporting the event that, as recently as 2019, the company had been criticised for failing to take down content from users such as Tommy Robinson, a far-right activist, 'who were careful to only post videos that were within the rules of the platform, even as they more broadly engaged in behaviour that went far beyond what the service would allow'. Despite these actions, incel community remains influential online, and with 'loose or non-existent moderation policies, such as

4chan and 8kun, have sizeable cohorts, and smaller dedicated forums are able to set their own moderation policies' (Hern, 2021).

In a useful summary of the history and shifting ideologies of incel, Hoffman et al. note that since it was established in 1997 by (interestingly) a young woman, the group has fragmented, grown substantially, and become increasingly extreme and misogynistic. Originally a group comprising both men and women which gave individuals an outlet for voicing their frustrations over sexuality and dating, incel developed its own culture which was reflected in its online forums, and particularly the two platforms 4chan founded in 2003, and Reddit, founded in 2005, which encouraged the expression of extremist declarations in order to engender visibility (Hoffman et al., 2020: 566). This served to create a feedback loop of outrageous statements that created a spiral of reactions and responses that concealed their 'true aggressiveness', a behaviour which has been tagged trolling or 'shitposting' (Hoffman et al., 2020: 566). Until less than a decade ago, the authors say, there existed two incel groups, one that continued to support those that were lonely and frustrated and those that were becoming increasingly militant and hostile to women. The more extreme elements of the latter eventually gravitated to another site where the rhetoric and messaging grew increasingly strident, overwhelmingly male-dominated and increasingly aggressive in its use of language and stated goals. As Hoffman et al. explain, in time, new forums proliferated on sites such as 4chan and Reddit and became more extreme and drowned out previous discussions and debate about inceldom, while attracting militants especially from the subreddit r/incels. They note that while Reddit banned this subreddit and a more heavily moderated version called r/braincells in September 2019, forums continued to spread across the platform and 4chan and have migrated to online community gaming forums like Discord or have established dedicated websites like incels.com and incels.net. The authors note that 'Although Reddit has reduced the ability to congregate en masse online, extremist threads regularly surface before getting banned' (Hoffman et al., 2020: 567).

The history of incel illustrates that technologies and online communities co-evolve and are mutually dependent, and that groups espousing hate and violence cannot be constrained by the restrictions imposed by specific platforms. Radicalised communities can shift platforms or establish their own platforms and/or craft their communications in order to avoid algorithmic detection. Research undertaken in 2021 revealed how right-wing extremist groups have been able to rapidly adapt to social media companies' efforts to increase scrutiny and moderation of their content (Bogle, 2021). This research, which was based on an analysis of nine Australian Telegraph channels that shared right-wing extremist content between 1 January 2021 and 15 July 2021, found that the companies' policies that explicitly prohibit the use of their services for hate speech were often unclear and not uniformly enforced. Crucially, the study found that right-wing groups had moved to alternative online content platforms and had been able to use a diverse range of mechanisms to raise funds, including the use of monetisation tools and cryptocurrencies (Bogle, 2021). The very architecture of the internet and the platforms it supports enables this to happen, the result being that Big Tech companies are hamstrung in their efforts to address online harm and abuse. Indeed, these efforts are contrary to their business model which, as noted, is premised on the assumption of being able to 'attract eyeballs' in order to extract value from users' data.

In the UK at least, responses to the harms posed by incel culture have focused on education in schools, such as initiatives to 'tackle the risks from incel culture through the relationships, sex and health education (RSHE) curriculum', as reported in the wake of the mass shooting in Plymouth in August 2021 (Adams et al., 2021). This report said that teachers would be encouraged to incorporate discussion of incel culture within the curriculum and that teachers in Scotland were also undergoing training 'to recognize signs of young people being radicalised by incel ideas' and that Education Scotland would 'hold a video seminar next month on "incel ideology and how it can present on and offline"' (Adams et al., 2021). Interestingly, this report also referred to research commissioned by the Department of Education published in June 2021, which noted 'an increase in the past three to four years in referrals involving extreme right-wing ideologies', although many children 'switched between ideologies, making it difficult to categorise the risk and develop a response to it' (Adams et al., 2021). What has been missing from public discourse has been reference to the operation of the online emotional economy that enables groups like incel to develop their cultures, to raise funds, and to avoid detection by changing sites or accounts, creating new sites, and shifting to different communities.

In a report published by the United Nations in November 2020, it was noted that during the COVID-19 pandemic different violent non-state actors, including terrorists, right-wing extremists, and criminal organisations, had 'maliciously' used social media to advance their objectives (UNICRI, 2020). It was noted that these actors 'had taken advantage of the inherent characteristics of social media and messenger apps, where contents can be uploaded anonymously, instantly, and at no cost' (2020: 15). This included the use of 'internet memes', or visual content containing a phrase, image, or video, to attract followers, which may then spread from person to person via social media and apps. Crucially, the actors also exploit functions and services provided by mainstream social media platforms, including their algorithms which suggest expanding one's network and finding new contacts ('friends'), based on criteria such as education, mutual friends, and work. It was noted that extreme right-wing groups had taken advantage of these algorithms during the pandemic 'to contact "suggested friends" and recruit new members' (UNICRI, 2020: 16). Further, 'As a result, members of the violent extremist groups frequently participate in different forums and groups on social media in an attempt to radicalize individuals and find other groups or individuals with whom they share similar extremist views' (2020: 16). However, this report, like others, focuses mostly on technology options, such as the use of Big Data visualisation to identify the spread of misinformation, AI tools and platforms to detect fake news online, the use of mobile apps and chatbots using fact-checkers oriented to the general public, and web browser extension tools for the general public to verify the reliability of online news sites and influential social media accounts (2020: 18–23). While it is acknowledged that 'technology cannot solve the problem', the report offers no insight into Big Tech companies' role and responsibilities in relation to tackling online violence and harm.

Racist abuse online

The ineffectiveness of Big Tech companies' efforts to stop online abuse is evident with online-based racist abuse. This issue has received a great deal of coverage, especially in the wake of George Floyd's death in May 2020 at the hands of police officer Derek Chauvin and three other officers, and the subsequent Black Lives Matter demonstrations which were held in many countries in its wake. An article appearing in the *New York Times* in 2021 noted repeated failures by social media companies, particularly Facebook, to address racist abuse directed specifically at black soccer players in the UK. In the report, it was claimed that representatives of the organisations of UK soccer who met with Facebook/Meta in May 2019 to discuss the issue felt that the company had given them the 'brush-off', with executives telling them that 'they had many issues to deal with, including content about terrorism and child sex abuse' (Mac and Panja, 2021). In the article, it was noted that Facebook/Meta claimed to be making various efforts to address the issue, including making racist material harder to view on Instagram, its photo-sharing app, and letting 'users hide potentially harassing comments and messages from accounts and messages from accounts that either don't follow or recently followed them'. Instagram's global head of public policy, Karina Newton, was quoted: 'The unfortunate reality is that tackling racism on social media, much like tackling racism in society, is complex'. While the platform had 'made important strides, many of which have been driven by our discussions with groups being targeted with abuse, like the UK football community', company executives 'privately acknowledged that racist speech against English soccer players is likely to continue' (Mac and Panja, 2021).

In February 2021, the Football Association (FA), the governing body for the sport accused Mark Zuckerberg and Jack Dorsey, the CEOs of Meta and Twitter, respectively, of 'inaction' against racial abuse, and 'demanded that the companies block racist and discriminatory content' and implement 'user identity verification so offenders could be rooted out'. But, according to the head of corporate affairs for FA, 'we didn't get a response' (Marc and Panjay, 2021). Then in April of 2021, English soccer organisations, players, and brands instituted a four-day boycott of social media. Details of related demands can be found on the website KickItOut, which includes 'preventive filtering and blocking measures to stop discriminatory abuse being sent or seen', among other measures (KickItOut, 2021). In response, in the same month Facebook announced a privacy setting called Hidden Words, to filter out offensive words, phrases, and images, and Instagram 'began a test' that allowed some users in some countries to flag 'racist language and activity', which 'generated hundreds of reports' (Mac and Panjay, 2021). Following England's loss of the European Championship Final to Italy on 11 July 2021, the *New York Times* article noted, 'racist comments against the players who missed penalty kicks … escalated'. This led to a 'site event' at Facebook/Meta, 'eventually triggering the kind of emergency associated with a major system outage of the site'. Employers of Facebook/Meta had used internal forums to report the appearance of various racist commentary which was met with automated messages indicating that 'the posts did not violate the company's guidelines' (Marc and Panjay, 2021). Following this, a Facebook director reminded workers that the company 'had introduced the Hidden word feature' to filter out offensive words, and that 'It was the players' responsibility to use the feature'. Other executives in the company argued that if the company filtered certain words this might mean that they may be denied access to some important messages. In short, the case showed the company's limited response in not addressing issues regarding its business model by, for example, banning perpetrators of abuse, and/or substantially altering its algorithms to stop abuse, and instead shifting responsibility to the users themselves. It also served to highlight the difficulty of developing algorithms able to detect harmful or abusive comments, with some, such as 'Bro stay in Africa', for example, not violating the automated moderation system (Mac and Panja, 2021).

Racism, like sexism, ageism, and homophobia, is pervasive in society and often enacted in subtle ways. Efforts to tackle it through measures such as those described above are likely to be at best marginally effective and do not address the socio-cultural factors that sustain its practices. The difficulty in tackling this form of online harm and abuse is illustrated by a case, reported in the *Washington Post* in July 2021 involving a 16-year-old 'half-Black' girl, Nevaeh, who was discussed in her Snapchat group by 'mostly White students' at two local schools who held a 'mock slave auction on the social media app, "trading" their Black peers for money'. Navaeh was reported to have been 'sold' by others in the group for one hundred dollars but said 'in the end I was given away for free'. The Snapchat group, who called themselves 'slave trade' also 'saw a student share the messages "all blacks should die" and "let's start another holocaust", according to the screenshots obtained by The Washington Post' (Natanson, 2021). In this case, both Navaeh and members of the black community were subject to denigrating comments. However, efforts to address the abuse laid bare the complex issues at stake. Following the sharing of the messages, a school equity resolution condemned racism and vowed that public schools in the region would better educate its mostly white student body and teaching staff on 'how to live in a diverse country'. This was rejected by the mostly white conservative parents who felt that 'their children are being taught to feel ashamed of their Whiteness—and their country' (Natason, 2021). The article noted that the parents believed that 'the resolution amounts to critical race theory in disguise' (Natason, 2021).

As the case made clear, an entire community—in this case, people from a predominantly (90 percent) white background—may share values and ideologies that make it difficult to address such abuse. While some individuals may be held responsible for distributing messages and/or images, and perhaps even subject to criminal action, their actions may be implicitly supported or even condoned by a wider community as evident through its inaction, the adoption of a defensive posture, the trivialisation of the issue, or the diversion of blame. Technology is clearly a mechanism for reinforcing racism and amplifying the expression of race-based abusive messages or images. However, reliance on technology for addressing racism is bound to be ineffective in the absence of efforts to understand and change the predisposing conditions. This includes a culture that privileges some groups over others according to their perceived biophysical characteristics and a digital ecosystem that extracts profits from this privileging.

Harm, abuse, and the continuous interface

As Jonathan Crary (2014) argues, one of the goals of Facebook/Meta, Google, and other corporate enterprises is to normalise and make indispensable the idea of a continuous interface. He suggests while this is 'not literally seamless' it involves 'a relatively unbroken engagement with illuminated screens of diverse kinds that unremittently demand interest or response' (2014: 75). For Big Tech companies, success is 'measured by the amount of information that can be extracted, accumulated, and used to predict and modify the behaviour of any individual with a digital identity' (2014: 75). During the COVID-19 pandemic, the earnings and power of companies such as Google, Apple, and Microsoft have increased significantly as more people became reliant on the internet and digital devices for business and social connection (Albergotti et al., 2021; Amazon, 2021). Corresponding with the start of the COVID-19 pandemic, eSafety authorities reported an increase in reported negative online experiences, including exposure to serious harms. For example, in Australia in April 2020, the eSafety Commissioner reported on its webpage that 'Since early March, reports to eSafety about online harms have surged' and that 'In certain areas, such as image-based abuse ... they have almost doubled', which was thought to be likely attributed to 'the effect of widespread social lockdown' (eSafety Commissioner, 2021d). The webpage also noted that eSafety's investigations had revealed 'an upswing of coronavirus-related activity in the dark web' and that 'In one forum, paedophiles noted that isolation measures have increased opportunities to contact children remotely and engage their "passion" for sexual abuse via platforms such as YouTube, Instagram and random webchat services' (sSafety Commissioner, 2021d). COVID-19 has provided a kind of experiment for how the continuous interface operates in action, with citizens suddenly made reliant on their digital devices for work, education, and sociality. This has created the ideal conditions for the creation and nurturing of communities that enable the kinds of harm and abuse outlined in this chapter.

Conclusion

As I argued in this chapter, digital media play a critical role in shaping conceptions and experiences of harm and abuse, and official and community responses to the phenomenon. Digital media are perceived to present distinct risks in that they create options for action, including means for creating messages and images that may be easily and widely disseminated, and be persistent and permanent. Yet, the absence of definitional clarity regarding harm and/or abuse combined with a focus on technological quick 'fixes' and behavioural change (typically of users, parents, and guardians) serves to deflect attention from the operation of the platforms that predispose to harm and abuse. As noted, the internet is powered by algorithms that encourage and reinforce the expression of extreme emotions, including outrage and abuse, and provides the means for accessing software that may be used to create and manipulate images in ways that cause harm to some people (Chapter 1). In order to use online platforms 'free of charge', users' are required to consent (through agreeing to the platform's terms of use) to forfeit their personal data that feeds the algorithms that fuel these emotions and assist cultures that harness them to perpetrate harmful and abusive messages and images. As I have previously argued, citizens' relationship to digital technologies may be likened to a Faustian bargain in that what they surrender in order to use the technology, namely personal information, may be much greater than what they receive in exchange (Petersen, 2019). For individual users, the full implications of their pact with the technology provider may either be not fully understood, or only understood after the harms have occurred. This may include harms to themselves, including physical and verbal abuse and related impacts on their emotional health, or to their friends, family members, and own communities.

In Chapter 5, I discuss efforts to address digital media's negative impacts, especially in creating harm and abuse, focusing on the concept of digital wellness, which has gained growing currency in recent years. Before doing so, however, I consider digital media's more *positive* role, namely in engendering sociality and hope. As I have argued, digital media operate in more complex ways than is widely portrayed, namely, as either tools of distraction and/or of abuse or tools of empowerment or sociality. I uncover this complexity in analysing the online dynamics of hopeful discourse. One of the major promises of digital media is to empower users, to control their interactions and futures. In the next chapter, I will explain how digital media are being used both to engender and thwart hope, making reference to the examples of loneliness and the search for stem cell treatments.

References

Adams, R., Quinn, B. and Dodd, V. (2021) 'Teachers in England encouraged to tackle "incel" movement in the classroom', *The Guardian*, 21 August, https://www.theguardian.com/education/2021/aug/20/teachers-given-flexibility-to-tackle-incel-culture-in-lessons (Accessed 23 August 2021).

Albergotti, R., De Vynck, G. and Greene, J. (2021) 'Giants warn of delta disruption', *The Australian Financial Review*, 29 July: 16.

Amazon (2021) 'Amazon.com announces second quarter results', https://s2.q4cdn.com/299287126/files/doc_financials/2021/q2/AMZN-Q2-2021-Earnings-Release.pdf (Accessed 30 July 2021).

AP/Reuters (2021) 'Facebook changes name to Meta to focus on building virtual-reality "metaverse"', *ABC News*, 29 October, https://www.abc.net.au/news/2021-10-29/facebook-rebrands-as-meta-to-harness-virtual-reality-in-future/100578908 (Accessed 29 October 2021).

Ball, M. (2020) 'The metaverse: what it is, where to find it, who will build it, and Fortnite', *MatthewBall.vc*, 13 January, https://www.matthewball.vc/all/themetaverse (Accessed 9 August 2021).

BBC News (2021) 'Plymouth shooting: who were the victims?', https://www.bbc.com/news/uk-58202760 (Accessed 17 August 2021).

Bennett, T. and Wootton, H. (2021) 'Banks bolster frontline teams to tackle domestic violence', *The Australian Financial Review*, 9 September: 3.

Bogle, A. (2021) 'Buying and selling extremism: new funding opportunities in the right-wing extremist online ecosystem', *Policy Brief Report No. 49/2021*. Published August. Australian Strategic Policy Institute and International Cyber Policy Centre.

Centre for Countering Digital Hate (2021a) 'About CCDH', https://www.counterhate.com/about-us (Accessed 3 August 2021).

Centre for Countering Digital Hate (2021b) *Malgorithm: How Instagram's Algorithm Publishes Misinformation and Hate to Millions During a Pandemic.* https://252f2edd-1c8b-49f5-9bb2-cb57bb47e4ba.filesusr.com/ugd/f4d9b9_89ed644926aa4477a442b55afbeac00e.pdf (Accessed 29 August 2022).

Clegg, N. (2021) 'What the wall street journal got wrong', *Facebook*, https://about.fb.com/news/2021/09/what-the-wall-street-journal-got-wrong/ (Accessed 20 September 2021).

Commonwealth of Australia (2022) 'Social media and online safety', *House of Representatives Select Committee on Social Media and Online Safety*, March 2022, https://parlinfo.aph.gov.au/parlInfo/download/committees/reportrep/024877/toc_pdf/SocialMediaandOnlineSafety.pdf;fileType=application%2Fpdf (Accessed 3 June 2022).

Crary, J. (2014) *24/7: Late Capitalism and the Ends of Sleep.* Verso, London and New York.

De Vynck, G. and Lerman, R. (2021) 'Facebook and YouTube spent a year fighting covid misinformation. It's still spreading', *The Washington Post*, 22 July, https://www.washingtonpost.com/technology/2021/07/22/facebook-youtube-vaccine-misinformation/?utm_campaign=wp_post_most&utm_medium=email&utm_source=newsletter&wpisrc=nl_most&carta-url=https%3A%2F%2Fs2.washingtonpost.com%2Fcar-ln-tr%2F343a3df%2F60fc368f9d2fda945a15e117%2F5e86729bade4e21f59b210ef%2F50%2F70%2F60fc368f9d2fda945a15e117 (Accessed 28 July 2021).

Digital Rights Watch (2022) 'Why the online safety inquiry falls short (and why it matters)', 22 March, https://digitalrightswatch.org.au/2022/03/22/online-safety-inquiry-falls-short/ (Accessed 3 June 2022).

Dodds, I. (2021) 'Facebook hate speech controls violated rights, German court rules', *The Australian Financial Review*, 31 July–1 August: 13.

Eisenbrand, R. and Peterson, S. (2020) 'Metaverse—the full story behind the hottest buzzwork in the tech scene', *OMR*, September, https://omr.com/en/metaverse-snow-crash/ (Accessed 9 August 2021).

Engler, A. (2021) 'Fighting deepfakes when detection fails', 14 November, https://www.brookings.edu/research/fighting-deepfakes-when-detection-fails/ (Accessed 4 August 2021).

eSafety Commissioner (2021a) 'Know the facts about women online', https://www.esafety.gov.au/women/know-facts-about-women-online (Accessed 8 September 2021).

eSafety Commissioner (2021b) 'Cyberbullying', https://www.esafety.gov.au/key-issues/cyberbullying (Accessed 16 July 2021).

eSafety Commissioner (2021c) 'Image-based abuse', https://www.esafety.gov.au/key-issues/image-based-abuse (Accessed 16 July 2021).

eSafety Commissioner (2021d) 'COVID-19: online risks, reporting and response', https://www.esafety.gov.au/about-us/blog/covid-19-online-risks-reporting-and-response (Accessed 5 August 2021).

Fromm, E. (2010; orig. 1968) *The Revolution of Hope: Toward a Humanized Technology.* American Mental Health Foundation Books, New York.

GlobalKidsOnline (2021) 'Children globally rely on the internet during Covid19', http://globalkidsonline.net/covidunder19-summit/ (Accessed 9 August 2021)

Harwell, D. (2020) 'A shadowy AI service has transformed thousands of women's photos into fake nudes: "Make fantasy a reality"', *The Washington Post*, 20 October, https://www.washingtonpost.com/technology/2020/10/20/deep-fake-nudes/ (Accessed 4 August 2021).

Hern, A. (2021) 'Social networks struggle to crack down on "incel" movement', *The Guardian*, 17 August, https://www.theguardian.com/media/2021/aug/16/social-networks-struggle-to-crack-down-on-incel-movement (Accessed 17 August 2021).

Hoffman, B., Ware, J. and Shapiro, E. (2020) 'Assessing the threat of incel violence', *Studies of Conflict and Terrorism*, 43, 7: 565–587.

Internet Watch Foundation (2021a) '"Grave threat" to children from predatory internet groomers as online child sexual abuse material soars to record levels', https://www.iwf.org.uk/news/%E2%80%98grave-threat%E2%80%99-children-predatory-internet-groomers-online-child-sexual-abuse-material-soars (Accessed 9 August 2021).

Internet Watch Foundation (2021b) '"Beyond heartbreaking" abuse as predators groom children to film siblings and friends', https://www.iwf.org.uk/news/%E2%80%98beyond-heart-breaking%E2%80%99-abuse-predators-groom-children-film-siblings-and-friends (Accessed 9 August 2021).

Internet Watch Foundation (2020a) '"Definite jump" as hotline sees 50% increase in public reports of online child sexual abuse during lockdown', https://www.iwf.org.uk/news/%E2%80%98definite-jump%E2%80%99-as-hotline-sees-50-increase-public-reports-of-online-child-sexual-abuse-during (Accessed 9 August 2021).

Internet Watch Foundation (2020b) '"Disturbing" rise in videos of children who have been groomed into filming their own abuse', https://www.iwf.org.uk/news/%E2%80%98disturbing%E2%80%99-rise-videos-of-children-who-have-been-groomed-into-filming-their-own-abuse (Accessed 9 August 2021).

Issac, M. (2021) 'Facebook wrestles with the features it used to define social networking', *The New York Times*, 25 October, https://www.nytimes.com/2021/10/25/technology/facebook-like-share-buttons.html?campaign_id=2&emc=edit_th_20211026&instance_id=43774&nl=todaysheadlines&regi_id=70510057&segment_id=72645&user_id=555b6d42a9884517ab975c86bed7dee1 (Accessed 29 October 2021).

Kang, C. (2021) 'Facebook "gets kids hooked, trades on hate"', *The Australian Financial Review*, 7 October: 11.

KickItOut (2021) '#STOPONLINEABUSE', https://www.kickitout.org/news/stoponlineabuse (Accessed 16 August 2021).

Lyons, K., Phillips, T., Walker, S., Henley, J., Farrell, P. and Carpenter, M. (2016) 'Online abuse: how different countries deal with it', *The Guardian*, 12 April, https://amp.theguardian.com/technology/2016/apr/12/online-abuse-how-harrassment-revenge-pornography-different-countries-deal-with-it (Accessed 27 July 2021).

Mac, R. and Panja, T. (2021) 'How facebook failed to stem racist abuse of England's soccer players', *The New York Times*, 11 August, https://www.nytimes.com/2021/08/11/technology/facebook-soccer-racism.html (Accessed 16 August 2021).

Mayes, T. (2011) 'We have no right to be forgotten online', *The Guardian*, 19 March, https://www.theguardian.com/commentisfree/libertycentral/2011/mar/18/forgotten-online-european-union-law-internet (Accessed 28 July 2021).

McLuhan, M. and Fiore, Q. (1967) *The Medium is the Massage: An Inventory of Effects*. Gingko Press, Corte Madera.

Merrill, J. B. and Oremus, W. (2021) 'Five points for anger, one for a "like": how facebook's formula fostered rage and misinformation', *The Washington Post*, 28 October, https://www.washingtonpost.com/technology/2021/10/26/facebook-angry-emoji-algorithm/ (Accessed 28 October 2021).

Namie, G. and Lutgen-Sandvik, P. E. (2010) 'Active and passive accompices: the communal character of workplace bullying', *International Journal of Communication*, 4: 343–373.

Natanson, H. (2021) 'It started with a mock "slave trade' and a school resolution against racism. Now a war over critical race theory is tearing this small town apart.', *The Washington Post*, 24 July, https://www.washingtonpost.com/local/education/mock-slave-trade-critical-race-theory/2021/07/23/b4372c36-e9a8-11eb-ba5d-55d3b5ffcaf1_story.html?utm_campaign=wp_post_most&utm_medium=email&utm_source=newsletter&wpisrc=nl_most&carta-url=https%3A%2F%2Fs2.washingtonpost.com%2Fcar-ln-tr%2F343d6e2%2F60fedcf59d2fda945a1931e5%2F5e86729bade4e21f59b210ef%2F8%2F70%2F60fedcf59d2fda945a1931e5 (Accessed 30 July 2021).

Ohlheiser, A. (2017) 'Erasing yourself from the internet is nearly impossible. But here's how your can try', *The Washington Post*, 10 February, https://www.washingtonpost.com/news/the-intersect/wp/2017/02/10/erasing-yourself-from-the-internet-is-nearly-impossible-but-heres-how-you-can-try/ (Accessed 28 July 2021).

Oremus, W. (2021) 'Facebook keeps researching its own harms—and burying the findings', *The Washington Post*, 16 September, https://www.washingtonpost.com/technology/2021/09/16/facebook-files-internal-research-harms/ (Accessed 17 September 2021).

Petersen, A. (2019) *Digital Health and Technological Promise*. Routledge, Abingdon and New York.

Pew Research Centre (2021a) 'The state of online harassment', https://www.pewresearch.org/internet/2021/01/13/the-state-of-online-harassment/ (Accessed 17 September 2021).

Pew Research Centre (2021b) 'Online harassment occurs most often on social media, but strikes other places, too', https://www.pewresearch.org/fact-tank/2021/02/16/online-harassment-occurs-most-often-on-social-media-but-strikes-in-other-places-too/ (Accessed 17 September).

Postman (2005; orig. 1985) *Amusing Ourselves To Death: Public Discourse in the Age of Show Business*. Penguin, New York.

Rackley, E., McGlynn, C., Johnson, K., Henry, N., Gavey, N., Flynn, A. and Powell, A. (2021) 'Seeking justice and redress for victim-survivors of imaged-based sexual abuse', *Feminist Legal Studies*, https://doi.org/10.1007/s10691-021-09460-8.

Raisingchildren.net.au (2021) 'School age: play, media and technology', https://raisingchildren.net.au/school-age/play-media-technology (Accessed 6 August 2021).

Salter, M. and Wong, W.K.T. (2021) 'The impact of COVID-19 on the risk of online child sexual exploitation and the implications for child protection and policing', *Research Report*, May, https://www.end-violence.org/sites/default/files/paragraphs/download/esafety%20OCSE%20report%20-%20salter%20and%20wong.pdf (Accessed 8 September 2021).

Satariano, A. (2021) 'An experiment to stop online abuse falls short in Germany', *The New York Times*, 23 September, https://www.nytimes.com/2021/09/23/technology/online-hate-speech-germany.html (Accessed 27 September 2021).

Stoilova, M., Livingstone, S. and Kharzbak, R. (2021) 'Investigating risks and opportunities for children in a digital world: a rapid review of the evidence on children's internet use and outcomes', *Innocenti Discussion Paper*, February 2021, https://www.unicef-irc.org/publications/pdf/Investigating-Risks-and-Opportunities-for-Children-in-a-Digital-World.pdf (Accessed 9 August 2021).

Stopbullying.gov (2021a) 'What is cyberbullying?' https://www.stopbullying.gov/cyberbullying/what-is-it (Accessed 22 July 2021).

Stopbullying.gov (2021b) 'Prevent cyberbullying', https://www.stopbullying.gov/cyberbullying/prevention (Accessed 4 August 2021).

Sullivan, M. (2021) 'Facebook is harming our society. Here's a radical solution for reigning it in', *The Washington Post*, 5 October, https://www.washingtonpost.com/lifestyle/media/media-sullivan-facebook-whistleblower-haugen/2021/10/04/3461c62e-2535-11ec-8831-a31e7b3de188_story.html?utm_campaign=wp_post_most&utm_medium=email&utm_source=newsletter&wpisrc=nl_most&carta-url=https%3A%2F%2Fs2.washingtonpost.com%2Fcar-ln-tr%2F34e1a9a%2F615c77ec9d2fda9d41fde1ff%2F5e86729bade4e21f59b210ef%2F26%2F74%2F615c77ec9d2fda9d41fde1ff (Accessed 8 October 2021).

UK Safer Internet Centre (2021) 'New national inquiry into "disturbing" rise of "self-generated" child sexual abuse material', https://www.saferinternet.org.uk/blog/new-national-inquiry-%E2%80%98disturbing%E2%80%99-rise-%E2%80%98self-generated%E2%80%99-child-sexual-abuse-material (Accessed 9 August 2021).

UNICEF (2020) 'Children at increased risk of harm online during global COVID-19 pandemic—UNICEF', 15 April, https://www.unicef.org/southafrica/press-releases/children-increased-risk-harm-online-during-global-covid-19-pandemic-unicef (Accessed 8 September 2021).

United Nations Interregional Crime and Justice Research Institute (2020) *Stop the Virus of Disinformation: The Risk of Malicious Use of Social Media During COVID-19 and the Technology Options to Fight It.* UNICRI, Torino, Italy.

Vaux-Montagny, N. (2021) 'Teenagers on trial for online abuse did it for laughs, subscribers', *The Sydney Morning Herald*, 23 June, https://www.smh.com.au/world/europe/teenagers-on-trial-for-online-abuse-did-if-for-laughs-subscribers-20210623-p583hu.html (Accessed 16 July 2021).

Wagner, K. (2021) 'Zukerberg says facebook's future lies in virtual "metaverse"', *Bloomberg Technology*, 29 July, https://www.bloomberg.com/news/articles/2021-07-29/mark-zuckerberg-explains-metaverse-vision-to-facebook-fb-investors-analysts (Accessed 2 August 2021).

Wells, G., Horwitz, J. and Seetharaman, D. (2021) 'The facebook files: facebook knows instagram is toxic for teen girls, its research shows', *The Wall Street Journal*, 15 September: A1.

Wootton, H. (2021) 'Victims failed by 'broken system': judge', *The Australian Financial Review*, 8 September: 3.

World Wide Web Foundation (2020) 'There's a pandemic of online violence against women and girls', 14 July, https://webfoundation.org/2020/07/theres-a-pandemic -of-online-violence-against-women-and-girls/ (Accessed 8 September 2021).

Zakrzewski, C., De Vynch, G., Masih, N. and Mahtani, S. (2021) 'How facebook neglected the rest of the world, fueling hate speech and violence in India', *The Washington Post*, 24 October, https://www.washingtonpost.com/technology/2021 /10/24/india-facebook-misinformation-hate-speech/?utm_campaign=wp_post _most&utm_medium=email&utm_source=newsletter&wpisrc=nl_most&carta-url =https%3A%2F%2Fs2.washingtonpost.com%2Fcar-ln-tr%2F3514e8a%2F61757f579 d2fda9d4121ca8d%2F5e86729bade4e21f59b210ef%2F8%2F72%2F61757f579d2fd a9d4121ca8d (Accessed 27 October 2021).

Zuboff, S. (2019) *The Age of Surveillance Capitalism: The Fight for a Human Future At the New Frontier of Power*. Profile Books Ltd, London.

4

HOPE ONLINE

Writing more than a decade before the launch of the World Wide Web, Starr Roxanne Hiltz and Murray Turoff predicted that in the future 'We will become the Network Nation, exchanging vast amounts of both information and social-emotional communications with colleagues, friends, and "strangers" who share similar interests, who are spread out all over the nation' (Hiltz and Turoff, 1978: 33). The authors' observations on the future networking possibilities of 'computer-mediated communications' seem prescient today. However, in the 1970s and 1980s, many computer scientists aimed to create collective intelligence and new network communities, which reflected the forms of sociability they were experiencing in their work and personal lives (Flichy, 2004). The choices they made regarding the use of their innovations were built into their technical design. According to Patrice Flichy, these early scientists were not only technology innovators but also *social innovators* who were part of a rapidly changing society where the first signs of 'connected individualism' were becoming evident (2004: 14). Their optimism carried through to the 1990s to the designers of the World Wide Web, such as Tim Berners-Lee, who has commented: 'The World Wide Web was originally designed as an interactive mode of shared information that people could exchange with one another and with their machines' (Flichy, 2004). When the World Wide Web browser was released to the public in August 1991, Berners-Lee sought to create a 'single global information space' that would empower users and unite populations around the world (Keen, 2015: 31). He and other computer scientists and entrepreneurs at the time saw their invention as an inclusive, democratising tool, that should and would in time be available to everyone. The vision included 'bottom-up design', unlimited access to the world's information, freedom from indiscriminate censorship and surveillance, and the promotion of universality with anyone able to publish anything on the internet (World Wide Web Foundation, 2021a). This vision was, in short, utopian.

DOI: 10.4324/9781003147435-4

Despite delivering many personal and social benefits, including enabling new forms of activism and helping efforts to find solutions to pervasive problems, the internet has fallen well short of the inventors' stated aspirations (Keen, 2015). As Keen observes, the internet was founded by 'naïve entrepreneurs' who shared the libertarian view that their invention would constitute 'a diverse, transparent and egalitarian place—a place that eschews tradition and democratizes social and economic opportunity' (Keen, 2015: 6). This view, he says, 'is common in Silicon Valley, where doing good and becoming rich are seen as indistinguishable and where disruptive companies like Google, Facebook and Uber are celebrated for their supposedly public-spirited destruction of archaic rules and institutions' (2015: 6). Instead, the internet had created new divides, new elites, new markets, and a new economy—in short, a new kind of capitalism that is 'anything but a cooperative venture' (2015: 33).

This chapter examines the hopes that have underpinned the development of digital media and that shape online behaviours. The technologies, systems, and practices of the internet comprise a political economy of hope that is sustained by many actors who hold often markedly different objectives and visions of the future. Despite holding diverse objectives and visions, however, they are largely united in their belief that digital media *will* enable meaningful social connections and provide the means for individuals to fulfil their aspirations. Yet for many users their online experiences often fall far short of their hopes for various reasons, including uncertainty about who and what to trust online, incursions on privacy, deception, and encountering harmful or abusive messages (Chapter 3). In what follows, I discuss the dynamics of the online hope economy, drawing on my own and other recent research on the role of digital media in addressing loneliness and in sustaining the market for clinically unproven treatments. In doing so, I aim to highlight the ways in which hope is bound up with visions of what digital media can offer and how this may create conditions that are far from 'empowering' for users and their communities. To begin, I should first clarify the concept of hope and its significance within the online emotional economy.

Hope and the online emotional economy

Hope is a complex emotion comprising a mixture of belief and expectation, as reflected in its formal definition: 'to want something to happen or to be true, and usually have a good reason to think that it might' (Cambridge Dictionary, 2021). While dictionary definitions provide a useful starting point for discussion, they are limited in implying that meanings are fixed and settled. Conceptions of hope vary through time and across contexts and are shaped by the dominant frameworks of knowledge. In the contemporary period, this knowledge is contributed largely by psychology, psychotherapy, and biomedicine, which has restricted understanding of the hope emotion's profound political significance (Petersen, 2015: 8–9). While different disciplines offer different conceptions of hope, there is general agreement on its *prospective* and *motivational* significance.

'Holding hope' conveys the belief that something *can* be done to improve one's current circumstance. In clinical practice, for example, health practitioners often seek to 'instil hope' in patients which is believed to positively impact the course of their recovery (Groopman, 2005). The opposite of hope is despair, or the belief that 'nothing can be done', which may lead to passivity or acceptance of one's current circumstances.

In the history of Western societies, one can identify a broad shift from a premodern, religious conception of hope linked to faith to a modern, secular, materialist conception linked to science and technology (Petersen, 2015: 35–42). The period of advanced liberalism or neoliberalism, beginning about 1980, has been dominated by an individualistic, strongly therapeutic conception of hope, involving strong belief in the empowerment and freedoms afforded by tech-nologies—particularly those that promote self-care and autonomy in different spheres of life (2015: 42–44). It is worth noting that the literature on hope from the late 1980s has been contributed largely by positive psychology and the work of writers such as Charles R. Snyder and his colleagues, who focused on hope as a cognition, namely, 'a positive motivational state' that is 'goal directed' (e.g. Snyder et al., 1991). Positive psychologists see themselves as part of a 'move-ment' focused on investigating the role of positive personal traits, such as future-mindedness, capacity for love and vocation, courage, and so on, which are seen as congruent with the promotion of civic virtues and the development of insti-tutions that support better citizenship: moderation, tolerance, altruism, and the inculcation of a strong work ethic (Seligman, 2002). This subfield of psychology has found favour among many policymakers in the United States, Australia, and other countries and is fully congruent with neoliberal philosophies and policies that aim to advance the personal qualities of entrepreneurialism, self-promotion, and self-care. Research generated by positive psychology has found application in policies and programs oriented to advancing 'subjective wellbeing' (Petersen, 2015: 45–46).

Digital technologies are archetype technologies of hope. They promise to liberate their users from the constraints of their physical and social environments and annihilate differences of time. This is perhaps most evident in contemporary healthcare where digital media are widely endorsed as technologies of health optimisation, risk management, and self-care (Petersen, 2019). Digital media offer users novel affordances or options to do things that they would otherwise be unable to do, or to do them more easily: connect with others, create public identities (personal profiles), forge new communities or further develop existing communities, generate their own forms of knowledge, self-track their move-ments through time and space, self-monitor their level of health and fitness, and undertake activist or advocacy pursuits of various kinds—for example, online crowdsourcing for funds and lobbying for changes in policy. Employing one or more of the various digital platforms available to them, users can create and pro-mote desired identities to accumulate the cultural and symbolic capital that con-tributes to social distinction and/or the accumulation of economic capital. The social influencer epitomises the idealised digital media-enabled 'empowerment' (Chapter 2). Digital media enable or facilitate forms of sociality founded on shared interests, goals, and experiences that provide the basis for emotional communities such as those formed by the chronically ill, people living with disabilities, informal carers, and lonely people, and/or their representative organisations. Within these communities, individuals exchange stories of illness, hardship, and recovery and work with others to fulfil their individual and collective hopes. In using these media, individuals often combine science-based knowledge and lay knowledge and became 'evidence-based activists' (Rabeharisoa et al., 2014).

Yet, while digital media technologies may appear to 'empower' their users, at least in a limited sense, their interactions occur in a complex ecosystem of ever-shifting relations of power (Chapter 1). The affordances that media offer users may be exploited by various state or non-state actors for political or financial ends. Some actors employ digital media to promulgate non-science-based views on health and medicine and to challenge credentialled expertise, as has been evident during the COVID-19 pandemic—the so-called infodemic referred to earlier (Chapters 1 and 3). In the online environment, hope is exploited via advertising that promotes products that promise to transform consumers' lives. As noted earlier, advertisers make extensive use of techniques to harness and manipulate people's emotions to sell products and services. The advent of digital advertising is seen to provide a depth of emotional engagement with audiences that is not achievable with older so-called legacy media. The potential for manipulation and exploitation inherent in internet-based communications was brought into sharp relief during the COVID-19 pandemic.

The COVID-19 pandemic and beyond

The COVID-19 pandemic increased reliance on and optimism for digital media—especially their potential to help manage risk and to sustain work and social connections during lockdowns and other restrictions—and served as the means to share messages of hope. At the same time, this increased reliance on digital media heightened fears about data harvesting, intrusions on privacy, online harms and abuse, the circulation of 'misinformation', rumours, and conspiracy theories, and the creation or worsening of social divisions (Chapter 3). A survey undertaken by the US Pew Research Centre between 30 June and 27 July 2020 (during the first year of the pandemic), with 915 technology innovators and developers, business and policy leaders, researchers and activists found that the 'broad and nearly universal view is that people's relationship with technology will deepen as larger segments of the population come to rely more on digital connections for work, education, healthcare, daily commercial transactions and essential social interactions'. Some referred to this as the 'tele-everything' world (Anderson et al., 2021). Assessments of this increased reliance on technology were mixed. Negative developments cited included worsening inequality 'as the tech-savvy pull ahead of those who have less access to digital tools and less training or aptitude for exploiting them and as technological change eliminates some jobs'; enhanced power of Big Tech firms as they exploit their market advantages and use of AI 'in ways that seem likely to further erode the privacy and autonomy of their users'; and the growing spread of misinformation 'as authoritarians and polarized populations wage warring information campaigns against their foes'. Many respondents also foresaw 'unstoppable manipulation of public perception, emotion and action via online disinformation—lies and hate speech deliberately weaponized in order to propagate destructive biases and fears'. One concern voiced was 'significant damage to social stability and cohesion and the reduced likelihood of rational deliberation and evidence-based policy-making' (Anderson et al., 2021: 3).

Despite expressing these concerns, the Pew survey respondents were hopeful that changes induced by the COVID-19 pandemic *will* deliver many benefits, including technology enhancements in AI and augmented and virtual reality which would 'allow people to live smarter, safer and more productive lives, enabled in many cases by "smart systems" in such key areas as healthcare, education and community living' (Anderson et al., 2021: 4). When asked for their views on what the 'new normal' might look like in 2025, respondents' views were divided, with 47 percent saying that life will be 'mostly worse' for most people than it was before the pandemic, and 39 percent saying that it will be 'mostly better' than pre-pandemic. Another 14 percent said that they did not see people's lives in 2025 being much different in that year from how they were before the pandemic (2021: 4). As the authors of the report note, the study was undertaken before the 2020 presidential elections and before COVID-19 vaccines had been approved—events which may have affected the findings.

The mixed assessments of respondents in this report—which is based on only a snapshot of views—reflect the ambivalence that typically surrounds technologies, discussed earlier, but which may have been exacerbated by pandemic-induced lockdowns and other restrictions. This ambivalence is reflected in a growing 'techlash', resulting from people's disillusionment with the online environment, especially Big Tech's data-harvesting practices and intrusions on privacy and their failure to tackle the dissemination of fake news, misinformation, and the various forms of online abuse described in the last chapter. Yet, while Big Tech companies seem to have made some effort to address these concerns, as explained in Chapter 3, they have been reluctant to substantially change the algorithm-driven systems that underpin the attention economy. These tensions, I suggest, will likely intensify as digital media technologies come to play an increasing role in people's lives in the post-COVID-19 future, with more individuals working at home, the development of hybrid working patterns, the rapid advance of new tracking and surveillance devices, such as QR codes, and vaccination passports and certificates, the mainstreaming of digital technologies in medicine and healthcare, and the growing use of virtual and augmented reality.

In October 2021, Mark Zuckerberg announced that Facebook was rebranding as Meta, underpinned by his vision of the totally immersive experience of the metaverse, a science fictional conception involving 'the seamless blending of virtual and physical reality' (McArdle, 2021), or 'a network of always-on virtual environments in which many people can interact with one another and digital objects while operating virtual representations—or avatars—of themselves' (Ratan and Lei, 2021). The timing of Zuckerberg's announcement may be explained by the decline of Facebook's user base, which has been attributed to the rising popularity of the video-sharing platform TikTok during the COVID-19 pandemic-induced lockdowns (Chapter 2). In Zuckerberg's depiction, the metaverse will be an amalgam of the online world and virtual and augmented reality, allowing users to select photorealistic avatars that may be used for different purposes, such as for work meetings or spending time with friends and family (Velazco, 2021) (Chapter 1). Significantly, neither in his announcement nor in subsequent communications has Zuckerberg provided any indication of how the numerous concerns raised about the operations of Facebook and Instagram will be addressed. I suggest that these concerns may be exacerbated as users are exposed to newer, more extensive means of sensory and emotional manipulation, including immersive forms of advertising.

The CEOs of the Big Tech companies whose visions have guided the development of the internet seem largely unfazed by the litany of concerns raised thus far. While Tim Berners-Lee has become disillusioned with the direction the internet has taken since it was launched, his public communications reveal no substantial shift in his original vision or its informing libertarianism. The World Wide Web Foundation, which Berners-Lee co-founded with Rosemary Leith in 2009, has as its stated goal to 'advance the open web as a public good and a basic right' (WWWF, 2021b). A blurb on its webpage announces: 'To deliver digital equality, we aim to change government and business policies for the better'. It goes on to mention the foundation's belief that everyone has a right of access to the internet and to 'use it freely and fully' and that it had helped 'unlock the benefits of the web for hundreds of millions of people' (WWWF, 2021b). In 2019, Berners-Lee unveiled a 'global plan to save the web from political manipulation, fake news, privacy violations and other malign forces that threaten to plunge the world into a "digital dystopia"' (Sample, 2019)—practices that worsened during 2020 and 2021 as COVID-19 ravaged many countries. The plan was reported to have the support of 150 organisations, including Microsoft, Twitter, Google, and Facebook/Meta, along with a digital rights group Electronic Frontier Foundation. On the foundation's website, it is noted that in the month following the launch over 1,000 organisations had backed the contract. A link takes one to 'Contract for the Web' which states that to achieve its goals, governments, companies, civil society, and individuals 'must commit to sustained policy development, advocacy, and implementation of the Contract text' (WWWF, 2021c). In this depiction, the internet is an essentially benevolent ecosystem that has been corrupted by malevolent actors and can be 'saved' by adherence to the 'principles' outlined in the charter, for example, by governments 'ensur[ing] everyone can connect to the internet', and 'respect[ing] and protect[ing] people's fundamental

online privacy and data rights' and by companies 'mak[ing] the internet affordable and accessible to everyone' (WWWF, 2021c). These principles are couched
in broad terms and are idealistic and naïve in disregarding the workings of politics and power, especially the power of Big Tech companies and their control
over the internet and its operations.

As explained in Chapter 1, the internet is a socio-technical system that is sustained by the labours of many actors. These include the behind-the-scenes 'ghost
workers' and 'front-stage' workers such as influencers and ordinary citizens that
benefit in one way or other from its use (Chapter 2). These actors, along with the
website and app designers, digital marketers, data scientists, e-commerce specialists, and the many businesses and organisations that support their activities and
advertise their goods and services online, help sustain the idea that the internet
is fundamentally a democratic, liberatory ecosystem that provides the means for
people to fulfil their aspirations. For Big Tech companies that control the internet and the many companies that profit from the attention economy, sustaining
hope in the internet's potential is crucial. This is where advertising plays a major
role, in keeping users engaged in the ways outlined in Chapter 2. In the face of
the growing 'tech lash', advertisers have sought to develop ever-more sophisti-
cated and subtle means to attract and retain their audiences. For many individuals, including those seeking companionship and patients with chronic conditions
and their families, digital media are likely to be a source of great hope. They offer
24/7 connection with others and ready access to vast repositories of information.
Yet, while the cultural, symbolic, and material benefits afforded by these online
engagements may be significant and valued, the longer-term consequences may
be incalculable, including the loss of privacy, identity theft, surveillance, and
threats to mental health (Petersen, 2019: 107). Certain categories of user, such as
those who experience loneliness or who live with a chronic, debilitating illness,
may be especially vulnerable to these online risks.

Digital media, loneliness, and social capital

Of the various promises attached to digital media, 'social connection' is par-
amount. In announcing that Facebook was rebranding itself as Meta, Mark
Zuckerberg commented: 'we are a company that builds technology to connect
people' (AP/Reuters, 2021). This connection may be especially valued by those
who experience intermittent or ongoing loneliness, which is an experience common to many people, and may be acute among certain groups of people such
as the chronically ill and those with limited opportunities for close or intimate
social relationships when this is desired. In recent years, many official reports on
loneliness have proposed the use of digital technologies, alongside other measures, to address experiences of loneliness. Moreover, various online resources
now exist to assist the isolated and lonely and/or to help people to 'connect',
including Good Karma Networks, One Good Street, Gather my crew.org, and
the Reddit platform Forever Alone, Together! Before proceeding much further,

I offer some comments on the framing of 'loneliness', a term that is often ill-defined or used in a confusing way. One consequence of this is that there is a lack of consensus on the dimensions of the purported 'problem' and the required 'solution'. In the academic literature, loneliness is conceived in somewhat different ways and is often equated, incorrectly, with 'social isolation'—a term which itself is often ill-defined. Living by oneself and/or lacking ongoing intimate social relationships is widely believed to predispose to loneliness—which is not necessarily the case. This may reflect negative social evaluations of solo living. Some people may choose to live alone and, even if they do not, this is not always accompanied by feelings of loneliness. As with many other areas of emotional life, loneliness has been largely understood via a psychological, psychotherapeutic, or biomedical lens, which has limited understanding of the factors that predispose to lonely experiences as well as the responses to the phenomenon. These disciplines and fields of practice are generally inattentive to the socio-cultural and politico-economic conditions that shape the emotional lives of individuals, groups, and communities. Sociologically, much can be learnt from how societies construct loneliness, such as the anxieties that attach to rapid social and technological change and the unintended consequences of the pursuit of certain policies and programs.

Studies of loneliness tend to rely on one-off surveys that aim to 'measure' lonely experiences using scales such as the UCLA Loneliness Scale. These studies show a recent increase in the incidence of reported loneliness among certain sections of the population, such as the young and the elderly. Because studies provide only a snapshot of a complex and a constantly evolving socio-cultural phenomenon, reliance on them without understanding the context-specific expressions and experiences of loneliness can be misleading and dangerous. They may lead to interventions that are unnecessary, may cause harm to those involved, and fail to address the conditions that shape people's lives that predispose them to experiencing such feelings. In one common definition, loneliness is an 'unwelcome feeling of lack or loss of companionship, which happens when there is a mismatch between the quantity and quality of the social relationships that we have, and those we want' (Campaign to End Loneliness, 2021). Because the experience of loneliness is subjective, it does not lend itself to straightforward 'measurement' via the use of scales or other quantitative approaches. The experience will vary according to many socio-cultural factors. However, it will likely be salient for those who through birth or social circumstances have limited opportunities for social interaction, perhaps because they are born with a stigmatised condition or identity, do not have or no longer have a partner when this is desired, or they reside or work in a place where the opportunities for interaction are limited, such as living in a remote region or a healthcare or aged care facility. The commonly used phrase 'the loneliness epidemic' is often used to convey the widespread nature of the experience but is unhelpful and potentially misleading in its suggestion of contagion and invites individualised and medicalised responses. The focus of research and policy on certain 'at-risk' groups, such as young people and the elderly, in this context implies that these groups may be more susceptible to the 'infection' of loneliness. Social anxieties about loneliness arise during a period when the institutions of civil society in many countries have been eroded and many people feel disconnected from and undervalued within their communities. In the view of the influential US political scientist Robert Putnam, writing more than 20 years ago, such experiences are indicative of the erosion of 'social capital'. Because Putnam discussed the potential role of the then nascent internet in countering the decline of 'connectedness', his work is worth close examination in light of recent advances in digital media.

Social capital and the internet

Putnam examined the importance of social capital—the 'social networks and norms of reciprocity and trustworthiness that arise from them'—for individuals' sense of connection or companionship (2000: 18). In Putnam's view, social capital characterises contexts of dense social networks. The 'generalised reciprocity' that he believed characterises the possession of social capital manifests in many ways with many different uses. As Putnam explains, social capital is not just a private good but also a public good, and its absence affects *whole communities*. One's extended family, he argued, represents a form of social capital, as do those who share activities in public spaces and not-so-public spaces such as the internet and professional acquaintances (2000: 20). Putnam was writing in the early years of the internet and before the rise of social media—and against the backdrop of the growing influence of neoliberal philosophies and policies, which have found favour in many countries since 1980 (Harvey, 2005). Putnam observed what he believed was the disintegration of social bonds in the previous few decades that had characterised 'the first two-thirds of the twentieth century' (2000: 27). He explored various possible explanations for this loss of social capital, including overwork, urban sprawl, 'the welfare state and women's revolution', television, and 'the growth of mobility to the growth of divorce' (2000: 27). Putnam did not refer specifically to 'neoliberalism' (or 'advanced liberalism'), which is now often linked to the decline in social capital, but he did wonder whether 'big business, capitalism, and the market' was a 'primary cause of declining civic engagement in contemporary America' (2000: 282). While he rejects the idea that market capitalism *per se* leads to 'social disconnectedness', he acknowledged that 'the gradual but accelerating nationalization and globalization of our economic structures' 'may have more validity' (2000: 282). He argued, for example, that 'The replacement of local banks, shops, and other locally based firms by far-flung multinational empires often means a decline in civic commitment on the part of business leaders' (2000: 282–283).

Putnam believed that 'the internet', 'small groups', and 'social movements', were 'three apparent counterexamples to the decline of connectedness' (2000: 27). In Putnam's view, the internet had the potential to simultaneously bridge groups across geography, gender, age, and religion and bond them along educational and ideological lines. As he noted, 'bonding and bridging are not "either-or" categories into which social networks can be neatly divided, but 'more or less' dimensions along which we can compare different forms of social capital' (2000: 27). Putnam poses the question, 'how is our society affected by the explosive growth in telecommunications in recent years, especially the Internet ... . Could new "virtual communities" simply be replacing the old-fashioned physical communities in which our parents lived?' Adding: 'In short, how do small groups, social movements, and telecommunications qualify our judgement about declining social connectedness and civic engagement?' (2000: 152). Putnam expressed his amazement at the rapid uptake of the inter-net in the US population, which he thought was 'substantially greater than that of almost any other consumer technology in history—rivalled only by the television' (2000: 173). However, he wondered whether 'virtual social capital' was 'a contradiction in terms'—responding that 'there is no easy answer' espe-cially in light of the 'flawed conjectures' about the social implications of the telephone (2000: 174).

In Putnam's assessment, 'few things can be said with any confidence about the connection between social capital and Internet technology'. However, 'The timing of the Internet explosion means that it cannot possibly be causally linked to the crumbling of social connectedness' (2000: 174). Putnam notes that activi-ties such as meeting, giving, visiting, and so on, had begun to decline before the internet. Moreover,

> By the time that the Internet reached 10 percent of American adults in 1996, the nationwide decline in social connectedness and civic engage-ment had been under way for a least a quarter of a century. Whatever the future implications of the Internet, social intercourse over the last several decades of the twentieth century was not simply displaced from physical space to cyberspace. The Internet may be part of the solution to our civic problem, or it may exacerbate it, but the cyberrevolution was not the cause.
>
> *(2000: 174)*

Putnam also dismissed the notion that the early users of the internet were less civically engaged than others, arguing that the social networks based on com-puter-mediated communication could be organised, as they often were, on shared interests rather than shared space. He speculated that users could be self-selected in that the internet may attract 'reclusive nerds' or 'civic dynamos' who are then 'sedated' (2000: 175). Given the evidence available to him then, however, Putnam believed that 'It is much too early to assess the long-run social effects of the Internet empirically', proposing instead to avoid a dystopian or utopian prognosis and to speculate that they would likely enhance communication and that 'their net effect will be to enhance community, perhaps even dramatically'. He noted, 'Social capital is about networks and the Net is the network to end all networks' in their potential to 'remove barriers of time and space' (2000: 175).

In short, Putnam was mostly optimistic about the potential of the internet to build social capital and thus enhance social connectedness. However, he believed that computer-mediated interactions *by themselves* did not promote social capital. Indeed, computer-mediated interactions, he noted, contained 'a poverty of cues' that inhibited interpersonal collaborations and trust, especially when the interaction was anonymous and was not embedded in a social context (2000: 176). He noted that while internet-based interactions were 'good for sharing information, gathering opinions and debating alternatives', they were poor for building trust, with participants being 'less inhibited by social niceties and quicker to resort to extreme language and invective'. Internet-based interactions, he observed, provided more scope for 'cheating and reneging' since 'misrepresentation and misunderstanding are easier' (2000: 176). He believed that widespread use of computer-mediated communications needed to be complemented with more frequent face-to-face interactions; that this was ultimately more conducive to the building of social capital. In his view, 'social capital may turn out to be a *prerequisite for*, rather than a *consequence of*, effective computer-mediated communication' (2000: 177; emphases in original). The internet, he thought, was predisposed to 'cyberbalkanisation', which may limit people's communications among those who share their interests regardless of where they live and other interests they may have—although he acknowledged that this was not restricted to the internet. While he recognised that this facility to easily share interests was a great attraction of the internet, he also saw it as a threat to bridging social capital in restricting users' outlets. Interaction in cyberspace, he observed, is 'single stranded' and 'Local heterogeneity may give rise to a more focused virtual homogeneity as communities coalesce across space' (2000: 8). Real-world interactions, he argued, encourage people to confront diversity, both demographic and in terms of interest and outlook. The anonymity and fluidity of the virtual world encouraged what he described as '"easy in, easy out", "drive by" relationships' (2000: 177).

Many of Putnam's predictions concerning the potential of the internet to remove barriers of time and space and to bridge and bond groups ring true today with the proliferation of online communities bound by common interests and emotions. In an Australian Research Council-funded project on patients' use of digital media undertaken between 2017 and 2020, involving qualitative interviews with 50 Australians with either HIV/AIDS, motor neurone disease, and breast cancer communities, my colleagues and I found that our respondents highly valued digital media for building connections and sharing stories with other patients. They said that they appreciated the potential the internet offered to connect with others at any time and to use the functions of Facebook, their commonly used platform, to maintain privacy, which was evident among those from HIV/AIDS communities due to the stigma that attaches to this condition. Many mentioned the isolation they felt living with a chronic illness which affected their day-to-day lives and identity and sense of belonging in the world. For them, this was one of the main reasons for using digital media; to try to make some connections and to regain something that they had lost or that had altered irreversibly. This experience was poignantly expressed by one of our respondents, a chronic pain activist:

> I think what it's [digital media's] done for me, really, is connected me with old friends. Even primary school friends. And I get a sense of belonging again … . Because the thing with chronic illness is you lose your identity and … you create a new one, but I lost who I am. I lost all my people … through being unwell. So, in that way, I can be someone again whether it's real or not.

Yet, while our respondents were generally optimistic about digital media, their comments also revealed ambivalence, which was reflected in concerns about the risks they faced when going online, which included trolling, deception, and confronting inappropriate, biased, or untrustworthy information and unwelcomed marketing (Petersen et al., 2020). Their comments showed not only awareness of the many risks they faced when online but also that they had been subject to one or more of the practices they described. Many were cautious in their online interactions and said that they made efforts to confirm the veracity of information and the trustworthiness of the sources they encountered, for example, by checking a number of sources, or confirming information with a trusted authority offline.

Given our research findings, Putnam's comments, especially the inadequacy of the internet in building trust and the potential for balkanisation, 'virtual homogeneity', 'misrepresentation', and 'cheating', seem prescient. He rightly questioned whether internet-based interactions could ever substitute for in-person encounters, given the 'poverty of cues' online—an issue much debated as Zoom and other video platforms gained ascendance during COVID-19. Putnam was writing some years before the launch of Facebook (in 2004) and other social media platforms, which have been widely criticised for creating 'echo chambers' of self-reinforcing opinion and contributing to the rapid spread of 'misinformation' and 'fake news'. At the time Putnam was writing, few would have envisaged the global dominance achieved by Facebook/Meta and other Big Tech companies—now among the most powerful in the world—and the considerable influence of their algorithm-driven systems that fuel extreme emotions that are now of great concern to many people (Chapters 1 and 3). As noted, these companies profit from the expression of extreme views and the various forms of harm and abuse that their platforms encourage.

While Putnam acknowledged that the internet per se would not build social capital, his view on the *potential* contributions of the internet, however, now seems overly optimistic. Technology-based interventions alone are insufficient to address widespread experiences of social disconnection. Indeed, reliance on digital media to 'solve' the complex phenomenon of loneliness carries the danger of diverting attention from the measures needed to strengthen civil society. The turn to technological solutions to complex socio-political problems may *reinforce* rather than reduce experiences of loneliness. In the view of some scholars, such as Sherry Turkle (2015), digital media undermines the very conditions for sociality and 'meaningful' conversation (e.g. Turkle, 2015). According to Hannah Arendt (1951), writing in the aftermath of the Nazi atrocities, the loneliness of a highly atomised society provides the foundation for the 'formation of mass attitudes' that have underpinned the rise of totalitarianism. In her view, totalitarian domination 'bases itself on loneliness, on the experience of not belonging to the world at all, which is among the most radical and desperate experiences of man' (1968; orig.1951: 199). While it would be wrong to directly link a particular set of practices or outcomes with experiences of loneliness, it is worth considering whether the expression of extreme emotions online has some basis in widely shared experiences of social disconnection and exclusion. Given the workings of the attention economy and its commercial underpinnings, it is difficult to envisage the internet per se advancing the kind of civic engagement and social connectedness that Putnam believed was essential for building trust and mutual support. The algorithm-driven systems that fuel extreme emotions and the personal comparisons that lead to the undermining of self-esteem have been shown to have deeply polarising effects and are antithetical to the ideals of a social capital-rich society.

Digital media and new treatment markets

While the internet's impacts on social connection, and its role in addressing loneliness, will no doubt continue to be debated among academics, policymakers, service providers, and media commentators, its significance in sustaining new medical treatment markets is clear. The internet has provided the conditions for a thriving market of cosmetic and anti-ageing treatments and enhancements of various kinds, complementary and alternative therapies, and 'treatments', the clinical efficiency and safety of which is uncertain. The sale of clinically unproven interventions that are marketed as 'treatments' via the internet is rife. It is a market buoyed by promise and hope for improved health and/or appearance or delayed ageing or the reversal of ageing. It is a market sustained by the hopes of many actors: patients and their carers who look forward to treatments that have the potential to improve their lives, scientists who 'keep hopes alive' through their constant promises to deliver new therapies in the unspecified future, and providers who aim to profit from the sale of claimed treatments to those who are willing and able to pay for them. The implications of citizens' ready access to such 'treatments' are far-reaching, including financial and physical harm to those submitting themselves to them, risks to the public's health and, in the longer term, potential loss of confidence in science. This is most evident with purported stem cell treatments whose clinical effectiveness and safety is often unclear.

Stem cells are seen to hold great promise in biomedicine due to their potential to regenerate diseased or damaged tissue by creating new cell types. These cells may be derived from embryonic material or the sample of a patient's blood—so-called autologous stem cells—which are processed in a laboratory and then injected into the patient. There are long-standing religious and ethical objections to the use of embryos in stem cell research; hence, much attention has focused on adult stem cells or induced pluripotent stem cells (iPSC) which share some of the same attributes as embryonic stem cells but do not involve the destruction of embryos. Because the stem cell treatment market is largely unregulated, the provenance of the stem cells is often difficult to determine. There is no easy way to confirm the origins of the stem cells used in the purported treatment or indeed whether the intervention uses stem cells. The methods used for storing and processing the cells are also often unclear. Except when used for a limited range of conditions, such as corneal transplants and bone marrow-based stem cell transplantation, stem cell treatments are assessed by scientists as being 'experimental' or clinically unproven, and hence potentially unsafe.

For patients and their families, the path from benchtop (research) to bedside (treatment) often proves painfully slow, with most research being in the early stages of proving safety with a small number of patients, using strict criteria of inclusion and exclusion which limits this option for many people. Huge investment in regenerative medical research along with frequent news coverage about 'breakthroughs' that have the potential to transform the treatment of currently untreatable diseases, however, has contributed to heightening many people's hopes. Meanwhile, providers of stem cell treatments have flourished, exploiting these hopes with promises of claimed treatments being advertised directly to people via the internet (Petersen et al., 2017: 4). Hope and promise have underpinned so-called stem cell tourism whereby individuals travel to another country, region, or jurisdiction to receive a treatment involving the use of stem cells otherwise not available to them where they live—usually because they are unapproved by their regulatory authorities. It is no coincidence that stem cell tourism gained public visibility soon after the launch of Facebook in 2004, which is a favoured social media platform for members of patient communities and is often mentioned as a source of information on stem cell treatments (Petersen et al., 2017: 42). As noted earlier, Facebook has enabled the formation of online communities that can control and build their membership, provide a platform for fundraising, and a means to curate messages, often of hope.

Stem cell tourism has expanded rapidly since about 2006, with the first media reports on the phenomenon published that year. In this report, stem cell therapy was described as 'an experimental technique' (Montlake, 2006). The impacts of the COVID-19 pandemic on the stem cell tourism market, and on health and medical travel in general, will likely be unknown for many years. However, travel restrictions posed by COVID-19 during 2020 and 2021 seem not to have curtailed demand for health and medical travel in general. Indeed, during the pandemic, countries keen to attract tourists and companies seeking to profit from tourism opportunities were offering trips to countries where individuals could secure a COVID-19 vaccination and enjoy the benefits this confers, especially vaccine passports—a phenomenon dubbed vaccination tourism (Petersen, 2021). According to a tourism market report published in 2021, companies offering medical tourism were resuming their operations following restrictive containment measures and were, as one report described it, 'adapting to the new normal' (EinPresswire, 2021). The report noted that the medical tourism market was expected to grow from $19.79 billion in 2020 to $40.03 million in 2025, or a growth rate of 16 percent. Market reports of this kind are published regularly, which underlines the perceived commercial opportunities offered by the economy of hope. Information on stem cell tourism specifically is hard to come by, but it is likely that patients seeking stem cell therapies may do so in their home countries. Since the beginning of the pandemic, cell-based interventions were proposed or investigated as potential therapies for COVID-19 patients. One study uncovered 79 clinical trials involving stem cell interventions exploring their potential for targeting COVID-19 symptoms—only about a quarter of which met the criteria of being randomised, double-blinded, and placebo-controlled (Kim and Knoepfler, 2021). Moreover, the COVID-19 results for the cell therapy trials indicated that their anticipated impact was low. Yet, despite this lack of evidence of clinical effectiveness, some US 'unproven stem cell clinics' began new marketing centred on COVID-19. Another article which assessed ethical and communication issues arising from the above studies concluded that they 'exhibit troubling signs of "pandemic research exceptionalism"—where the urgency created by crisis conditions may justify reliance on small studies undertaken with haste—much like the broader effort to develop COVID-19 therapeutics' (Turner et al., 2021: 2).

Growing access to the internet, the rise of direct-to-consumer advertising, and the availability of relatively cheap airfares have enabled those who otherwise have limited treatment options to look for promising new therapies in another country or region. In an Australian Research Council (ARC)-funded study undertaken between 2012 and 2015, my colleagues and I examined the politico-economic and socio-cultural factors that underpin stem cell tourism (Petersen et al., 2017). The study involved interviews with Australian patients and carers, and Australian-based researchers (sometimes also clinicians), scientists, and some local providers of alleged stem cell treatments—100 interviews in all. Twenty-four of these were with those who had undertaken stem cell treatments and/or their carers (sometimes interviewed together), and 27 who had contemplated doing so but at the time of the interview had not yet decided to pursue a treatment for various reasons, including holding reservations and being still at the stage of exploring options. The overseas travellers had visited clinics in various countries, including China, India, Thailand, Israel, Germany, Panama, Mexico, and the United States. Our study also involved fieldwork in China and Germany. During their interviews, the patients and/or carers often mentioned the importance of other patients' personal stories, found on Facebook, or gained via personal contact with others, in making their treatment decisions. Facebook and other social media provide new tools for patients to learn about alternative treatment options themselves without consultation with a doctor or another third party, and to share their stories, sometimes ones relating supposedly miraculous improvements following treatment. Using digital media, many patients are able to directly contact providers through their webpages and, in some cases, undertake a recognisance trip to learn first-hand about treatments and what they involve.

While the use of the term 'tourism' is common in media reports on those who travel for stem cell therapies, it is problematic, suggesting as it does some recreational activity accompanying therapy, which is not the case in most instances. These treatments are typically undertaken by people who suffer severe, often life-threatening conditions and have few if any conventional treatment options available to them and hold high hopes for what stem cell therapies may offer (Petersen et al., 2017: 8–9). These individuals indicated that it was important for them to explore all avenues, with one saying that 'doing nothing was no option'. Sometimes, this treatment may be sought in their own country, and hence involve little travel. During the period of our study, a growing number of clinics began to advertise so-called autologous treatments, involving the use of cells derived from adipose tissue from the patient's own body, for various conditions such as arthritis, migraines, and other diseases and illnesses (Munsie and Pera, 2014). The Australian providers of these autologous stem cell treatments commented that patients tend to have 'unrealistic' expectations, with one describing it as 'the cult of the magic bullet … [the belief] that stem cells is going to be the be-all and end-all of everything' (Petersen et al., 2017: 168). Dismissing patients' or carers' (who are often parents) expectations in this way, however, fails to account for the significance of hope in the lives of those who often have severe, life-limiting conditions and few options available to them.

The patients and carers whom we interviewed indicated to us that they generally do so because they feel that they had been offered 'no hope' by their doctors and have been abandoned. In contemporary healthcare, considerable emphasis is given to the use of advanced medical technologies, particularly treatments that offer the prospect of controlling debilitating symptoms or slowing the progression of disease. News reports frequently include stories of medical research that has the potential to lead to 'breakthrough' treatments, such as genetics and stem cell therapies. Through the 1990s and 2000s, many of these stories pertained to genetic-based treatments and, in the wake of the mapping of the human genome in 2000, 'personalised' medicine. This coverage contributed to heightened expectations and the production of hype regarding developments (Petersen, 2001, 2011). As noted, this hype has been contributed to by scientists themselves in their effort to highlight the significance of their work and thus attract funding. Scientists often work in organisations that provide news releases which are delivered to news media electronically but held under embargo as part of scientists' efforts to establish control over the timing and impact of news to their advantage. For journalists, news releases are considered a primary source since the information comes from original informants. Most large research organisations and universities nowadays have public relations units, and these would seem to provide a large proportion of the content of mass media (Macnamara, 2014). However, with the growing use of social media, scientists have often struggled to control the circulation of science news which may flow rapidly via the internet, where it may contribute to heightening optimism. For patients and their families, these media also provide the means to exchange stories and to raise funds and lobby for treatments that many feel they have been denied, and to make direct contact with providers who advertise their products and services online.

There are various paths by which patients gain treatment, which tend to be pursued following fruitless encounters with doctors and/or other healthcare professionals. Patients and/or their carers often find providers themselves online, whom they then contact to make further enquiries and sometimes visit to undertake their own investigations of the clinic itself and to garner impressions of the provider and to learn more about what is involved in treatment. Many seek advice from friends, family members, and people they have met through work or other avenues. However, many individuals will encounter enthusiastic supporters of stem cell treatments online, some of whom are part of patient communities—what might be called 'communities of hope'—that create their own positive narratives about stem cell treatments and challenge official, regulatory-focused discourses of risk-benefit and trust (Petersen et al., 2017: 192). As part of our study, we examined the case of one online activist—an individual living with multiple sclerosis—whose quest to embark on a stem cell treatment in Russia achieved prominence following her appearance on the *60 Minutes* television program in 2014 (Petersen et al., 2016). There are many highly publicised cases of this kind involving either celebrities such as sports stars or movie stars, or ordinary individuals who have achieved a public profile through their media appearances or online lobbying efforts. However, this case served well to uncover the intricacies of how traditional media and social media may interact to lend profile to an issue and help shape public discourse on a controversial new treatment. As our analysis revealed, social media may provide ordinary citizens with the tools to curate stories and shape public discourse in ways that would have been difficult, and perhaps not possible, before the internet.

As a colleague and I found in an earlier study, the webpages of the providers who advertise stem cell treatments offer stories of hope and recovery, which are difficult to verify, and often contain information and images that promise or lend the impression of clinical competence, efficiency, and trustworthiness (Petersen and Seear, 2011). The websites we analysed suggested that virtually any condition is treatable with a stem cell therapy if one is prepared to travel and can pay. The use of patient stories and blogs, along with interactive content such as videos, and links to scientific articles and news stories serve to provide a persuasive narrative of the healing power of stem cell therapies. Moreover, the sites offer prospective patients and their carers numerous assurances of the safety of treatments and the promise of being able to gain control over their lives. They use a personalised style that leaves the impression that the providers are caring and acting with the patients' interests as their primary concern. Some providers' websites say they offer patients 'the gift of opportunity', while most use the word 'hope' in advertisements, such as 'new found hope'. In our study, we found that patient testimonials, recounting miraculous recoveries, appeared on most of the websites we examined, and often used blogs or videos lending an air of 'authenticity' and 'relatability' to stories—using techniques that are common in the history of advertising (Chapter 2). On the other hand, advertisements leave much unstated and unresolved. They offer no firm assurances about longer-term outcomes of treatments and what constitutes 'success' from claimed treatments, whether there are any likely adverse outcomes, and are often vague about the costs of travel to receive treatment, which is likely to include accommodation, meals, and assistance with care. In our ARC study, and informally, we found that adverse outcomes from treatment did occur, although patients were often reluctant to disclose such information to others, with some expressing to us 'off the record' that they felt embarrassed about their decision to undertake treatment. As this study revealed, the costs of overseas travel and accommodation can be significant, especially for those who decide to undertake a second or subsequent treatment, which is not uncommon. The costs for healthcare systems in treating patients who suffer adverse outcomes or who may return to their home countries with antimicrobial resistant organisms are incalculable—and generally not recorded in current systems for documenting adverse outcomes of medical treatments.

It is not known what, if any role, online advertising plays in patients' and carers' decisions regarding clinically unproven stem cell therapies. The effectiveness of advertising *in general* and digital advertising specifically has been questioned (Chapter 2). Those whom we interviewed often mentioned websites as sources of information, but they also gained information from other sources, including friends, family members, work colleagues, and other parties. Respondents often showed acute awareness of the dangers of relying on providers' websites. However, our study highlighted that some individuals are prepared to undertake treatments generally based on unverified claims. Those who live with chronic conditions, such as multiple sclerosis, motor neurone disease, or cystic fibrosis, generally have few conventional therapeutic options available to them and may be especially likely to pursue these treatments and be vulnerable to the persuasive messages of advertising.

According to many scientists, healthcare professionals, policymakers, and regulators, stem cell tourism is fuelled by patients' unrealistic or 'false' hopes which are exploited by malicious actors. In interviews, these groups often spoke of the dangers of 'cowboys' or 'charlatans' spruiking treatment of dubious value or that are unsafe. Yet, this depiction of 'the problem' denies the role played by scientists, policymakers, the media, and patients themselves and their families, in the economy of hope through contributing to a promissory discourse that may predispose some individuals to taking risks that they may not otherwise take. Depictions of this kind are common in science and serve in policing the boundaries of science by deeming certain nonauthorised knowledge and practices illegitimate (Gieryn, 1999). The portrayal serves to reinforce the perception that there is a clear line between 'real' science, involving clinical trials and a linear path to drug or treatment approval, and 'fake' science, which bypasses this process, which is often not the case. Indeed, pre-approval access or 'compassionate access', whereby patients with life-threatening diseases or seriously debilitating conditions and no approved treatment options can gain unapproved treatments illustrates the permeability of this border (e.g. European Medicines Agency, 2021). This portrayal denies the critical role played by digital media in both advertising these treatments and providing the means for ordinary citizens to learn about and access them. While digital technologies are widely promoted as tools for empowering patients and improving their lives, as the stem cell tourism example illustrates, they do so in ways that have the potential to cause harm.

Conclusion

From its beginning, the internet has been underpinned by high hopes. The designers of the internet believed that their invention would serve as an inclusive, democratising tool that would empower their users and unite people around the world. Yet, the hopes of the mostly male, relatively privileged engineers and entrepreneurs were underpinned by a naïve libertarianism and technological determinism that is blind to the workings of power and inequality and to the potential for innovations to be used in ways different to those envisaged. As I noted, digital media technologies often either fail to produce the promised benefits or enable practices that have the potential to produce harm. The internet and digital platforms that it has given rise to have been designed in ways that were bound to frustrate the hopes of their users and create or exacerbate the problems and social divisions that have become increasingly evident in recent years. The algorithm-driven systems that make the internet seem smart and accessible often narrow rather than broaden views and encourage and reinforce the expression of certain emotions. Further, they may contribute to creating *false* hopes, that is, hopes based upon an improbable outcome (Rettig et al., 2007). As Rettig et al. have shown with reference to the case of a seemingly promising new treatment for breast cancer that ultimately proved ineffective, consensus can quickly develop around a technology based upon an unrealistic set of expectations, which may be encouraged by faulty or incomplete information, or an unwillingness of people to accept the limits of science (2007: 286). The Big Tech companies that are responsible for creating systems and technologies that directly or indirectly cause harm and abuse thus far are disinclined to redesign their algorithms which may go some way to alleviating the problems they have created or contributed to since this would undermine their business model based upon the harvesting of personal data. But is this the only available or viable option? In the next chapter, I examine some other responses, focusing on 'digital wellness' which have been proposed as a panacea for addressing some of the harms posed by the internet, such as the mental health problems associated with increased screen time during the COVID-19 pandemic. What does 'digital wellness' entail and is it likely to be effective in addressing some of the issues identified in this and earlier chapter, or is it simply a diversion from more substantial changes?

References

Anderson, J., Rainie, L. and Vogels, E. A. (2021) 'Experts say the "new normal" in 2025 will be more tech-driven, with more big challenges', https://www.elon.edu/u/imagining/wp-content/uploads/sites/964/2021/02/Elon-Pew-Digital-Life-2025-After-Covid-Outbreak.pdf (Accessed 22 October 2021).

AP/Reuters (2021) 'Facebook changes name to meta to focus on building virtual-reality "metaverse"', *ABC News*, 29 October, https://www.abc.net.au/news/2021-10-29/facebook-rebrands-as-meta-to-harness-virtual-reality-in-future/100578908 (Accessed 29 October 2021).

Arendt, H. (1968; orig. 1951) *Totalitarianism*. Harcourt, Brace and World, Inc., New York.

Cambridge Dictionary (2021) 'Hope', https://dictionary.cambridge.org/dictionary/english/hope (Accessed 15 September 2021).

Campaign to End Loneliness (2021) 'About loneliness', https://www.campaigntoendloneliness.org/about-loneliness/ (Accessed 3 November 2021).

EinPresswire (2021) 'Global medical tourism market trends, strategies, and opportunities in the medical tourism market 2021–2030', https://www.einnews.com/pr_news/551333727/global-medical-tourism-market-trends-strategies-and-opportunities-in-the-medical-tourism-market-2021-2030 (Accessed 23 September 2021).

European Medicines Agency (2021) 'Compassionate access', https://www.ema.europa.eu/en/human-regulatory/research-development/compassionate-use (Accessed 19 October 2021).

Flichy, P. (2004) 'Connected individualism between digital technology and society', *Réseaux*, 124, 2: 17–51.

Gieryn, T. F. (1999) *Cultural Boundaries of Science: Credibility On the Line*. The University of Chicago Press, Chicago.

Groopman, J. (2005) *The Anatomy of Hope: How People Prevail In the Face of Illness*. Random House, New York.

Harvey, D. (2005) *A Brief History of Neoliberalism*. Oxford University Press, Oxford and New York.

Hiltz, S. R. and Turoff, M. (1978) *The Network Nation: Human Communication Via Computer*. Addison-Wesley Publishing Company, Inc., Reading, MA.

Keen, A. (2015) *The Internet Is Not the Answer*. Atlantic Books, London.

Kim, M. and Knoepfler, P. S. (2021) 'Anticipated impact of stem cell and other cellular medicine clinical trials for COVID-19', *Regenerative Medicine*, 16: 525–533, https://doi.org/10/2217/rme-2021-0025

Macnamara, J. (2014) *Journalism and PR: Unpacking 'Spin', Stereotypes and Media Myths*. Peter Lang Publishing, Pieterlen and Bern.

McArdle, M. (2021) 'Opinion: the metaverse may be coming. But don't expect it from Mark Zuckerberg', *The Washington Post*, 31 October 2021, https://www.washingtonpost.com/opinions/2021/10/30/metaverse-may-be-coming-dont-expect-it-mark-zuckerberg/?utm_campaign=wp_post_most&utm_medium=email&utm_source=newsletter&wpisrc=nl_most&carta-url=https%3A%2F%2Fs2.washingtonpost.com%2Fcar-ln-tr%2F3527b35%2F617ec10b9d2fda9d412eba72%2F5e86729bade4e21f59b210ef%2F54%2F72%2F617ec10b9d2fda9d412eba72 (Accessed 1 November 2021).

Montlake, S. (2006) 'Stem cell tourism', *South China Morning Post*, https://www.scmp.com/article/550313/stem-cell-tourism (Accessed 23 September 2021).

Munsie, M. and Pera, M. (2014) 'Regulatory loophole enables unproven autologous cell therapies to thrive in Australia', *Stem Cells and Development*, 23 (S1), 34–38.

Petersen, A. (2001) 'Biofantasies: genetics and medicine in the print news media', *Social Science & Medicine*, 52, 8: 1255–1268.

Petersen, A. (2015) *Hope in Health: The Socio-Politics of Optimism*. Palgrave Macmillan, Basingstoke.

Petersen, A. (2019) *Digital Health and Technological Promise: A Sociological Inquiry*. Routledge, London and New York.

Petersen, A. (2021) 'Vaccine vacations: countries cashing in on the quest for COVID jabs', *Monash Lens*, 8 April, h.edu/@politics-society/2021/04/08/1383050/covid-1 9-vaccine-tourism-profiting-from-desperation (Accessed 27 September 2021).

Petersen, A., MacGregor, C. and Munsie, M. (2016) 'Stem cell miracles or Russian roulette?: patients' use of digital media to campaign for access to clinically unproven treatments', *Health, Risk and Society*, 17, 7–8: 592–604.

Petersen, A., Munsie, M., Tanner, C., MacGregor, C. and Brophy, J. (2017) *Stem Cell Tourism and the Political Economy of Hope*. Palgrave Macmillan, London.

Petersen, A., Schermuly, A. and Anderson, A. (2020) 'Feeling less alone online: patients' ambivalent engagements with digital media', *Sociology of Health and Illness*, 42, 6: 1441–1455.

Petersen, A. and Seear, K. (2011) 'Technologies of hope: techniques of the online advertising of stem cell treatments', *New Genetics and Society*, 30, 4: 329–246.

Putnam, R. D. (2000) *Bowling Alone: The Collapse and Revival of American Community*. Simon & Schuster, New York.

Rabeharisoa, V., Moreira, T. and Alrich, M. (2014) 'Evidence-based activism: patients', users' and activist groups in knowledge society', *BioSocieties*, 9, 2: 111–128.

Ratan, R. and Lei, Y. (2021) 'What is the metaverse? 2 media and information experts explain', *The Conversation*, August 12, https://theconversation.com/what -is-the-metaverse-2-media-and-information-experts-explain-165731   (Accessed 3 November 2021).

Rettig, R. A., Jacobson, P. D., Farquhar, C. and Aubry, W. M. (2007) *False Hope: Bone Marrow Transplantation for Breast Cancer*. Oxford University Press, Oxford.

Sample, I. (2019) 'Tim Berners-Lee unveils global plan to save the web', *The Guardian*, 25   November,   https://www.theguardian.com/technology/2019/nov/24/tim -berners-lee-unveils-global-plan-to-save-the-internet (Accessed 9 September 2021).

Seligman, M. (2002) 'Positive psychology, positive prevention, and positive therapy', in C. R. Snyder and S. J. Lopez (eds) *Handbook of Positive Psychology*. Oxford University Press, New York.

Snyder, C. R., Irving, L. and Anderson, J. R. (1991) 'Hope and health: measuring the will and the ways', in C. R. Snyder and D. R. Forsyth (eds) *Handbook of Social and Clinical Psychology: The Health Perspective*. Pergamon, Elmsford.

Turkle, S. (2015) *Reclaiming Conversation: The Power of Talk in a Digital Age*. Penguin Press, New York.

Turner, L., Munsie, M., Levine, A. D. and Ikonomou, L. (2021) 'Ethical issues and public communication in the development of cell-based treatments for COVID-19: lessons from the pandemic', *Stem Cell Reports*, 16: 1–10, https://doi.org/10.1016/j.stemcr .2021.09.005

Velazco, C. (2021) 'Mark Zuckerberg just laid out his vision for the met averse. These are the five things you should know', *The Washington Post*, 28 October. https://www .washingtonpost.com/technology/2021/10/28/facebook-meta-metaverse-explained/ (Accessed 30 August 2022).

World Wide Web Foundation (2021a) 'History of the web', https://webfoundation.org/about/vision/history-of-the-web/ (Accessed 10 September 2021).

World Wide Web Foundation (2021b) 'About us', https://webfoundation.org/about/ (Accessed 9 September 2021).

World Wide Web Foundation (2021c) 'Contract for the web', https://contractfortheweb.org/ (Accessed 9 September 2021).

5

DIGITAL WELL-BEING

People's experiences of digital media are complex and often ambivalent. Many eagerly embrace smartphones, apps, and other devices and enjoy their affordances, including instant connection with others from virtually anywhere, anytime along with access to a vast pool of goods and services. Employing the vast array of technologies now available to them, individuals can do things they might not otherwise be able to do or do them more easily than they could in the pre-internet era: controlling the times and terms of interactions with friends, family, and those in our various communities; creating and sharing vast amounts of information; receiving personalised messages; working collectively with different groups to effect change; curating a preferred online identity; and using one or more of the numerous online platforms available to accumulate cultural and economic capital. In doing so, media users may feel 'empowered' or in control of their lives. Yet, virtually all users, regardless of their level of usage, will be compelled to negotiate the constant demands and intrusions of technology and the affordances they offer. There is a fine line between 'feeling in control' and 'losing control' of one's use of technology and, for some people, it would seem, the former can tip over into the latter and become compulsive or 'addictive'. This addiction, many experts claim, may cause anxiety, mood disorders, loss of sleep, depression, loss of self-esteem, loneliness, a diminishing social life, and 'withdrawal' symptoms or discomfort or anxiety when not 'connected' (so-called 'nomophobia'). In response, a growing number of so-called digital well-being or digital wellness initiatives have been developed that focus on changing users' relationships with technology, to bring them into 'balance'.

This chapter examines the phenomenon of digital well-being, highlighting its various implications. Over the last 20 years, an expanding number of digital well-being products and services have been advertised on the promise that they will assist individuals to develop a 'healthy' relationship with technology. The Big

DOI: 10.4324/9781003147435-5

Tech companies themselves have developed apps and devices and offer ideas and tools 'to help people find a better balance with technology'—although the question of what this might entail in practice is rarely articulated (e.g. Google, 2021). The concepts of digital well-being and digital wellness have gained growing popularity since around 2008 in the wake of the launch of Facebook and other social networking services. During this period, authorities have expressed concerns about the increasing amount of time people, especially children, spend online. The question of how best to balance the benefits of internet use while limiting the harms that may result from claimed excessive or inappropriate 'screen time' is now prominent in debates about the impacts of digital media. The onset of the COVID-19 pandemic and related lockdowns when more people spent time online has not just resulted in increased focus on the concept of digital well-being but also attracted the interest of companies in the related commercial opportunities. Since many discussions and many initiatives have focused on 'internet addiction' (sometimes called 'technology addiction'), I begin by examining the rise of this phenomenon and how it has been constructed, before considering the responses. 'Addiction', I suggest, is a commonly used metaphor for explaining the imperatives and compulsions of a digitally mediated age and underpins a thriving economy oriented to addressing people's purported well-being needs.

The rise of 'internet addiction'

Growing concerns about users' levels of media use, especially when this becomes compulsive, or 'addictive', has paralleled rising levels of access to the internet and social media platforms. The origins of the term 'internet addiction' can be traced back to 1995 when a psychiatrist Ivan Goldberg posted a humorous entry on the subject in PsychCom.net (Perdew, 2015: 24). As Perdew explains, Goldberg 'crafted it to look like an entry in the DSM' [Diagnostic and Statistical Manual], a publication of the American Psychiatric Association, which provides a comprehensive list of classifications of officially recognised psychiatric disorders. The creation of this fictious disorder on Goldberg's bulletin board was subsequently met with a flood of stories from others narrating tales of '"remaining caught in the Net" and seeking help with their condition' (Dalai and Basu, 2016). According to Dalai and Basu, in the same year, a clinical psychology student undertook research on the psychological factors shaping computer use and independently coined 'addictive use of the internet'. The author then published a report, 'Internet addiction: emergence of a new clinical disorder' in 1996 based on an illustrative case, which was subsequently widely cited. This was then followed by the publication of other articles with 'Internet addiction' in their titles, with an accelerating number to a total of 1561 articles cited in PubMed using the term by 2015/16—which is deemed a phenomenal growth in just 20 years (Dalai and Basu, 2016: 62–63).

An analysis of Google's Ngram search engine for book sources reveals a dramatic increase in the use of the term 'internet addiction' from about 2006—that is, soon after the launch of Facebook in 2004 which was soon followed by other social media—which has continued its steep upward trend to 2019 (the last date available for an Ngram analysis). Recent years have seen an increasing number of books with 'internet addiction' (or sometimes 'technology addiction') in their titles. These include recently: David Greenfield's *Overcoming Internet Addiction for Dummies* (2021); Katajun Lindenberg et al.'s *Internet Addiction in Adolescents* (2021); Emaline Friedman's *Internet Addiction: A Critical Psychology of Users* (2020); the Information Resources Management Association's *Internet and Technology Addiction: Breakthroughs in Research and Practice* (2019); Kathryn Vercillo's *Internet Addiction* (2020); Kimberly Young's and Nabuco de Abre's *Internet Addiction in Children and Adolescents* (2017), and Nathan Driskell's *Internet Addiction, Kicking the Habit: 30 Day Plan to Take Back Your Life* (2016). These books are diverse in their foci and assumed audience, with some targeting parents, some offering guidance to 'addicts', and others written largely for scholars, especially psychologists. Few of the books surveyed question the use of 'internet addiction', except for Friedman's book, above, which offers a critique of the concept, drawing on the work of the philosopher Gilles Deleuze and the psychoanalyst Felix Guattari. One of the above authors, Driskell, describes himself in an advertisement for his book as a 'former internet Addict who spent six years of his life trapped within an online game' and that 'After choosing to escape his online world, he decided to become a therapist so he can help others with this addiction' (Amazon, 2021).

Many writings, policies, and program centre on children and young people's dependence on or 'addiction' to technology—continuing long-standing concerns about the impacts of electronic media on children's minds, beginning with television (Chapter 1). A 2019 OECD report, *Educating 21st Century Children: Emotional Well-Being in the Digital Age*, however, questioned the use of 'internet addiction' or other similar terms to describe children's claimed problematic online use (Burns and Gottschalk, 2019). The report noted in reviewing the evidence that there is a 'disconnect between research and policy/practice' and that 'There is little evidence suggesting that a significant number of children/adolescents are dependent on devices to the extent that they are at risk of significant negative health outcomes, or that they experience a significant impairment in a major area of their lives, the definition of addiction (Burns and Gottschalk, 2019: 26). It also commented that terms like 'internet addiction' are 'misleading' in that they potentially create social stigma that is 'unhelpful in supporting children and young people with "problematic interactive media use"', and 'obscures the growing evidence that individuals who already suffer anxiety or depression are more prone to engage in problematic use of technology'. In the authors' view, it is difficult to determine causality, and interventions are most likely to be effective when they address both online and offline concerns (Burns and Gottschalk, 2019: 268).

Notwithstanding the growing use of 'internet addiction', the behaviour so described has not (yet) been recognised by the World Health Organization as being a 'disorder' and is not listed in the Diagnostic and Statistical Manual of

Mental Disorders (DSM-5), the world health professions' handbook, or the International Classification of Diseases (ICD-11). However, 'internet gaming disorder' or 'video game addiction' is recognised by the World Health Organization as a medical condition and included in the International Classification of Diseases in 2018 (WHO, 2018a). In 2018, a WHO media release noted that 'excessive use' of the 'internet, computers, smartphones and other electronic devices' 'often has negative health consequences' and that in some countries the magnitude of the problem was 'a significant public health concern' (WHO, 2018b). Further, it noted that since 2014, in response to concerns by professional groups, WHO collaborating centres, academics, and clinicians, had been conducting various related activities including a series of meetings with experts in medicine and addiction, with one focusing on gaming and gambling disorders (WHO, 2018b). It is worth mentioning that the use of 'disorder' to describe some forms of gaming behaviour, and the distinction of gaming from other internet or smartphone-based behaviour, has been questioned by some behavioural experts (Park, 2019).

In 2017, the National Institutes of Health in the United States funded the first study on internet addiction—focusing specifically on online gaming—which was reported to 'determine the best form of treatment'. An article reporting on this research, 'Internet addiction is sweeping America, affecting millions', commented that the findings 'may help determine whether online gaming should be listed in the Diagnostic and Statistical Manual of Mental Disorders as a true mental health disorder' (Booth, 2017). Internet addiction, the article noted, is a global disorder and has received more attention in some countries than in the United States, such as South Korea, China, and Japan, which have major internet gaming industries. In South Korea, for example, the government was reported to have sponsored about 200 counselling centres and hospitals with programs servicing those who are addicted and had trained 1,000 counsellors. In Japan, the government is reported to have introduced 'internet fasting camps' offering young addicts counselling in a tech-free environment, while China had 'more than three hundred treatment centers (China officials there estimate 10 million teenagers are addicted)' (Booth, 2017).

In short, despite the lack of scientific consensus on whether a certain level and/or pattern of internet use should be described as constituting an 'addiction', authorities in many countries have responded to it as such, with concerns centred on young users. Like the addictions of alcohol, heroin, cocaine and other drugs, and gambling, 'internet addiction' is seen as calling for a biomedical response, namely, 'treatment' and support for those who have lost control or are 'hooked', and/or suffer 'withdrawal' symptoms. Moreover, in line with approaches to other addictions, the focus is resolutely on the user (who is often, albeit implicitly, blamed) and their relationship with the object of addiction, in this case, technology, especially their level and pattern of use. With some other addictive products, like heroin and cocaine, authorities have banned them, or, in the case of alcohol, tobacco, or gambling, the product or activity is often heavily regulated. But with 'internet addiction', it is the individual user, whose behaviour and relationship with the addictive product is deemed to be problematic, that is the primary target of interventions.

Responses to 'internet addiction'

The dominant framing of 'addiction' ascribes responsibility to the individual user or, in the case of children, their parents or other guardians who are offered technological assistance to monitor the individual's media use—which ignores the substantial efforts made by Big Tech companies to attract users and keep them engaged ('hooked'), and clicking and purchasing. Technology companies have designed their devices, platforms, and systems, to appeal and, for some individuals, their engagements reach a level that is judged by some experts and authorities to be problematic and in need of intervention. As noted, children are seen as especially vulnerable to this form of addiction and many of the innovations mentioned are directed at controlling their 'screen time'. The comments of Anna Lembke, a psychiatrist and professor at Stanford University and author of *Dopamine Nation: Finding Balance in the Age of Indulgence* (2021), reflect both this framing of 'the problem' and 'the solution':

> A patient of mine, a bright and thoughtful young man in his early 20s, came to see me for debilitating anxiety and depression. He had dropped out of college and was living with his parents. He was vaguely contemplating suicide. He was also playing videogames most of every day and late into every night. Twenty years ago the first thing I would have done for a patient like this was prescribe an antidepressant. Today I recommend something altogether different: a dopamine fast. I suggest that he abstain from all screens, including videogames, for one month.
>
> *(Lembke, 2021)*

This suggested technology abstinence, or 'digital detox', is a common 'prescription' for this 'craving' or 'disorder' and diverts attention from the complexity of the issues and the interests of those with a stake in how they are framed. In the above example, the problem is constructed as having a biophysical basis, an excess of dopamine, a chemical that resides in the brain that is believed to affect one's emotional well-being ('makes one feel good'). As a government health information website explains, 'Having the right amount of dopamine is important both for your body and your brain' (HealthDirect, 2021). Having 'too much' dopamine, it notes, 'is linked to being more competitive, aggressive and having poor impulse control [and] it can lead to conditions that include ADHD, binge eating, addiction and gambling' (HealthDirect, 2021). As Lembke explains, when people engage in activities they enjoy, like playing video games, 'the brain releases a little bit of dopamine and we feel good' but, as neuroscience has discovered, 'pleasure and pain are processed in the same parts of the brain' and while the brain tries to keep them in balance once it 'tips in one direction' this balance is 'hard to restore'. If one keeps returning to the source of pleasure, namely video games, then 'the brain's set-point for pleasure changes' and 'we need to keep playing games, not to feel pleasure but just to feel normal'. As soon as one stops, symptoms of withdrawal kick in, as happens with any addictive substance: 'anxiety, irritability, insomnia, dysphoria and mental preoccupation with using my drug, otherwise known as craving' (Lembke, 2021). Conceptions of 'internet addiction', like substance addiction and gambling addiction are heavily influenced by neuroscientific and biochemical understandings of the body that ignore the socio-cultural and politico-economic contexts within which problems arise and are defined. The use of the language of addiction and references to being 'hooked' and to 'addictive' technology are now common in both academic research and media portrayals of users' engagements with digital media, and the term even appears in some otherwise critical analyses of digital media, for example, Adam Alter's (2017) *Irresistible: The Rise of Addictive Technology and the Business of Keeping Us Hooked*. The metaphor of addiction is firmly embedded and familiar in the wider culture, as are the responses, which focus on 'treating' heavy ('hooked') users or promoting 'well-being' or 'wellness'—making the idea relatively easy to communicate and sell.

While responses to 'internet addiction' generally focus on the individual and their relationship to technology, some commentators blame technology companies for *creating* the problem by measuring product success by the number of users (Baskaran, 2019). Support for this view is provided by different sources including those who have worked for Big Tech companies. Industry veterans, such as Tristan Harris and colleagues who offer insider accounts in *The Social Dilemma* (Chapter 2) and the Facebook employee-turned-whistleblower, Frances Haugen, who testified to the US Senate subcommittee in 2021 (Chapter 3), have helped expose Big Tech companies' hidden practices including incentivising their employees to design features that ensure that users stay on their platforms. Evidence of the existence of these practices, while compelling, does not 'prove' that they 'cause' 'addiction' or other claimed problematic online behaviours. Technologies may be designed to engage their users, but users deploy technologies in often unpredictable ways, their practices being shaped by potentially numerous factors including gender, ethnicity, age, level of ability, the users' ideological commitments, and the time and context of their technology use. Users may deploy only certain functions or features of their technologies or use these on only certain occasions or with certain devices or use ad blockers and/ or opt out of tracking (Chapter 2). However, some people, especially those who are heavily reliant on digital media due to, say, living with a debilitating chronic illness, or having restricted in-person social contacts or limited immobile, may be especially predisposed to media's manipulations (Chapter 4).

Big Tech companies have responded to criticisms of the operations of their technologies or systems by offering mostly *technological* solutions such as control features and apps to monitor and limit users' time spent online, such as Apple's Screen Time, Google's Family Link and Digital Wellbeing, and TikTok's 'Screen

Time Management' and 'Restricted Mode'. Other companies, large and small, such as Qustodio, ActionDash, SPACE, Digitox, Zario, and Tracky, have also made apps available to download for free. These tools can be used to set boundaries on usage and can be limited to certain times of the day, and time limits can be applied to specific kinds of app, such as social networks (Deloitte, 2019). These offer features which help users track their smartphone usage, and app usage, and understand how much time they spend on their phone. Some include 'digital limit reminders' or 'overuse alarms' and/or parental controls. These apps employ psychological theories of behaviour change to engender a kind of panoptic self-monitoring—and the guilt and self-blame that follows from the failure to reduce one's technology usage. The app-based response reflects the responsibilisation that is a hallmark of contemporary neoliberal politics that prevails in many societies. Individual users are ascribed responsibility for monitoring their own technology engagements and finding their own 'balanced' relationship with technology. The SPACE App is advertised as 'a personalised behaviour change programme design to help you think about how you use your phone and how it affects your life', with the stated mission 'to help millions of people to find their phone/life balance' (SPACE, 2021a). A link on SPACE App's website takes one to a page, 'Digital wellbeing is the next environmentalism', where the author, Georgia Powel, explains the difficulty of establishing consensus on the concept of digital well-being given that this 'is personal', including all areas of people's lives, each of which is 'highly multidisciplinary', and that the 'technology landscape is changing at an unprecedented rate'. Writing in 2019, Powel notes that ten years earlier, 'iPhones had only existed for a year, and the app store had only just launched', and that in the previous five years the number of apps had rapidly grown to 'three million for Android and over two million on iOS' which 'help us do more online than ever before' and 'have to be better than ever at keeping our attention' (SPACE, 2021b). As Powel argues, these factors in combination explain 'why there are no consistent recommendations' on digital well-being, including 'how much screen time children should have' (SPACE, 2021b). Despite this absence of consistent recommendations on digital well-being, apps are advertised on the basis that they *are* effective tools for managing one's relationships with technology—with some advertised as helping users 'break phone addiction' and better managing their screen time. While they may assist some individuals to change their digital media use, their value within the wider population is questionable, with no reliable evidence to support their claimed benefits.

A 2019 Deloitte report on smartphone uses, based on a UK survey of a representative sample of over 4,000 consumers aged 16–75, concluded that while 'Screen time trackers are readily accessible [and] easily customisable' they are 'rarely used, even among self-declared over-users' and that 'The overwhelming majority (92 per cent) of over-users do not use screen time tools' (Deloitte, 2019: 11). (In the study, 'over-use' was not quantified, but rather left to the respondents to decide.) The Deloitte report also noted that other techniques for curbing usage, while more widespread—such as making the phone inaudible, 'presumably to mute acoustic alerts'—were ad hoc and perhaps less effective (2019: 12). Little is known about the experiences of those who do use these apps, apart from what can be learnt from online user reviews which reveal many criticisms of their operations. For example, users' reviews on Google's Digital Wellbeing app include (in order of appearance): 'Horrible. The app does whatever it wants. God forbid you don't have auto update off or you will have this app take control ...' (26 October 2021); 'Sneaky little invasive app ...' (27 September 2021); 'Spyware. Android is just increasingly becoming spyware ...' (15 November 2021); 'My issue is: I'm unable to install this application. I'm unable to disable this application ...' (1 November 2021) (Google Play, 2021). Other apps, such as Apple Screen Time, have received similarly negative user reviews or mixed assessments, with some users complaining that they include 'bugs' that seem unable to be fixed or that the app affected the operations of their other apps, or created other problems such as wasting time sorting out issues (see, e.g. App Store, 2021).

In TikTok's response to the many concerns raised about the operations of its app—especially that it steers its mostly young users towards videos that keep them scrolling sometimes towards content that promotes suicide or self-harm—the company offers 'Screen Time Management and Restricted Mode' via its Privacy and Settings (under a section labelled 'Digital Wellbeing'). This allows users or their parents or guardians to control screen time and content which they judge not be appropriate. However, in December 2021, a columnist from the *New York Times* claimed to have obtained an internal company document about the workings of TikTok's algorithms that indicates that these efforts to limit users' engagements come into direct conflict with the company's business goals. According to the columnist, the document was produced for non-technical specialist employees to help explain how the algorithm works and provides insight into 'the company's understanding of human nature—our tendency towards boredom, our sensitivity to culture cues—that help explain why it's so hard to put down' (Smith, 2021). The document explains in frank terms the company's 'ultimate goal' of adding active users and that to achieve it 'it has chosen to optimize two closely related metrics in the stream of videos it serves—"retention"—that is, whether a user comes back—and "time spent"'. In short, 'The app wants to keep you there as long as possible' (Smith, 2021). In addition to the amount of watch time, videos are scored according to three items of data, namely, likes, comments and playtime, and an indication that the video has been played. The recommender system then gives scores to videos based on this equation and provides users with videos with the highest scores. As the columnist notes, other nuances, such as cultural references, detected by the algorithm, are then used to 'feed' users' content that will keep them engaged (Smith, 2021).

In 2022, TikTok came under scrutiny for fuelling 'witch hunts' of those who have undertaken alleged misdeeds on other platforms. A case was reported of a man named Caleb being 'mobbed' by TikTok users after a female posted comments about him on the dating app Hinge claiming that he had 'love-bombed' her; that is, initially demonstrating affection and then 'ghosting' them after a couple of dates. The article reporting the case noted that after the posting 'hordes of commenters and content creators' joined in the attack. It noted: 'Someone posted his address, phone number and workplace' and 'A woman joked about heckling him at a coronavirus testing line that she heard he was waiting at'. Further, 'Calls have been made for him to be "run out of the city"' (Paúl, 2022). Casey Fiesler, a specialist in technology ethics and policy at University of Colorado Boulder, who is cited in the article, notes that content on TikTok was more likely to go viral than on other social media platforms because its highly personalised algorithm 'fuels its "For you" feed and determines which videos appear on a person's screen' (Paúl, 2022). As the article explains, 'Recommendations are based on followed accounts, videos that are liked or shared as well as a person's own content'. Great engagement is also encouraged by trending sounds and hashtags—features which 'make it easier for content to quickly amass thousands of views' (Paúl, 2022).

As noted in Chapter 3, Instagram has been criticised for employing an algorithm that provides recommendations for extreme and harmful content and for being responsible for creating body image and mental health problems among teenage girls. In response to the latter criticism, in December 2021, the company announced that it would start offering 'take a break' reminders if users had been scrolling on the social media app too long (Hunter, 2021). In the news article, it was reported that the company indicated that this was one of a range of features that it is rolling out 'to keep teens safer and healthier online' and that these would 'include unspecified restrictions on what content is algorithmically recommended to teens and soon-to-come tools for parents to view and manage the time their teens spend on the app' (Hunter, 2021). Users would receive a 'break prompt' 'ping' after 10, 20, or 30 minutes of scrolling and 'suggest they switch activities' and that, while the feature was not set to default, 'teens would get notifications encouraging them to set the reminders'. Other features include allowing users to 'mass-delete past posts, comments and likes to better manage their online presence' and to 'limit unwanted contact from strangers by preventing them from tagging teens in comments or posts'. Guardians would be allowed to monitor teens' time online and set limits, while teens would have 'the option to notify their parents when they report someone for inappropriate behaviour on the app' (Hunter, 2021). The company was said to be also 'experimenting with alerts for teens who spend too much time "dwelling" on posts about a single topic', which follows criticisms of the company for 'serving to teens potentially harmful posts including on diet and weight loss information and content promoting eating disorders'. As with TikTok, the options offered by these features conflict with the company's business model which is oriented to keeping teens engaged on their platform. Critics argued that the timing of the announcement was a 'smokescreen' created by the company to draw attention from issues they did not want highlighted at an upcoming hearing before the US Congress which would focus on 'the company's impacts on young people' (Hunter, 2021).

Given growing evidence of Big Tech company's efforts to keep users engaged, critics argue that technological responses of the kind outlined above, involving controls on screen time and/or content, are insufficient to curb harms and abuse and have called for further measures; however, these measures also often entail the use of technologies or alterations of their design. For example, it has been suggested that companies should be required to conduct assessments of the impact on users of time spent online, of product misuse, and of algorithmic bias, especially in relation to young people; establish design principles and codes of ethics for designers; and appoint independent authorities such as an ombudsperson, to oversee product design (Baskaran, 2019). History is filled with examples of efforts to solve technology-related problems, including those related to their use, employing other technologies and/or changing their users' relationships to them, particularly through legislative and educative efforts. A classic example is the use of seatbelts and airbags in cars to mitigate the risks of traffic accidents, combined with road safety messages encouraging people to drive more safely. Another example is the proposal to use so-called carbon capture and storage and other technologies to curb the greenhouse gases that contribute to human-induced climate change, in tandem with efforts to encourage citizens to alter their energy use and consumption practices. While technologies and their users can play an important role in managing or mitigating risks—in the latter example, rapidly rising sea levels, damaging storms, recurring droughts and fires, and other impacts—and/or minimising the harms, this will do little to address the predisposing economic, political, and social conditions that led to the problem in the first place. For these examples, this includes a history of prioritising the 'freedoms' of personalised forms of transport over more inclusive forms of public transport, and the use of carbon-based technologies of production over other, more energy efficient, sustainable options, respectively. Likewise with the purported 'addictions' that are linked to the extensive use of digital media.

The concept of digital well-being

As noted, 'digital well-being', or 'digital wellness', is often proposed as the response to alleged addictive technology by changing media users' relationships to technologies; to bring them into a 'healthy balance'. An Ngram analysis reveals that there were no references to 'digital well-being' or 'digital wellness' in books printed before 2008 after which the use of the terms increased substantially up until 2019, the last year available for analysis via this search engine. Like many concepts in health and medicine, however, the term has evolved to embrace a diverse array of practices, many of which entail the use of technologies, and some which do not, or use them in combination with non-technology-based interventions. It is worth considering some definitions of the term before turning to examine some specific initiatives. As I explain, recent years have seen a growing market of 'digital well-being' and 'digital wellness' products and services. Many companies have become concerned with the question of how to harness attention productively while not causing harm to their employees and users of their services. Both Big Tech and smaller companies themselves benefit from this focus on digital well-being, which offers an opportunity for them to develop and sell new products and services while, in effect, avoiding scrutiny of their own systems and practices which are *designed* to keep users engaged.

It is difficult to find a generally accepted definition of 'digital well-being' or 'digital wellness'—terms so vague and all-encompassing that they defy easy definition. One can find no definition of these concepts on the websites of government departments or agencies overseeing digital health, public health, and mental health, where one would expect to find a definition; for example, the Australian government's Department of Health's Healthdirect health advice service; Australia's mental health well-being support service, Beyond Blue; the Australian Digital Health Agency; the UK's Department of Health and Social Care; and US Department of Health and Human Services. The World Health Organization, which has a primary role for international health, does not define the terms. While the WHO mentions the role of 'digital health' in supporting 'equitable and universal access to quality health services' and 'mak[ing] health systems more efficient and sustainable, enabling them to deliver good quality, affordable and equitable care', there is no specific reference to 'digital wellbeing' (WHO, 2021a). However, the WHO has identified the mental health implications of online gaming as an issue of concern. Given changes in people's routines wrought by the pandemic, in November 2021, the WHO announced: 'In order to help inspire millions of online gamers to lead an active lifestyle and look after their mental health', WHO has encouraged online gaming companies to invite their users to take WHO's #HealthyAtHome challenge. The website includes recent related initiatives such as World Mental Health Day and the use of characters in games (Playrix Homescapes and Gardenscapes) 'remind[ing] players about the importance of taking care of their mental health by reducing stress, supporting loved ones, and fostering and maintaining social contacts' (WHO, 2021b).

Definitions of 'digital well-being' or 'digital wellness' appear on the websites of some non-government or charitable organisations, particularly those focusing on children's online safety. An example is the UK Safer Internet Centre, a partnership of childnet (which produces resources and undertakes policy work on children's online safety), Internet Watch Foundation (which is devoted to helping child victims of sexual abuse), and SWGfl (South West Grid for learning) (a UK charity committed to ensuring children benefit from, but are not harmed by technology). According to the Centre, 'digital wellbeing or online wellness' (the terms are used synonymously) are 'essentially about having an awareness of how being online can make us feel and looking after ourselves and others when online. This can include recognising the impact being online can have on our emotions, mental wellbeing and even on our physical health and knowing what to do if something goes wrong' (UK Safer Internet Centre, 2021a). Additionally, it notes, 'Our digital wellbeing can be influenced by the choices we make online, the content we see, the interactions we have with others and even how long we spend engaging with technology and the internet'. It then cites reports that confirm that 'those who spend extended amounts of time online are more likely to see upsetting content, receive abuse comments or send abuse to others' (UK Safer Internet Centre, 2021a). A link on the website takes users to a blog, 'Supporting young people with digital wellbeing this summer' which notes: 'Your child's digital wellbeing refers to how being online affects their mood, emotions, and safety. Lots of different parts of life online can affect digital wellbeing such as screen time, gaming, and online relationships' (UK Safer Internet Centre, 2021b). Childnet's straightforward definition states: 'Digital wellbeing is about recognising the way going online makes us feel and knowing how to manage this' (Childnet, 2021). These definitions which pertain to children imply that 'digital well-being' is a subjective state that may be influenced by either the quantity or quality of online engagements and the decisions of the user. As Childnet's website makes clear, 'Self-care' online is deemed crucial: 'Self-care is about actively taking steps to protect your own wellbeing. This could be limiting the negative impact of the things you see online by unfollowing or blocking particular types of content; seeking out more positive experiences online; balancing your time online with offline activities that help you recharge, get some space and feel better'. It goes on: 'Self-care is different for everyone but lots of young people have told us they enjoy: going outside and getting some exercise, spending time with friends and family, taking a long bath, listening to music, reading, baking or other similar hobbies' (Childnet, 2021). The site includes various advice and tips regarding one's online experiences presented in a question-answer format; for example, 'Is going online good for me?', 'Why does going online sometimes make me feel bad?', 'How can I make my experience online more positive?', and 'What tools exist to help me manage my digital wellbeing?'

As the websites of these organisations make clear, parents and carers are ascribed a major responsibility for ensuring that children develop a 'healthy' relationship with digital media. The UK Safer Internet Centre's blog, above, offers a series of 'Digital Wellbeing Tips' for parents and carers: 'Talk to your child about how being online makes them feel', 'Help your child to have a healthy balance and enjoy time offline too', 'Encourage your child to know the warning signs', 'Set boundaries and use wellbeing tools together', and 'Help your child to stay critical online'. The unstated assumption is that digital well-being is part of responsible parenthood and that parents who fail to fulfil their duties in assisting children to achieve a 'healthy balance' in their digital media use are being irresponsible and hence blameworthy. The UK has a strong charitable sector much of which focuses exclusively or strongly on children's health and well-being, including the Save the Children Fund, the Children's Society, Coram, and Joseph Rowntree Foundation, and the policies and programs of the above organisations no doubt partly reflect the country's long tradition of the some-times-paternalistic approach to children's welfare. However, growing attention to 'well-being' in general, like 'happiness', has been of growing policy interest in many areas, including business, healthcare, and education, being often buttressed by the evidence of positive psychology which has had considerable influence in many countries (Chapter 4). Given the widespread receptiveness to these concepts, it is hardly surprising that businesses have sought to capitalise on them as digitalisation has gained pace.

Dimensions of the digital well-being market

The digital well-being industry services a substantial and rapidly growing market of products and services with many dimensions, some oriented specifically to addressing 'internet addiction', some to the health of the growing number of online workers, and others to broader issues of well-being that use digital technologies—or some combination of these elements. Because digital media are now integrated into many people's lives, a vast range of experiences or practices may be encompassed by or related to 'digital well-being' or 'digital wellness'. In recent years, a growing number of organisations, initiatives, and businesses oriented to addressing digital well-being/wellness have been launched. In what follows, I consider some examples of the products and services that are advertised. The range of products, services, and practices encompassed by 'well-being' is broad and seemingly ever-expanding. As I will show, the concept may include various elements, which is evident with the Digital Wellbeing Institute (2021a), a self-described 'learning platform' that offers certification programs and courses, which I examine in some detail shortly. First, it is instructive to consider how conceptions of 'well-being' have changed since the World Health Organization employed the term in its founding documents many decades ago.

According to the principles laid out in the preamble to the WHO's Constitution, which entered into force in 1948, 'well-being' is a multidimensional concept that underpins 'health' in its widest sense; that is, 'Health is a state of complete physical, mental and social well-being and not merely the absence of disease or infirmity' (WHO, 2021c). The Constitution document makes some references to 'well-being' that make clear that it is an outcome of collaborations between various actors and stakeholders from Member States. The document also notes that all States have a common interest in achieving the promotion and protection of health which is 'fundamental to the attainment of peace and security and is dependent upon the fullest co-operation of individuals and States' (WHO, 2021c). The WHO's Constitution was developed in the aftermath of the Second World War, when death, illness, and suffering were the outcome of an *absence* of cooperation and of conflict. In the document, the concept of well-being remained unelaborated and continues to be so in the many reports and news releases that can be found on the WHO's website. Increasingly, however, 'well-being' is used synonymously with 'wellness', or a quality of life that is intrinsically valuable to *a person*, or what is *judged by them* to be in their self-interest (Crisp, 2017; my emphasis). In contemporary philosophy, 'well-being' is mostly used 'to describe what is non-instrumentally or ultimately good *for* a person' (Fletcher, 2021; emphasis in original). As Fletcher explains, in popular usage, 'well-being' usually relates to health, but from a philosophical perspective this is not all that matters for one's well-being, which may also include 'negative' aspects of their life and self-interest or, as he puts it, 'what is in the interest of myself, and not others' (Fletcher, 2021). This all-encompassing, individualistic conceptualisation of 'well-being' has allowed scope for different groups with different interests and agendas—particularly psychologists and psychotherapists and those drawing on their knowledge—to appropriate the term and use it to suit their own purposes. The individualistic conception of well-being is congruent with the neoliberal focus on the entrepreneurial self and self-responsibility. In some instances, those using the term appear to be adopting the narrow conception of 'subjective well-being' or individual happiness rather than using it in a broader sense as originally deployed by the WHO. Notwithstanding these definitional ambiguities, it is clear that 'digital well-being/wellness' has become big business and the basis for a lucrative, and seemingly expanding, market.

Official websites of businesses and other organisations provide only limited insight into their operations and the networks that sustain them. Being the public face of their operations, their websites trade on promise—in the case of digital well-being/wellness industries, to address technology-related problems—and appeals to claimed expertise, reputation, credibility, and trustworthiness. Often their stated goals involve the merging of business venture and utopian aspiration. In some instances, their language borders on the esoteric, mystic or 'new age'. In examining these websites, however, one can learn much about the companies' self-representations, the range of products and/or services they offer and to whom they are advertised, the range of expertise they rely on, the marketing techniques they employ, and the kinds of companies or groups that have a stake in the digital well-being/wellness market.

The Digital Wellness Institute's website is informative in this regard. On its 'About Us' page, it notes that the company 'exists to equip leaders and change-makers with tools to assess and address digital wellness in order to foster a more positive digital culture around the world' (Digital Wellness Institute, 2021b). Its entry on Linkedin states in its 'About Us':

> The Digital Wellness Institute uses the Digital Flourishing™ Model to teach holistic health and wellness. Drawing on theoretical frameworks from positive psychology, traditional psychology, sociology, and data science, programs offered by the Institute equip mental health practitioners, educators and organizational leaders with research-based solutions and tools to embody and teach digital wellness.
>
> *(Digital Wellness Institute, 2021c)*

It will be noted that 'digital flourishing' is trade-marked and is obviously what is being sold. On the institute's website there appears an illustration of what is dubbed a 'Digital Flourishing™ Wheel', with different elements, including 'Physical health, 'Mental health', 'Relationships', 'Communication', 'Environment', 'Productivity', 'Digital citizenship', and 'Quantified self' organised in a concentric circle, with the 'Digital Flourishing™ Wheel' logo in the centre. There is no explanation of how the elements interrelate and how they contribute to 'digital flourishing'. However, Myrth™, a company that claims to have links with the Digital Wellness Collective and describes itself as 'a female founded and run mental health startup ... built for digital wellness, social wellbeing, self-care, mental health and better habit building' (Myrth, 2021a), explains: 'digital wellness' exists along a continuum, from no engagement with tech to 'minimalism, to digital flourishing, to overuse, to dependence or addiction'. It continues: 'In this framework, digital flourishing is the sweet spot right in the middle, and where you can perform your personal and professional roles optimally. It allows you to be a good community member while still having time and resources for yourself, too' (Myrth, 2021a). It might well be asked: what is the problem that the Institute claims to address? On the Institute's 'Home' page appears the prominent banner 'Stating the facts', under which appears 'Together, we're prioritizing wellbeing in a fast-paced world', with accompanying information on 'The Digital Revolution', referring to the impacts of the pandemic associated with 'a shift to remote work and more digital access than ever before', and 'Digital Empowerment' explaining how the Institute 'has helped hundreds of organizations'.

It is informative to note the expertise described on the Digital Wellness Institute's website. They include an 'entrepreneur building technology startups and media companies'; 'instructor'; 'international speaker and leading expert in digital wellness', 'Bestselling author of The Future of Happiness', 'TEDx Speaker' and 'Featured professor in Oprah's Happiness course'; and a 'consultant' and 'strategist' (Digital Wellness Institute, 2021b, c). The Institute offers courses, including 'Certification Program' and a 'Digital Wellness 101 Mini Course'—the latter partnering with 'the #1 ranked online university in Canada, PowerED™ by Athabasca University' (Digital Wellness Institute, 2021d). The institute also advertises 'Speaker Requests' and its website suggests that this is oriented to businesses. The blurb refers to the challenges facing executives such as balancing health concerns with real-time communications with a remote workforce and 'driving productivity' which lead employees to face 'unprecedented levels of burnout, stress, and anxiety' (Digital Wellness Institute, 2021e). The Institute says that 'Leaders need help solving these problems now' and that it can help through offering 'a variety of keynotes and workshops designed to equip leaders and practitioners with research-based tools and strategies to teach and achieve greater digital wellness (Digital Wellness Institute, 2021e). In its advertising, the Institute trades strongly on the psychotherapeutic benefits that will be derived from participation in its courses and from listening to its speakers.

The Institute offers an all-embracing definition of 'digital wellness' that leaves much scope for interpretation and different interventions:

> the optimum state of health and well-being that each individual using technology is capable of achieving. It is a way of life, while using technology,

that promotes optimal health and well-being in which body, mind, and spirit are integrated by the individual to live more fully within the human, natural, and digital communities.

(Digital Wellness Institute, 2021a)

The reference to 'a way of life', 'optimal health and wellbeing' and integration of 'body, mind, and spirit', and so on, resonates with the contemporary neo-liberal emphasis on self-determination, holistic care, healthy living, and health optimisation. The Institute appears to have a long-standing investment in the digital wellness market that is not restricted to young consumers. According to this organisation's website, its origins can be traced back to Apple's launch in 2018 of its first digital wellness tool (now Screen Time) and removal of 'several other amazing wellness apps in the App store' which led to 'a petition [being] circulated to garner more than two thousand signatures which led to the successful reinstatement of these well-being apps' and subsequent establishment of 'the world's first trade association for digital wellness, dubbed the Digital Wellness Collective' (Digital Wellness Institute, 2021b). As explained, this initiative gave rise to 'the explicit need for an education and training body dedicated to equipping leaders with a common definition of digital wellness and a set of research-based metrics and skills for achieving a more positive digital culture'. Then, in March 2020, as the COVID-19 pandemic took hold and many people began to rely on digital media during lockdowns, 'the Collective formally reorganized as the Digital Wellbeing Institute and launched its flagship certificate program'. As the website explains, the Institute's stated goal is 'To educate 25 million people about strategies for digital flourishing within 5 years' (Digital Wellness Institute, 2021b).

Digital Wellness Day

The Digital Wellness Institute hosts 'Digital Wellness Day', described on the event's website ('Overview' page) as 'a nonprofit initiative fiscally sponsored by HAPPI' (Helping Awesome Parents Parent Intentionally) (Digital Wellness, Day, 2021a). The first such event was hosted in May 2020, presumably to capitalise on increased reliance on digital technology during the lockdowns of the COVID-19 pandemic. A press release for the 2021 event claimed that the previous year's 'inaugural Digital Wellness Day reached 1.2 million people worldwide, and this year over 10 million are expected to participate in virtual gatherings around the globe' (Digital Wellness Institute, 2021f). It also noted that 'COVID-19 triggered dramatic social-economic changes, resulting in many of us working from home and socializing remotely in a virtual world', and that 'Digital Wellness Day is a catalyst for exploring and sharing how we can evolve and flourish in this context of living and working, and encourages diverse audiences to publicly share their ideas and experiences regarding achieving digital wellbeing' (Digital Wellbeing Institute, 2021f).

According to its stated mission, 'Digital Wellness Day raises global attention for mental, physical, emotional health, and safety when using digital devices. It's a chance to rethink when, where, why, and how we interact with technology to ensure we are using it for its best and highest purposes' (Digital Wellness Day, 2021a). The event's homepage, includes a large banner advertising the forthcoming event, with an 'impact report' (noting '7,697,427 people reached, 77 public-facing events held, 4 languages'), videos of past events, and information on sponsors, which includes organisations or companies that purport to specialise in digital wellness or responsible technology use (e.g. bonfire digital wellness, tech wellness, LookUp, The Social Dilemma), media and media education companies (Greater Good Science Centre, Media Done Responsibly), university-based science centres or education providers (The Greater Good Science Centre, University of California, Berkeley, PowerEd™, Athabasca University), a wellness app company (Daily Haloha) and a company that makes personalised handcrafted keepsakes (Cades and Birch) (Digital Wellness Day, 2021b). A 'Resources' page includes a link to a 'Digital wellness certificate program', along with a 'Digital Wellness Toolkit', offering various information, advice and tips along with a 'digital flourishing survey' and a 'free, digital wellness check-up' and information on an introductory course ('1.5 hours + a digital badge'); 'Digital wellness bingo for adults and kids; a free e-book download (for those with a Kindle reader) of 'Digital wellness: your playbook for thriving in the remote work era' (Digital Wellness Day, 2021c). Another page, lists 'Speakers' with a diverse array of backgrounds and specialisms, including health professionals (e.g. wellness instructors, psychologists), media organisations, developers of software and devices, technology consultants, representatives of technology companies (e.g. IBM), youth organisations, and various digital wellness advocates (e.g. Intentionally Unplugged, Cyber Civics, Digital Wellness Institute). Visitors to the website are also invited to donate to Digital Wellness Day, with a fee of '3,025 of $333,333 goal' (Digital Wellness Day, 2021d).

The digital well-being/wellness market is largely US-based and -focused and the nature and scope of related interventions reflect the values and aspirations of the more affluent sections of its population who spend much of their time online as workers in the rapidly expanding digital economy. Many if not most are required, as part of their employment, to be 'consumer-focused' and adopt the kinds of emotional management styles described by Hochschild in her classic study of airline hostesses undertaken four decades ago (Hochschild, 1983). However, much has changed in the world of work since Hochschild undertook her seminal study, including the rise of many digitally based enterprises whose fortunes rest on their public image and the employment of staff whose values and outlooks closely align with their own (Chapter 1). These values include the ability to conduct oneself in an entrepreneurial way, recover from setbacks, learn from one's mistakes, and exhibit toughness in the face of adversity; in short, 'resilience'. Individuals are often employed for these personal skills and attributes along with the ability to exhibit empathy and the capacity to emotionally 'connect' with clients and audiences (who may also be clients) (Chapter 2). Digital well-being/wellness initiatives are promoted as engendering these skills and qualities in order that one may 'flourish'.

Digital wellness apps

While they are difficult to neatly categorise, the companies that market 'digital well-being/wellness' are mostly in the business of selling digital devices or apps that purportedly assist people to self-manage their health and other aspects of their life. These include especially personal apps that assist behavioural changes (e.g. self-monitoring/tracking devices) and platforms that help individuals with decisions about weight loss, diet, and chronic disease management. These apps and platforms are part of a burgeoning market of what may be described as 'digital health' technologies (Petersen, 2019). They are advertised not only to consumers but also to health professionals, businesses, and governments, to help them assist their staff to achieve their 'well-being goals'. One company wellteq advertisers with the rather grandiose sounding slogan 'Empowering people to be healthier and happier', with the by-line 'From prevention to intervention, wellteq supports health journeys by coaching better wellbeing habits' (wellteq, 2021a). The company, which claims to be global with offices in 32 countries, is clearly oriented to businesses: 'Create a healthier and happier workforce. Data-driven employee health and wellbeing technology that helps you create a healthier and happier workforce' (wellteq, 2021b). The website also states: 'Personalised digital health technology for your employees to make lasting behaviour changes. Powerful analytics for your business to create a healthier workplace' (wellteq, 2021b). It also includes a banner 'For employers', 'For insurers', and 'For partners and resellers' outlining the various benefits for them, including workplace engagement, productivity, building brand loyalty, and 'increased reach' (wellteq, 2021b). Another banner, appearing on its 'About Us' page, states that 'Our solutions are based on 'user-centred design principles' and that 'A proprietary personalised engine captures each user with content specific to their profile and health risk assessment for maximum user engagement and outcomes'. Moreover, 'We constantly stay on the edge of innovation, bringing you the latest in technology and health tech improvements'. Finally, the reassurance is offered about data privacy, cybersecurity, and governance, noting that 'We take as much pride in protecting your information as we do in improving your health' (wellteq, 2021a). Assurances of data privacy and security appear on many company websites, reflecting recognition that many people are concerned about this issue in the age of mass data harvesting and theft. wellteq also lists on its website 'some amazing healthcare providers' it has 'teamed up' with 'to deliver you and end-to-end wellness solution'; they include a business start-up (Doctor Anywhere), a company specialising in smartphone-based human-scanning technology (Advanced Human Imaging), a company offering health analytics and blood testing services (iScreen), a mobile cognitive assessment platform (Sanovix), a manufacturer of GPS devices (Garmin), a multichannel digital health technology company (Well Health), an online psychology counselling service (Lysn), a personal training and coaching company (UFIT), and a global risk management, insurance brokerage, and advisory company (Willis Towers Watson).

This list of companies reflects some of the diverse interests in the digital well-being/wellness market and the kinds of technologies that are finding application. Digital health and well-being technology is now a huge and rapidly growing sector of healthcare, much focused on self-care and home-based care. One can gain some insight into the state and likely future direction of this market by viewing the offerings of the Consumer Electronics Show (CES) held in Las Vegas in January every year, which is seen as offering a window on trends in digital health and wellness technologies. In his comments on the 2020 CES event, Digital Health editor-in-chief, Jon Hoeksma, noted that

> a diverse array of start-ups big and small, established big consumer brands such as Amazon and Apple, Proctor and Gamble and Johnson and Johnson, were demonstrating their parts of this digital health 'eco-system of eco-systems', the fastest growing segment of the giant tech show.
>
> *(Hoeksma, 2020)*

As Hoeksma observed, digital health was 'moving from hospital to people's homes' with a vast array of 'digital tools and data to support people in their own homes for long-term conditions, behavioural change, mental health and wellness, including sleep' (Hoeksma, 2020). Hoeksma was writing just before the COVID-19 pandemic begun which has turbocharged the field of digital health and well-being, with many technologies marketed to those who were soon to become heavily reliant on digital media during lockdowns and other restrictions on social interactions.

Nurturing 'resilience'

Organisations and companies that market 'digital health/well-being' make many references to the goal of assisting people to 'thrive' and be 'resilient' in the digital age. The National Institute for Digital Health and Wellbeing, a US-based self-described 'not-for-profit organisation' states:

> Our mission is to help individuals, families, schools, organizations and our planet to thrive in the new, challenging landscape of the Digital Age. By offering education, resources, prevention services, treatment and training to schools, individuals, therapists and organizations, we can build a healthier, more resilient and purposeful planet that uses technology as a tool—and does not become the 'tool of tools' (as the transcendentalist philosopher Henry David Thoreau said over 100 years ago).
>
> *(NIDHW, 2021a)*

The institute offers education, resources, and training, as well as certification for therapists, and claims to have members from various disciplines including psychology, education, science, advocacy, philanthropy, and 'everyday people who are concerned about our species and how it has been affected by technology' (NIDHW, 2021a). On its 'Certifications' link, reference is made to the various problems facing 'our youth' including 'increased rates of ADHD, depression, suicidal thoughts, anxiety, sleep irregularities, thought disorder and stunted social skills'. It goes on: 'Our goal is to provide safe and effective strategies to work with kids hijacked by tech addiction' (NIDHW, 2021b). This page includes the steps required to complete in order to obtain certification and 'Our target audience', which is extensive and includes: counsellors, social workers, psychologists, marriage and family therapists, addiction professionals, case managers, occupational therapies, and other professionals who work with children (NIDHW, 2021b).

One company, Digital Wellness, which has offices in New York, London, and Sydney, advertises itself as being 'passionate about empowering the worldwide wellness revolution'. It goes on to note that 'This passion—combined with our digital expertise—has led us to become world leaders in delivering innovative online weight loss solutions' (Digital Wellness, 2022). Reading down its 'About Us' page, one discovers a timeline illustrating 'Over 30 years in heritage of weight loss'. This indicates that the company rebranded as 'Digital Wellness' in 2020 from the founding company name 'SP Health'. The timeline indicates that the company was launched in 1980 by 'The Penn family who were pioneers of the Australian weight loss market, rapidly growing Weight Watchers in Australia and bringing aerobic dancing to the nation'. Weight Watchers was later (in 1999) bought by a private equity firm, followed by the launch of a company 'SP Health' in 2006 with 'a goal to create the world's best online weight loss platforms'. Then, in 2015, it 'partnered' with CSIRO [Australia's Commonwealth Scientific and Industrial Research Organisation] to 'launch the CSIRO Healthy Diet Score'. In 2021, the company launched its 'new Maho Clinic Diet' (Digital Wellness, 2022). The company has obviously sought to capitalise on its history in weight loss initiatives and general interest in well-being/wellness to rebrand itself as 'Digital Wellness' during a period of increased use of digital media during the COVID-19 lockdowns.

Young people

As noted, young people and children have been a prime focus of digital well-being/wellness initiatives and provide the basis for a huge market of products and services. One youth-focused organisation, bonfire digital wellness, states as its mission 'to ensure that everyone **feels seen and heard**, is **positively motivated to achieve their potential**, and **maintains healthy habits**, including a **productive relationship with technology**' (bonfire digital wellness, 2021a; emphases in original). The website of bonfire explains that the organisation is a 'collective team' that has 'worked with thousands of students, and has seen firsthand the benefits of providing a sense of warmth and positivity that allows them to feel safe, supported, and confident'. It goes on to explain that 'We've also had some of our best memories around a bonfire, chatting with family and friends, having meaningful conversations, planning our future, or just hanging out and having fun' and that bonfire aimed to recreate this community and collaborative culture for members, 'providing continuous ember to ignite and sustain their potential' (bonfire digital wellness, 2021a). On its 'Approach' page, it is explained that bonfire is 'not anti-tech, screens, or gaming', and that 'screens are here for good, and there are quite a lot of benefits technology affords us, but there are a lot of risks as well. As with many things in life, the key is balance'. To help site visitors understand their message, bonfire presents a 'Healthy Screen Time Pyramid' which provides 'a guide for balanced and productive screen time' (bonfire digital wellness, 2021b). At the top of the pyramid there appear images of 'binge-watching', 'seeking validation', and 'gossip' which are marked 'Less'. As one proceeds down the pyramid, one is directed to other activities, including 'news', 'gaming', 'documenting', and 'sharing' marked with 'some', then moving lower to other activities, such as 'hobbies' civil engagement, 'community', and 'connecting' marked 'More', and finally, at the bottom of the pyramid appear 'creativity', 'inspiration', 'skill-building', 'discovery', and 'learning', marked with 'Most' (bonfire digital wellness, 2021b). On the same page, some comments highlight the challenges posed by 'the COVID crisis' which 'clearly has increased technology's impact on all our lives' and, while it acknowledges the 'positive experiences' notes that 'without proper balance, they can also create negative outcomes'. It then refers to three documentaries released in 2020, 'clearly laying out the digital minefield our kids are playing in', with hyperlinks to *Social Dilemma* (referred to in Chapter 2), *Childhood 2.0*, and *Screened Out*. Finally, a 'Membership' link takes one to a page that explains that the organisation offers personalised coaching for children, group classes (which includes content on 'digital citizenship' and 'working on productive screen time habits') and details and costs of membership plans (bonfire digital wellness, 2021c).

The onset of the COVID-19 pandemic created new opportunities for companies hoping to capitalise on 'digital well-being/wellness', with many services oriented specifically to young people. One such company is EVERFI, an education technology company that claims to 'work with young adults to teach them critical skills', including 'work readiness' and health and wellness, and collaborates with 25,000 schools in the United States and Canada, as well as 1,700 colleges and universities in the United States, the UK, Canada, and UAE, including Stanford and Ivy Leagues. Launching the Digital Wellness Network in 2019, Jon Chapman, the co-founder and president of EVERFI spoke about the challenges facing young people today with digital media, which both offered benefits and contributed to them feeling depressed, isolated, and lonely today. One of these challenges, Chapman said, was 'how do we give them [young people] the know-how, the hard skills to be safe online … but how do we combine with an understanding of the soft skills, the social and emotional understanding of how they are interacting with technology online'. Adding: 'At EVERFI we call that digital wellness' (Chapman, 2019). The Digital Wellness Network is described as a 'public-private coalition of corporations, nonprofits, and educators committing to mitigating the negative impact of unhealthy technology use by empowering students to make safe and healthy decisions about technology' (EVERFI, 2021a). The stated aims of the Network focus on its commitment to 'empowering youth with the "rules of the road" that will help them remain respectful and balanced as they utilize technology'. The website entry notes that the Network 'supports and funds the activation of EVERFI's digital wellness and online safety course, Ignition … [which] demonstrates to students the benefits of a digital community and resources while teaching learners to successfully navigate challenges inherent in the digital space' (EVERFI, 2021a). The site also outlines the 'Partnership Benefits', including research and impact reporting and marketing and communication plans 'supported by EVERFI that showcases your investment in digital wellness education' (EVERFI, 2021a).

It is evident from the webpage that EVERFI is keen to attract partners, which arguably provides not just funding but a profile to the business. Some representatives of the partner companies appear in an accompanying video. The CEO of one company Take-Two Interactive, a US video game holding company, explains that he felt that they could 'help make a difference in not only educating students on the best way to use technology in a more respectful way and to give them life skills that they can take with them forever'. A representative of another partner, the executive director of ESA (Entertainment Software Association) Foundation, an organisation that supports programs that use video games to benefit students, schools, and charities (ESA Foundation, 2021) points out that at the foundation 'we talk a lot about developing future innovators and creators and video game-makers. I feel it is extremely important that not just those students, but all students have what is often referred to as twenty-first century skills and, if they're going to join the workforce of tomorrow it is extremely important that they understand how to safely and respectfully navigate online not just for their own personal self but also for their professional lives' (EVERFI, 2021a). It is interesting that these companies, with interests in video gaming should be part of these digital wellness initiatives given the attention that has been focused on the purported addictions that gamers suffer. The focus of EVERFI on 'empowering youth' through education and the development of what it calls 'social-emotional learning skills' addresses what is now widely accepted as a widespread addiction, namely online gaming, but uses the very same technologies and some of the same techniques in its advertised teaching practices. For example, the company's 'Free digital lessons', 'Financial literacy for kids' is advertising as using 'interactive and game-based learning' which 'immerses students in real-time financial scenarios that focus on skill building and responsible decision-making'. As explained, 'This gamified course features an engaging storyline, diverse set of characters, and interactions & activities to teach students fundamental financial topics in a fun and engaging way' (EVERFI, 2021b).

'Responsible' technology use and 'digital distraction'

With many companies relying extensively on digital technologies, 'responsible' technology use has become a commonly stated corporate goal. Responsible technology use means changing workers' relationships with technologies in ways that both benefit them and the organisation's, or business's goals. 'Focus' is recognised as important to business success and that digital distraction among staff can adversely affect productivity. Employees' attention may be split between different tasks, or they may spend time surfing the internet or engaged in non-productive activities such as WhatsApp texting or 'facebooking', or else be distracted by incessant pings on mobiles and desktop screens (see, e.g. Nielsen, 2021). Such distractions, it is argued, sap time and energies, leading workers to perform at a sub-optimal level. A McKinsey study found that the average 'interaction worker' spent an estimated 28 percent of the work week managing email, and that improved communication and collaboration through use of social technologies could raise the productivity of workers by 20–25 percent (Chui, et al., 2021). Some writers speak of an 'epidemic of digital distraction', with one noting that 'Every time you pull away from a project to check your phone or Twitter fee, it takes 1,395 second (23+ minutes) on average to regain your focus' (Solis, 2019). In some assessments, distraction results in part from access to 'too much information' creating an 'information overload' (or 'information glut', 'infoxication', or 'data smog') which 'occurs when the information available exceeds the processing abilities of the individual in the time available' (IORG, 2021). Recognising employers' concerns about attention distraction and other harmful effects of digital connections, including on businesses' bottom-lines, companies offer services to assist them to become more 'responsible'.

The close links between being 'responsible' and being productive online is clear with Sentient Digital, which claims to 'help you [being the employer] to put responsible technology and digital wellbeing into practice'. Listed under a banner headed 'Our Clients', Sentient Digital's website says, 'We work with companies who know that responsible technology is good business; with start-ups leading the way in digital wellbeing; for leaders who want their teams to stay in control of technology' (Sentient Digital, 2021a). The company advertises consulting to organisations and government 'to help them understand digital wellbeing & responsible technology and to develop their corporate & technology strategies accordingly'. Sentient Digital says it also works with start-ups that build digital well-being products and 'innovators who are experimenting with new business models to make responsible technology a reality' (Sentient Digital, 2021b). On its 'Research' page, it is explained that 'We work with researchers and academics around the world to better understand technology habits, behaviour change and routes to digital wellbeing'. It goes on to note that digital well-being is a relatively new field and that more research is needed 'to better understand how our relationships with devices and apps affects us both as individuals and society'. And that 'In many cases, researchers lack access to timely, accurate and reliable data on how people are using their phones, and what this means for their emotions and behaviours'. It is explained that the research field is 'multidisciplinary' and that 'it is important to start amassing quantitative, as well as qualitative, studies to better understand our relationship with technology'. It goes on: 'With this research, we can come closer to a consensus on what digital well-being really means, so that we can better educate users, regulators, governments and technology companies accordingly' (Sentient Digital, 2021c). The company says it works with academic researchers and start-ups around the world and offers them support through consultancy and data gathering, and that this is accomplished via 'a partnership with screen-time app SPACE' (Sentient Digital, 2021c).

Sentient Digital also offers training through hosting workshops which 'help people to better understand the technology landscape, the attention economy and how some products are designed to keep us hooked' (Sentient Digital, 2021d). As the company's website elaborates,

> If we have purpose in our use of technology, we can connect, create and learn. But for a lot of us, using a device is not a conscious choice, it's a habit. It causes us to lose out on meaningful engagement with the 'real world' and the people in it. We also miss the creativity that come in idle moment, when our mind is free to wander.
>
> *(Sentient Digital, 2021d)*

As noted, in the workplace, the challenges of 24/7 life are 'all too apparent' including continual distraction, increases in stress, decreased productivity and 'the loss of true human connection'. The answer, it is suggested, is not avoidance of technology, which is 'not realistic and isn't even necessary', but rather 'being in control of when we use our devices' but that 'breaking out of any negative habits is challenging' and 'takes time' and that people 'need a helping hand to achieve a change in their digital behaviour'. Businesses, individuals, and families need to examine how they can ensure that technology 'enhances their lives rather than overwhelms them'. As the website states, 'We reflect on what is good and bad about how we use technology, on our own habit formation, and the triggers that lead us to behave in the ways we do'. It goes on to explain that 'phone/life balance is different for everyone' and that they 'provide employees with the right tools to support behaviour change in a positive, fun and sustainable way', which 'includes frameworks for digital wellbeing, like a value-based approach, or the 4C's Framework of Control, Connection, Content & Care' (Sentient Digital, 2021d). The company's training programs, it is noted, are often run-in partnership with Mind Over Tech, an organisation dedicated to changing 'digital habits' with the slogan 'Embrace technology with intention'. Mind Over Tech's website has a link to a 'digital habit lab' with a 'card deck of 50 bite-sized experiments to disrupt your digital habits' and 'Take control of your tech for increased wellbeing, creativity and productivity' with an announced launching date of February 2022.

Mind Over Tech also conducts talks and workshops, and its website includes links to a series of podcasts on various related topics (e.g. 'Being intentional moment-to-moment', 'Inner freedom', 'Generation Z and tech culture', 'Playful experiments with digital tools') and 'Posts', with various observations on digital life (e.g. 'My desk is an extension of my nervous system', 'My inbox is regularly breathtaking'). Mind Over Tech lists Google, Vodaphone, Accenture, Deloitte, KPMG, Slaughter and May, *The Telegraph* newspaper, and the Cabinet Office, on its website—presumably those to whom they offer services.

As noted, the onset of the COVID-19 pandemic has served to accelerate many trends in the digital well-being market and create new opportunities for the sale of various products and services. Enforced lockdowns during the early phases of the pandemic provided a captive audience for advertisers and heightened anxieties about people's (especially children's) screen time. One organisation, the Global Wellness Institute, which describes itself as 'a nonprofit organization with a mission to empower wellness worldwide by educating the public and private sectors about preventive health and wellness', and offers various year-by-year 'digital wellness initiative trends', documented a 'surge in online wellness services' in 2020, corresponding with the onset of COVID-19. For example, its website notes that the meditation app Headspace 'experienced as 19-fold jump in users completing a calming exercise'. Demand for these services, it is claimed, was in part driven by 'the public's desire to boost the immune system to contend with COVID-19', as well as 'the desire for human connection' resulting from social isolation-induced loneliness. The institute offers the prediction that 'online wellness services will continue post-COVID due to benefits of at-home servicing' (Global Wellness Institute, 2022a). The webpage includes a link to an article in *The Economist*, which reports that 'With millions stuck at home, the online wellness industry is booming' (Merchlinksy, 2020). One of the '2021 Trends' listed is the rise of 'digital self-care' during a period of restricted access to medical examinations during COVID-19. It is noted that 'As one of the positive aspects of COVID-19, more people have been reported to focus on their mental health, wellbeing, physical health and nutrition and increased their self-knowledge' (Global Wellness Institute, 2022a)—a claim supported by a reference to a report by PricewaterhouseCoopers' based on a survey of approximately '4,500 respondents across regions that were differently affected by the pandemic' (Lombardo, 2020). The Global Wellness Institute also coordinates the 'Digital Wellness initiative' whose aim, its website states, 'is to bring together thought leaders from wellness, healthcare, technology, government, and education to serve as a think tank evaluating research and advocating for policy and education on the healthy use and adoption of technology' (Global Wellness Institute, 2022b).

'Burn-out' and 'languishing' during the COVID-19 pandemic

A salient well-being issue arising during the COVID-19 pandemic was the exhaustion or 'burnout' reportedly suffered by many people as a result of grappling with the challenges of the pandemic itself, especially the massive disruptions to work, school, and personal and social life, and increased reliance on digital media. Another, related term that gained currency during COVID-19 was 'languishing'—a sense of 'stagnation and emptiness' (Grant, 2021)—the very opposite of 'flourishing' a concept which, as noted, is heavily promoted by the Digital Wellness Institute. According to the Australian-based mental health organisation, Beyond Blue, languishing is the feeling that 'you're not on top of everything but also not feeling really down'. As its website states, 'In a COVID-affected world, it's something many people are feeling right now' (Beyond Blue, 2022). Written during the period of restrictions and lockdowns in Australia, particularly Victoria, the webpage description elaborates:

> One of the key factors of languishing is that people might not notice that they are experiencing it. Reaching this point is a more gradual process than, for instance, someone who is flourishing but then finds themselves experiencing depression.
>
> *(Beyond Blue, 2022)*

During 2021, there were growing reports of many people reassessing their lives, and of workers quitting their jobs and starting new lives or new jobs—the so-called Great Resignation (Schwantes, 2021). According to one survey, involving 1,000 US-based employees, the 'vast majority' (40 percent) of people left their last job 'feeling burned out and unappreciated and sought new positions with organizations that invest in their well-being' (Limeade, 2022). Many left their position without having a job lined up. Events outside the workplace, such as the COVID-19 pandemic, were reported as exacerbating burn-out during the previous 20 months. Employees who were attracted to their current position valued it for 'the ability to work remotely (40%) and other forms of flexibility', which included 'not been restricted to complete job responsibilities during set work hours'. Those who had made the shift, reported being generally happier that they had done so, with many (22 percent) receiving 'a boost in feeling cared for as an individual by their new employer compared with their previous employer' and were more comfortable disclosing a mental health condition to their new employer' compared with their previous employer (Limeade, 2022). As one media commentator noted, with reference to these findings and other observations during COVID-19, 'burn-out' has become a commonly used word used to talk about work-related problems (Malesic, 2021).

While COVID-19 brought prominence to 'burn-out', the term has a long history, stretching as far back as 1969 when the phenomenon was identified in a research paper reporting the experiences of treatment staff at a rehabilitation centre for young adult offenders (Malesic, 2021). As Malesic notes, in the early 1970s, the term then began to be used to describe the experiences of those involved in the care and treatment of others, which involved an 'attitude that combines sympathetic concern with clinical objectivity', which can prove to be emotionally draining (Malesic, 2021). It was suggested at the time that 'Detachment is a protective strategy' which, if it becomes extreme, can lead to experiences of 'burn-out'. Malesic suggests that henceforth the term 'burn-out' became a 'cultural buzzword' which has continued to this day, but with its use rising and falling over time and corresponding with the economic development of the countries involved. In 2019, they note, 'burn-out' was classified as a 'syndrome' by the World Health Organization in its International Classification of Diseases. In some countries, including Sweden and Finland, a diagnosis of 'burn-out' can entitle those so labelled to be paid time off and gain sickness benefits or qualify for participation in paid rehabilitation workshops along with intensive individual and group activities such as counselling, exercise, and nutrition classes (Malesic, 2021). However, during COVID-19 there were growing reports of front-line health staff suffering burn-out as a result of grappling with rising numbers of patients in hospitals in intensive care units suffering often life-threatening illnesses (e.g. Leo, et al. 2021). Some healthcare workers were reported to be not only exhausted but emotionally detached from their patients. According to one of the leading scholars in the field, Cristina Maslach, 'burn-out' is 'a psychological syndrome emerging as a prolonged response to chronic interpersonal stresses on the job' (Maslach and Leiter, 2016). Maslach developed a 'Burnout Inventory', which was a psychological assessment involving 22 symptom items to measure occupational burn-out (Maslach and Jackson, 1996–2016). In 2019, burn-out was classified by the World Health Organization as an 'occupational phenomenon' in the International Classification of Diseases (WHO, 2022). The WHO defines burn-out as 'a syndrome conceptualized as resulting from chronic workplace stress that has not been successfully managed'. Is not a medical condition and is restricted to the occupational context, and is characterised by three dimensions: 'feelings of energy depletion or exhaustion; increased mental distance from one's job, or feelings of negativism or cynicism related to one's job; and reduced professional efficiency' (WHO, 2022). Interestingly, the syndrome is generally associated with professional work involving interaction with people, such as physicians, nurses, doctors, social workers, and teachers (De Hert, 2020). But in contemporary societies, many individuals arguably are prone to 'burn-out', including those working as front-line, often poorly paid service workers in the hospitality sector and the aged care sector, and the online-based workers (including call centre staff) and others responsible for handling customer and client enquiries online and offline. These workers undertake emotional labour and it is a kind of labour that is often under-acknowledged and under-valued—a large proportion undertaken by women and those from poorer (often cultural and linguistic minority) communities. But being typically employed in precarious employment they tend to lack the level of resources and institutional support available to professionals.

Conclusion

'Digital wellbeing/wellness' is a phenomenon oriented to and mostly benefitting the relatively rich, privileged professionals who can afford to pay for the advertised products and services. Like many other aspects of COVID-19, the pandemic brought to light or exacerbated inequalities, and served to expose the limits of the individualistic and consumeristic focus of the contemporary 'well-being' phenomenon. This includes the intensive focus on the self, and related social comparison which it fuels. As noted, in the WHO's original conception, 'wellbeing' is multidimensional and is achieved via the collaborations of various actors and stakeholders from Member States. The use of technologies and the kinds of interventions *may* play some role in improving people's health in a digital age but the focus on changing individuals' relationships to technologies, especially by changing their behaviours, and the pursuit of the kinds of profit-generating 'digital well-being/wellness' initiatives pursued thus far, will have little effect on changing the conditions that impact 'well-being' in its broadest sense.

There have been relatively few criticisms of the value of a technology response to 'digital wellness' (Waterfield, 2018)—a phenomenon that has achieved wide currency as has its assumed opposite, namely 'digital addiction'. As I have argued, 'digital wellness' has come to constitute a massive industry oriented to addressing the compulsions of a digital media age involving more than the sale of apps and devices. This industry comprises 'attention merchants' who have developed an extensive repertoire of techniques developed over a long period of time oriented to catching our eye, cultivating our tastes, and influencing our consumption (Wu, 2016). I discussed some of this history in earlier chapters, especially in Chapter 2, and the step change in the techniques of harvesting attention associated with the rise of programmatic advertising. There are few areas of contemporary life unaffected by the influence of advertising. Yet, the conditions that have enabled this pervasive advertising—and the emotional economy upon which it relies—are undergoing significant change for reasons I explain in the next and final chapter.

References

Amazon (2021) 'Advertising for internet addiction: kicking the habit: 30 day plan to take back your life', https://www.amazon.com.au/Internet-Addiction-Kicking-Habit -Plan-ebook/dp/B01LYD5MQ9 (Accessed 19 November 2021).

App Store (2021) 'App store preview, ratings and reviews', https://apps.apple.com/us/ app/screen-time-parental-control/id1055315077 (Accessed 10 December 2021).

Baskaran, A. (2019) 'The role of technology companies in technology addiction', *Sustainalytics*, 16 July, https://www.sustainalytics.com/esg-research/resource/ investors-esg-blog/the-role-of-technology-companies-in-technology-addiction# _edn5 (Accessed 24 November 2021).

Beyond Blue (2022) 'Let's talk about languishing', https://coronavirus.beyondblue.org .au/COVID-normal/supporting-personal-wellbeing/lets-talk-about-languishing ?gclid=CjwKCAiAp8iMBhAqEiwAJb94z_FlWAq1u_PUacAigYvillj9kQ_RyDr75t _rASa_4JFYn3nt2TaDLBoCrdoQAvD_BwE (Accessed 21 January 2022).

Bonfire Digital Wellness (2021a) 'Why bonfire?', https://bonfiredw.org/about (Accessed 16 December 2021).

Bonfire Digital Wellness (2021b) 'The bonfire effect', https://bonfiredw.org/approach (Accessed 16 December 2021).

Bonfire Digital Wellness (2021c) 'Membership', https://bonfiredw.org/membership (Accessed 16 December 2021).

Booth, B. (2017) 'Internet addiction is sweeping America, affecting millions', *Modern Medicine*, 29 August, https://www.cnbc.com/2017/08/29/us-addresses-internet-addiction-with-funded-research.html (Accessed 19 November 2021).

Burns, T. and Gottschalk, F. (eds) (2019) 'Educating 21st century children: emotional well-being in the digital age', *Education Research and Innovation*. OECD, Paris, https://doi.org/10.1787/b7f33425-en.

Chapman, J. (2019) 'Generation "connected": promoting digital wellness', *YouTube*, posted on EVERFI webpage 'Empower students to be safe and healthy online', https://everfi.com/networks/digital-wellness-network/network-launch/ (Accessed 16 December 2021).

Childnet (2021) 'Digital wellbeing', https://www.childnet.com/young-people/secondary/digital-wellbeing (Accessed 13 December 2021).

Chui, M., Manyika, J., Bughin, J., Dobbs, R., Roxburgh, C., Sarrazin, H., Sands, G. and Westergren, M. (2021) 'The social economy: unlocking value and productivity through social technologies', *McKinsey Global Institute*, 1 July 2012, https://www.mckinsey.com/industries/technology-media-and-telecommunications/our-insights/the-social-economy (Accessed 24 December 2021).

Crisp, R. (2017) 'Well-being', *The Stanford Encylopedia of Philosophy*, Metaphysics Research Lab, Stanford University, https://plato.stanford.edu/entries/well-being/ (Accessed 14 December 2021).

Dalai, P. K. and Basu, D. (2016) 'Twenty years of internet addiction....*Quo Vadis?*', *Industrial Psychiatry Journal*, 27, 1: 61–66.

De Hert, S. (2020) 'Burnout in healthcare workers: prevalence, impact and preventive strategies', *Local and Regional Anesthesia*, 13: 171–183.

Deloitte (2019) 'Global mobile consumer survey: UK cut plateauing at the peak. The state of the smartphone', https://www2.deloitte.com/content/dam/Deloitte/uk/Documents/technology-media-telecommunications/deloitte-uk-plateauing-at-the-peak-the-state-of-the-smartphone.pdf (Accessed 10 December 2021).

Digital Wellness (2022) 'About us', https://www.digitalwellness.com/about-us/about-us/ (Accessed 18 January 2022).

Digital Wellness Day (2021a) 'Overview: our mission', https://summit.digitalwellnessday.com/about/ (Accessed 23 December 2021).

Digital Wellness Day (2021b) 'Home', https://digital-wellness-day.heysummit.com/ (Accessed 23 December 2021).

Digital Wellness Day (2021c) 'Resources', https://digital-wellness-day.heysummit.com/resources-20/ (Accessed 23 December 2021).

Digital Wellness Day (2021d) 'Donate', https://charity.gofundme.com/o/en/campaign/digitalwellnessday (Accessed 23 December 2021).

Digital Wellness Institute (2021a) 'What is digital wellness', https://www.digitalwellnessinstitute.com/ (Accessed 30 November 2021).

Digital Wellness Institute (2021b) 'Our story', https://www.digitalwellnessinstitute.com/about-us (Accessed 30 November 2021).

Digital Wellness Institute (2021c) 'Digital wellness institute—about us', https://www.linkedin.com/company/digital-wellness-institute (Accessed 2 December 2021).

Digital Wellness Institute (2021d) 'Mini course', https://www.digitalwellnessinstitute.com/dw-101 (Accessed 2 December 2021).

Digital Wellness Institute (2021e) 'Speaker requests', https://www.digitalwellnessinstitute.com/speaker-requests (Accessed 1 December 2021).

Digital Wellness Institute (2021f) 'Press release: international digital wellness day will be celebrated globally on May 7, 2021', 12 April, https://www.pr.com/press-release/834388 (Accessed 23 December 2021).

Driskell (2016) *Internet Addiction, Kicking the Habit: 30 Day Plan to Take Back Your Life*. Independently Published.

ESA Foundation (2021) 'About', https://esafoundation.org/about/ (Accessed 16 December 2021).

EVERFI (2021a) 'Empowering students to be safe and healthy online', https://everfi.com/networks/digital-wellness-network/ (Accessed 16 December 2021).

EVERFI (2021b) 'Free for teachers and students', https://everfi.com/courses/k-12/financial-literacy-elementary-students/ (Accessed 20 December 2021).

Fletcher, G. (2021) 'Well-being', *The Stanford Encyclopedia of Philosophy* (Winter 2021 Edition) https://plato.stanford.edu/entries/well-being/#Bib (Accessed 1 December 2021).

Friedman, E. (2020) *Internet Addiction: A Critical Psychology of Users*. Routledge, London and New York.

Global Wellness Institute (2022a) 'Digital wellness initiative trends', https://globalwellnessinstitute.org/initiatives/digital-wellness-initiative/digital-wellness-trends/ (Accessed 18 January 2022).

Global Wellness Institute (2022b) 'Digital wellness initiative', https://globalwellnessinstitute.org/initiatives/digital-wellness-initiative/ (Accessed 18 January 2022).

Google (2022) 'Digital wellbeing experiments', https://experiments.withgoogle.com/collection/digitalwellbeing (Accessed 18 November 2022).

Google Play (2021) 'Apps, digital wellbeing', https://play.google.com/store/apps/details?id=com.google.android.apps.wellbeing&hl=en_AU&gl=US&showAllReviews=true (Accessed 10 December 2021).

Grant, A. (2021) 'There's a name for the blah you're feeling: it's called languishing', *The New York Times*, 19 April, https://www.nytimes.com/2021/04/19/well/mind/covid-mental-health-languishing.html (Accessed 21 January 2022).

Greenfield, D. (2021) *Overcoming Internet Addiction for Dummies*. John Wiley & Sons, Inc., Hoboken.

HealthDirect (2021) 'Dopamine', https://www.healthdirect.gov.au/dopamine (Accessed 17 November 2021).

Hochschild, A. R. (1983) *The Managed Heart: The Commercialization of Human Feeling*. University of California Press, Berkeley.

Hoeksma, J. (2020) 'Key CES digital health and wellness tech trends to watch', *digitalhealth*, 14 January, https://www.digitalhealth.net/2020/01/key-ces-digital-health-wellness-tech-trends/?utm_source=Digital+Health+Main+Newsletter+List&utm_campaign=d0ac0153db-DHNEWS_16_1_20&utm_medium=email&utm_term=0_5b35787700-d0ac0153db-105009693 (Accessed 16 December 2021).

Hunter, T. (2021) 'Instagram is touting safety features for teens. Mental health advocates aren't buying it.', *The Washington Post*, 7 December, https://www.washingtonpost.com/technology/2021/12/07/instagram-teen-health/?utm_campaign=wp_post_most&utm_medium=email&utm_source=newsletter&wpisrc=nl_most&carta-url=https%3A%2F%2Fs2.washingtonpost.com%2Fcar-ln-tr%2F357710a%2F61afa65e9d2fdab56bb91299%2F5e86729bade4e21f59b210ef%2F59%2F72%2F61afa65e9d2fdab56bb91299 (Accessed 10 December 2021).

Information Overload Research Group (2021) 'IO basics', https://iorgforum.org/io-basics/ (Accessed 24 December 2021).

Information Resources Management Association (2019) *Internet and Technology Addiction: Breakthroughs in Research and Practice*. IGA Global, Hershey, PA.

Lembke, A. (2021) 'Digital addictions are drowning us in Dopamine', *TECHI*, 13 August, https://techiai.com/digital-addictions-are-drowning-us-in-dopamine/ (Accessed 21 December 2021).

Leo, C. G., Sabina, S., Tumolo, M. R., Bodini, A., Ponzini, G., Sabata, E. and Mincarone, P. (2021) 'Burnout among healthcare workers in the COVID 10 era: a review of the existing literature', *Frontiers in Public Health*, 29 October, https://www.frontiersin.org/articles/10.3389/fpubh.2021.750529/full#:~:text=https%3A//doi.org/10.3389/fpubh.2021.750529

Limeade (2022) 'The great resignation update: limeade employee care report', https://www.limeade.com/resources/resource-center/limeade-employee-care-report-the-great-resignation-update/?utm_source=newswire&utm_medium=press_release (Accessed 21 January 2022).

Lindenberg, K., Kindt, S. and Szász-Janocha, C. (2021) *Internet Addiction in Adolescents: The PROTECT Program for Evidence-Based Prevention and Treatment*. Springer, New York.

Lombardo, C. (2020) 'COVID-19 is accelerating digital and self-care trends', *Strategy*, 5 July, https://strategyonline.ca/2020/07/09/covid-19-is-accelerating-embrace-of-digital-and-self-care/ (Accessed 18 January 2022).

Malesic, J. (2021) 'Burnout dominated 2021. Here's the history of our burnout problem', *The Washington Post*, 1 January, https://www.washingtonpost.com/history/2022/01/01/burnout-history-freudensberger-maslach/ (Accessed 21 January 2022).

Maslach, C. and Leiter, M. P. (2016) 'Understanding the burnout experience: recent research and its implications for psychiatry', *World Psychiatry*, 15, 2: 103–111.

Maslach, C. and Jackson, S. E. (1996–2016) *Maslach Burnout Inventory Manual*. 4th edition. Mind Garden, Inc., Menlo Park, CA.

Merchlinksy, C. (2020) 'With millions stuck at home, the online wellness industry is booming', *The Economist*, 4 April, https://www.economist.com/international/2020/04/04/with-millions-stuck-at-home-the-online-wellness-industry-is-booming (Accessed 18 January 2022).

Myrth (2021a) 'Frequently asked questions. What is Myrth?', https://www.getmyrth.com/about-myrth (3 December 2021).

Myrth (2021b) 'Digital flourishing: how it differs from digital minimalism', https://www.getmyrth.com/myrthblog/digital-flourishing-how-it-differs-from-digital-minimalism (Accessed 3 December 2021).

National Institute for Digital Health and Wellness (2021a) 'Landing page', https://www.nidhw.org/ (Accessed 17 December 2021).

National Institute for Digital Health and Wellness (2021b) 'Certifications', https://www.nidhw.org/certifications/ (Accessed 15 December 2021).

Nielsen, A. (2021) 'How to measure and regulate the attention costs of consumer technology', *Tech Stream, Brookings*, 4 November, https://www.brookings.edu/techstream/how-to-measure-and-regulate-the-attention-costs-of-consumer-technology/ (Accessed 24 December 2021).

Park, A. (2019) '"Gaming disorder" is now an official medical condition, according to WHO', *Time*, 29 May, https://time.com/5597258/gaming-disorder-icd-11-who/ (Accessed 17 November 2021).

Paúl, M. L. (2022) 'Couch guy to West Elm Caleb: inside the making of a TikTok "villain"', *The Washington Post*, 23 January, https://www.washingtonpost.com/technology/2022/01/23/west-elm-caleb-tiktok/?utm_campaign=wp_post_most

&utm_medium=email&utm_source=newsletter&wpisrc=nl_most&carta-url=https%3A%2F%2Fs2.washingtonpost.com%2Fcar-ln-tr%2F35d62e2%2F61ed85339d2fda14d7040149%2F5e86729bade4e21f59b210ef%2F46%2F70%2F61ed85339d2fda14d7040149 (Accessed 2 June 2022).

Perdew, L. (2015) *Internet Addiction*. Abdo Publishing, Minneapolis.

Petersen, A. (2019) *Digital Health and Technological Promise*. Routledge, London and New York.

Schwantes, M. (2021) 'During the great resignation, the biggest obstacle to management success is too many meetings, says research', *Inc.*, 11 November, https://www.inc.com/marcel-schwantes/during-great-resignation-biggest-obstacle-to-management-success-is-too-many-meetings-says-research.html (Accessed 21 January 2022).

Sentient Digital (2021a) 'Home page', https://www.sentientdigitalconsulting.com/ (Accessed 21 December 2021).

Sentient Digital (2021b) 'Consulting', https://www.sentientdigitalconsulting.com/consulting (Accessed 21 December 2021).

Sentient Digital (2021c) 'Research', https://www.sentientdigitalconsulting.com/research (Accessed 21 December 2021).

Sentient Digital (2021d) 'Training', https://www.sentientdigitalconsulting.com/training (Accessed 22 December 2021).

Smith, B. (2021) 'How tiktok reads your mind', *The New York Times*, 5 December, https://www.nytimes.com/2021/12/05/business/media/tiktok-algorithm.html?campaign_id=2&emc=edit_th_20211206&instance_id=47080&nl=todaysheadlines&regi_id=70510057&segment_id=76207&user_id=555b6d42a9884517ab975c86bed7dee1 (Accessed 10 December 2021).

Solis, B. (2019) 'Our digital malaise: distraction is costing us more than we think', 19 April, https://blogs.lse.ac.uk/businessreview/2019/04/19/our-digital-malaise-distraction-is-costing-us-more-than-we-think/ (Accessed 24 December 2021).

SPACE (2021a) 'SPACE homepage', https://findyourphonelifebalance.com/ (Accessed 22 December 2021).

SPACE (2021b) 'Digital wellbeing is the next environmentalism', https://findyourphonelifebalance.com/news/2019/8/1/digital-wellbeing-is-the-next-environmentalism (Accessed 22 December 2021).

UK Safer Internet Centre (2021a) 'Digital wellbeing', https://www.childnet.com/parents-and-carers/hot-topics/digital-wellbeing (Accessed 29 November 2021).

UK Safer Internet Centre (2021b) 'Supporting young people with digital wellbeing this summer', 19 August, https://saferinternet.org.uk/blog/supporting-young-people-with-digital-wellbeing-this-summer (Accessed 1 December 2021).

Vercillo, K. (2020) *Internet Addiction*. ABC-Clio, LLC, Santa Barbara.

Waterfield, S. (2018) 'Is "digital wellness" really the answer?', *Forbes*, 6 June, https://www.forbes.com/sites/pheewaterfield/2018/06/06/is-digital-wellness-really-the-answer/?sh=32bc5306451c (Accessed 21 February 2022).

wellteq (2021a) 'About us', https://wellteq.co/about/ (Accessed 15 December 2021).

wellteq (2021b) 'Creating a healthier and happier workforce', https://wellteq.co/ (Accessed 15 December 2021).

World Health Organization (2018a) 'Inclusion of "gaming disorder" in ICD-11', https://www.who.int/news/item/14-09-2018-inclusion-of-gaming-disorder-in-icd-11 (Accessed 17 November 2021).

World Health Organization (2018b) 'Public health implications of excessive use of the Internet and other communication and gaming platforms', 13 September, https://www.who.int/news/item/13-09-2018-public-health-implications-of-excessive

-use-of-the-internet-and-other-communication-and-gaming-platforms (Accessed 29 November 2021).

World Health Organization (2021a) 'Global strategy on digital health', https://apps .who.int/iris/bitstream/handle/10665/344249/9789240020924-eng.pdf (Accessed 13 December 2021).

World Health Organization (2021b) 'Online games encourage players to stay mentally and physically healthy at home', https://www.who.int/news/item/16-11-2021 -online-games-encourage-players-to-stay-mentally-and-physically-healthy-at-home (Accessed 13 December 2021).

World Health Organization (2021c) 'Constitution of the world health organization', https://apps.who.int/gb/bd/pdf_files/BD_49th-en.pdf#page=6 (Accessed 13 December 2021).

World Health Organization (2022) 'Burnout an "occupational phenomenon": international classification of diseases', https://www.who.int/news/item/28-05-2019 -burn-out-an-occupational-phenomenon-international-classification-of-diseases (Accessed 24 January 2022).

Wu, T. (2016) *The Attention Merchants*. Atlantic Books, London.

Young, K. and Nabuco de Abreu, C. (2017) *Internet Addiction in Children and Adolescents: Risk Factors, Assessment and Treatment*. Springer, New York.

6

DIGITAL MEDIA AND FUTURE EMOTIONAL LIFE

What is the likely direction of the evolution of digital media—and what might this mean for future emotional life? Digital media are being developed at such a rapid pace that predicting the path of their development, let alone the likely related implications, is hazardous. However, given the potentially profound personal and social consequences of their operations and use, it is crucial to attempt to do so. Sociologists, media scholars, digital activists, and others who are concerned about the impacts of media on people's lives can play a critical role by analysing the major trends and issues in media development and use. In doing so, they will need to challenge entrenched views on media technologies. Many people today take for granted the affordances of these technologies such as ready access to digital platforms and apps and their ability to rapidly create knowledge and share experiences. Mobile phones and other internet-connected devices are now so pervasive and easy to use that they tend to be viewed as part of the natural order of things; as an inexorable outcome of 'progress' and unaffected by the workings of politics, power, and commercial influence. But they have been *designed* to seem natural, to fit seamlessly into people's lives, by offering features and functions that attract users and retain their attention to enable their data to be harvested and monetised by corporations. In the previous chapters, I described the techniques and the algorithm-driven technologies and systems that underpin the so-called attention economy. This economy relies on the emotional labours of many actors, working 'front-stage' on digital platforms as ordinary users or as influencers and behind-the-scenes as curators, moderators, and user-experience and user-interface researchers, and thus may more usefully be described as an *emotional economy* (Chapter 2). In this concluding chapter, I summarise the main points of my argument, as outlined in the previous chapters, and consider some broad trends in the development of digital media as they potentially impact emotional life.

DOI: 10.4324/9781003147435-6

To begin, it is important to acknowledge that this book was written during the first two years of the COVID-19 pandemic and related lockdowns—a period of far-reaching change in many areas of life, including digital media development and use. The pandemic-induced lockdowns and increased reliance on digital platforms led to increased debate about media's implications, and about how best to regulate them to reduce their harms. The pandemic was the first pandemic to occur during the digital age, and the rapid spread of (mis-)information online has profoundly altered perceptions of pandemics and their control and the role of media technologies in communication. While the social restrictions reinforced appreciation of digital media's affordances, they also exposed their limitations as tools for sociality and the many risks they pose such as online abuse and harassment, the circulation of 'false news', the fostering of extremist views, cyberattacks, and identity theft, to name a few. I discussed some of these risks and the mechanisms that facilitate harm in earlier chapters. I also noted that the lockdowns provided enhanced opportunities for advertisers to test and document emotional responses to their advertisements as part of a broader effort to create a large emotion database. They enabled Zoom, TikTok, and other platforms to vastly expand their market, and massively increased the profits of Amazon, a company focusing on e-commerce, and demand for cloud computing, digital streaming, and artificial intelligence (Chapter 2).

Pandemic conditions may have helped consolidate the power of Big Tech companies, but they also contributed to highlighting many problematic aspects of their practices. As I noted, in 2021 and 2022, some whistleblowers, including ex-Google employee and president and co-founder of Center for Humane Technology, Tristan Harris, exposed Big Tech's practices of data harvesting and intrusions on privacy (for example, in the 2020 film *The Social Dilemma*) (Chapter 2). Facebook employee-turned-whistleblower Frances Haugen also provided testimony to a US Senate subcommittee in 2022 revealing her previous company's practices and the business imperatives that put concerns about profit, growth, and market share above users' welfare (Chapter 3). Yet, while these and other exposures of Big Tech's practices have helped raise public awareness of these issues, there has been little debate about the companies' role in the emotional economy and the creation of emotional regimes, and how the operations of these regimes impact the affective bonds that bind communities and that characterise social capital. Social capital has been severely eroded under neoliberal policies in recent decades—a period corresponding with the growing power and influence of Big Tech companies and their technologies, systems, and platforms. While there has been much debate about the various harms and abuses of digital media, some of which I described in the earlier chapters (especially Chapter 3), the questions raised by Putnam about the role of the internet in the formation or erosion of social capital more than two decades ago—before the launch of Facebook (in 2004) and other social media—remain largely unanswered (Chapter 4).

As I argued in Chapter 1, discussions about the role of digital media are often ahistorical and reflect visions of technologies and their effects that are long-standing in modern Western societies. They mostly overlook the complex operations of contemporary media which are governed by algorithms and the commercial priorities of Big Tech and exploit human agency and emotional labour for the purpose of profit maximisation. The early writers on electronic communications may have foreseen many of the issues raised by media analysts today, but they *understated* the role of human agency and the role of the emotions, and their work predates the rise of the attention economy and the now-ubiquitous programmatic advertising that is at the core of media operations (Chapter 2). I outlined key features of the online emotional economy, and the mechanisms deployed to attract users and keep them engaged—a subtle art in a world of many, constant distractions. Contemporary media rely on the contributions of specialist 'attention merchants' (Wu, 2016) to constantly develop new methods to 'attract eyeballs' who use the insights of psychology (especially nudge theory) and user-experience and user-engagement researchers to make media users' experiences effortless and satisfying. Clearly, Big Tech companies have much at stake in their efforts to capture and retain users' attentions—namely, their viability as businesses—and consequently are compelled to continually develop new techniques, technologies, and systems. Given the importance of 'connecting' with and retaining audiences, it should not be surprising that the trend has been for the development of ever more *immersive* user experiences, such as those envisaged by Mark Zuckerberg in the outline of his plans for the metaverse—a vision shared by other entrepreneurs who are keen to capitalise on his imagined digital utopia.

Anticipating what they believe will be the future of digital media development, companies are investing heavily in *affective* computing. Initiatives in this field, I noted, are expected to offer unprecedented control over users' emotions so that they may be manipulated for commercial gain (Chapters 1 and 2). Smartphones currently being developed by Apple, Samsung, and Huawei include AI features that offer users 'compelling and personalized experiences' such as user authentication, emotion recognition, and device management; the aim being to acquire new customers and retain current users (Jacobi, 2020). Companies are involved in a technological 'arms race' to develop innovations that will put them at the forefront of the effort to predict and control people's thoughts *and* emotions, and consequently their actions. Yet, as noted, the envisaged direction of future innovation is not inevitable since history shows that technologies often fail to develop as envisaged. The anticipated paths of digital media development may be disrupted for various reasons, including because the expected users reject them. Users, as indicated in Chapter 1, constitute a diverse group, and have different investments in technologies and their affordances, and employ technologies to pursue their own goals. They are exploited by or exploit the online emotional economy to varying degrees at different times. Understanding the dynamics of this economy and its vulnerabilities, I propose, is critical to any change agenda.

In the previous chapters, I introduced some key dimensions of digital media and the contemporary online emotional economy. However, there are many questions yet to explore. They include: how do online emotional regimes change over time—and what might this reveal about the broader workings of power in a digital age? How do the affordances of media shape emotional repertoires—the range of expected, encouraged, or tolerated emotions—and the manner and intensity of their expression? How are emotional communities sustained online—and how do they interact with offline communities? Are some platforms or forums especially prone to reinforcing extreme emotions, such as anger or hate (or, alternatively, kindness or love)—if so, why? My analysis also raises questions pertaining to the governance of technologies—some of which I will consider in this chapter. They include: what kinds of measures will ensure that technologies do not serve as tools of abuse? What responsibilities should Big Tech and other companies have to reduce harms—including those experienced by their own staff who moderate platforms and by the growing number of online influencers who contribute their emotional labours? Is self-regulation sufficient—or should it be complemented (or replaced) by other measures? Can technologies, systems, and platforms be *re-designed* to make them less harmful and engender users' trust? What scope is there for developing new models of the internet that are less centralised and non-exploitative? It is difficult to respond to these questions without having a vision of the kind of society desired, and how it might be realised. However, to date, debates about potential futures have been largely dominated and restricted by the socio-technical imaginaries of Big Tech companies and entrepreneurs, such as Mark Zuckerberg and Elon Musk, and other powerful actors, rather than by ordinary citizens who are significantly reliant on and are directly impacted by the operations of digital media. Having said this, it is clear that the momentum for change in media operations is gathering pace as more and more people become aware of the limitations of and risks posed by digital platforms and demand that Big Tech be held accountable for the operations of their technologies, systems, and platforms.

Challenging the power of Big Tech

The ability of Big Tech companies to maintain their control of the online emotional economy is pivotal to their viability and profitability, which explains why they have resisted demands to curtail their practices. The digital ecosystem is now highly concentrated and dominated by a relatively few powerful companies with huge resources, notably Google, Apple, Facebook/Meta, Amazon, and Microsoft. They must work to maintain their power and dominance over the digital ecosystem which is vulnerable to changes in 'market sentiment' and the erosion of community trust. If one is to challenge the influence of these companies, one first needs to recognise the reach of their power and influence in the global politico-economic order, as well as their commercial vulnerabilities. According to the Global 500 report, published in January 2022, tech remains the most valuable industry in the world. Apple is the 'world's most valuable brand title', valued at more than US$355 billion, closely followed by Amazon (US$350 billion) and Google (US$263 billion). This represents a year-on-year growth of 35 percent, 38 percent, and 38 percent, respectively, for the companies. The relatively new entrant, TikTok, is the world's fastest-growing brand, being up 215 percent on the previous year, and considered to be 'leading global revolution in media consumption' (Global 500, 2022). The popularity of the video platform Zoom, founded in 2011 and launched in January 2013, increased dramatically during the COVID-19 lockdowns, with its daily participants increasing from 10 million in December 2019 to 200 million in May 2020, and then to 300 million the following month (Iqbal, 2022). The growing influence of TikTok, Zoom, and other video platforms corresponding with the onset of the pandemic has been phenomenal and has facilitated the shift in practices of work, education, and sociality. Within a relatively short space of time, these technologies have come to dominate our social, economic, and emotional lives.

Yet, it is important to recognise that 'Big Tech' constitutes a diverse group of companies whose reliance on and investments in the online emotional economy vary considerably—as do their vulnerabilities to the dynamics of markets and 'consumer loyalty'. Google depends on advertising for the bulk of its revenue, and this is sensitive to market swings; for example, its revenue dropped at the start of the COVID-19 pandemic due to uncertainty but then rebounded as people adjusted to the 'new normal' and began to spend more time online (Globel 500, 2022). Apple, on the other hand, gains most of its revenue from the sale of products such as its iPhone, which accounts for about half its sales, and other products (e.g. iPads, iMacs, Macbooks) and services (Apple TV, Apple Pay); the company trades on its high brand value and attention to its customers, including privacy concerns in order to build trust (Global 500, 2022). Amazon's reputation rests on its logistics and the development of its own end-to-end supply chain through investment in different types of transport. TikTok, on the other hand, trades on its entertainment value and strong appeal to its Gen Z base (that is, those born between 1997 and 2012), but like other brands is rapidly expanding into the new services (Global 500, 2022). Meanwhile, traditional media brands such as Warner Bros, and CBS and NBC have seen recent declines in their value as consumers turn to social media platforms and on-demand streaming (Global 500, 2022). The ability of companies to quickly adapt to a rapidly changing market dynamics and consumer demands and tastes and to achieve and sustain the loyalty of its users is crucial, and may be affected by various factors, including privacy breaches and the ability to offer services that are distinctive and ensure users' loyalty and trust. This trust cannot be taken for granted and may quickly turn to distrust as Facebook found in the wake of the Cambridge Analytica scandal and a series of other controversies regarding its practices (Chapters 2 and 3).

Trust

Trust is fundamental to all communication. There are many definitions of trust, but it generally refers to a quality of a relationship between individuals, or between individuals and other phenomena such as businesses, technologies, or information sources. Scholars have identified typical aspects of a trusting relationship, including the possession of a certain disposition regarding another person or entity or an expectation regarding competence, reciprocity, and/or assistance to fulfil one's agency or needs in some way (Jones, 2021). Analysing trust in any context is challenging; having an intangible quality it eludes precise measurement. It is closely linked to another concept I introduced in Chapter 4, namely hope. As one dictionary entry explains, trust is defined as 'dependence on something future or contingent: hope' (Merriam-Webster, 2022). As I noted in that chapter, hope has underpinned the aspirations of the designers of the internet and nourishes and sustains its operations; yet the hopes of users of digital media are often unfulfilled or only partly realised. A growing number of highly publicised cases of data harvesting, privacy breaches, and deceptive, manipulative practices, has led many people to question the *trustworthiness* of Big Tech. While these companies and some commentators blame the decline of trust solely or largely on 'bad actors' (individuals and/or states) who misuse media for nefarious or abusive purposes, it has become increasingly evident that Big Tech's practices are largely responsible for the above problems and others. Consequently, measures that fail to tackle the dominance of Big Tech and the nature of its operations will be limited in reducing harm and unlikely to promote trust in companies or their technologies.

From Web 2.0 to Web 3.0, and beyond: Towards a more trustworthy internet?

As the internet developed and transformed from its relatively static Web 1.0 phase (from about 1990 to 2000), which enabled users to consume information created by publishers, to a more dynamic Web 2.0 environment (from about 2000 onwards), whereby ordinary users could create, upload, and share information (e.g. YouTube videos, crowdfunding platforms, blog posts, product reviews), many people assumed that the internet would become more trustworthy. Yet, Web 2.0 media has been shown to have fallen short of this espoused ideal: it has greatly enriched Big Tech companies, such as Meta and Google, which own some of the most widely used apps in the world via the exploitation of the emotional and physical labours of many people. Big Tech holds considerable control over users since they may choose to suspend or cancel their accounts or remove posted content, with users often having little recourse to reverse decisions. In some cases, the removal of content has been due to companies' content moderation processes including biases that inadvertently discriminate against some groups. In 2021, for example, Facebook censors were reported to have 'wrongfully removed and suppressed content by Palestinians and their supporters, including about human rights abuses carried out in Israel and Palestine during the May 2021 hostilities'— although it was claimed the company subsequently acknowledged the errors and attempted to correct some of them (Human Rights Watch, 2021). As explained in an article reporting the event, the protection of free expression on issues relating to Israel and Palestine is especially important given the restrictions on open discussion imposed by both Israeli and Palestinian authorities in the West Bank and Gaza, as well as by some other countries (Human Rights Watch, 2021). In 2022, whistleblowers claimed that Facebook/Meta deliberately blocked access to Australian government pages as part of a 'negotiating tactic' to pressure lawmakers as they debated making tech companies pay to host news articles (Hagey et al., 2022). The Facebook pages that were blocked included major health, corporate, sporting, and charity organisations, as well as emergency services including the Bureau of Meteorology and Fire and Rescue New South Wales, leaving many people without access to local health information about the COVID-19 pandemic (Dye and McGuire, 2021). Big Tech's inaction or delayed action in moderating or removing problematic content from their platforms has allegedly contributed to harm. In one case, reported in 2021, Rohingya people brought a class action against Facebook for $150 billion, 'alleging it helped perpetuate genocide in Myanmar' by failing to 'quickly stop the spread of hate speech and misinformation' against them, thereby contributing to the persecution and alleged genocide of the minority community in Myanmar (Cheng, 2021). Governments, too, may and often do control or ban platforms, or block access to and/or monitor content, such as China's use of its 'Great Fire Wall', and Russia's banning of Facebook and Instagram in March 2022 on the grounds that they were 'carrying out extremist activities' (Zuckerman, 2022). Whether it is Big Tech or governments that engage in these practices, diverse ordinary users are affected, and public discourse is restricted, which potentially creates risks, especially to those who rely on sites for information about decisions affecting health and personal or collective security. Undoubtedly, some restrictions are valid, as when posted material has the potential to cause harm to individuals or certain groups. The question of how to establish a balance between the 'free expression' (which is a problematic concept) and control of views and images is the subject of ongoing, often-heated debate with responses depending on the national and cultural context and the actors involved. What might be deemed objectionable by some people in one context may not be considered so in another. The difficulty, and arguably impossibility, of reconciling different positions on the above question is all too evident in the above debate about Facebook censors' removal of content produced by Palestinians and their supporters.

Decentralised media

One response to the risks posed by the centralised control of media and its content has been to propose systems that do not rely on platforms owned and controlled by Big Tech companies. The generally favoured alternative is *decentralised* media and models of 'open governance', that is, making online communications 'interoperable' without being held by a central server. The impetus for this decentralisation is partly if not largely driven by proponents of cryptocurrency and blockchain technology who wish to bypass centralised platforms and related regulatory scrutiny. This so-called Web 3.0 (or web3) phase of expected internet development, it has been argued, would ensure that users are not tied to any particular app or platform such as Facebook and are able to participate in 'peer-to-peer matrix' communication which gives users more control over the content available to them. It is suggested that this may involve, for example, screening out certain sources likely to include harmful content or controlling the inflow of random people or restricting communication to those with whom one has established a trusting relationship. The concept of the decentralised internet has been championed by the start-ups Matrix and Manyverse, among others. In some accounts, the use of blockchain technology—described as 'a database that lives across the network of computers rather than on one server' and thereby obviates control by a single person or organisation—would enable the building of systems that build trust (Edelman, 2022). In this conception, individuals would own their own data and decide what and with whom to share it. Moreover, they could take their data with them if they wish to change their service. Some decentralisation proposals build on the decentralised platform Scuttlebutt founded by a New Zealand sailor, Dominic Tarr, who claims to have come up with the idea while being at sea, after having experienced frustrations with using Facebook (LTB Network, 2019). The trend to decentralisation—described by some commentators as a 'movement'—is underpinned by a libertarian philosophy that is problematic in many respects—as I will explain shortly. It is supported by cryptocurrency and blockchain enthusiasts who wish to avoid banks and mainstream institutions, in whom many people lost trust after the Global Financial Crisis of 2007–2008. It also facilitates criminal activities, including money laundering, since it is designed to keep transactions private and difficult to trace and to avoid regulatory scrutiny (Sun and Smagalla, 2022). Critics of Web 3.0 argue that the concept is vague, captured by vested interests including criminal groups, and exploits the hopes of especially younger people who are poor, marginalised, and susceptible to the false promises of quick riches via the purchase of cryptocurrency (see, e.g. White, 2022). The Web 3.0 concept, I should add, is generally promoted by those in technology communities, whose visions are inspired by the prospect of radically redesigned technologies rather than broad social change.

Exposing Big Tech's deceptive practices, and their implications

While a more decentralised internet of some form may go some way to overcoming the dominance of Big Tech, it is difficult to envisage a substantial shift away from the current status quo in the short-to-medium term given companies' control of the digital ecosystem and the related regulatory framework that has evolved in response. The existing technologies, systems and platforms are so deeply integrated into economies and people's lives in many countries that 'path dependence' (or commitment to developing technologies in certain ways) has become established and innovations become 'locked-in' (or the standard) and difficult to alter. However, as mentioned, there is a strong momentum for change, which has been given impetus by highly publicised cases revealing companies' deceptive, manipulative practices, which may help shift public sentiment in favour of the adoption of more de-centred models of the internet. It is important to expose these practices, making clear their implications for users of digital media and for society more generally. Areas of particular concern so far are infringements on users' privacy and the use of deceptive design features, such as dark patterns (Chapters 1, 2, and 3).

Both these issues were brought to light in 2022, when it was reported that attorneys general 'from D.C. and three states' of the United States were suing Google for deceiving consumers in order to gain access to their location data. According to the report, it was alleged that 'the company made misleading promises about its users' ability to protect their privacy through Google account settings, dating from at least 2014' and that 'The suits seek to stop Google from engaging in these practices and to fine the company' (Zakrzewski, 2022). The article went on to note that it was also alleged that the company 'has deployed "dark patterns", or design tricks that can subtly influence users' decisions in ways that are advantageous for the business', which involved the design of products that 'repeatedly nudge or pressure people to provide more and more location data, "inadvertently or out of frustration"'—practice which, it was alleged, 'violates various state and D.C. consumer protection laws' (Zakrzewski, 2022). This alleged use of 'dark patterns', which lead users to make certain choices, has been known for some time yet remained unaddressed, and is part-and-parcel of how Google operates, according to a report on this practice published in 2018 based on research of 'a regular user experience' (Forbrukerrådet, 2018: 5) (Chapter 1). These 'dark patterns' or 'deceptive designs' are tricks used in websites and apps to make users do things that they may not have intended to do, such as buying or signing up to something. Those who design webpages or apps know that users do not read every word and skim read and make assumptions—and use what scholars in the field of human decision-making call heuristics or 'rules-of-thumb' to make decisions—and take advantage of this to exploit them (Chapter 2). Most users would be unaware of the extent to which they are manipulated when they go online, and it is in the interest of Big Tech companies for them to 'stay in the dark'.

The question of how technologies are designed is critical to their exploitative potential, as the above report explains:

> Through so-called 'dark patterns', deceptive design practices, users are nudged toward making choices that are in favor of the service-provider, and often against their own interests. Dark patterns come in many shapes, and encapsulate many different design practices. For example, the use of color, visibility and wording may serve to steer users toward choices that benefit the service provider. This can include misrepresenting the consequences of

a choice, by only focusing on certain aspects that put the service provider's preferred choice in a positive light. Similarly, information that might dissuade the user from opting in to a service can be withheld or hidden from view, giving users a skewed impression.

(Forbrukerrådet, 2018: 12)

As the report goes on to note, mobile phone users will often take the path of least resistance in order to expedite choices and may choose the least privacy-friendly option which is presented as

> part of the natural flow of a service. The strategic positioning of certain buttons or other functions or features can mean that users overlook privacy or security protections, or may unintentionally enable a setting without knowing that they have done so. Certain continuous prompts may also lead users to enable settings, which 'do not respect users' original choice and may wear out users and make them resign to clicking 'I accept' despite originally being reluctant.

(Forbrukerrådet, 2018: 12–13)

The report also identified other dark patterns that may be considered unethical, but part of the technology's design that works against the user's interest. Mobile devices, however, represent but one domain of design bias that operates against users.

Biases are 'baked into' the design of search engines, digital devices, platforms, and apps, as well as the algorithms that power them. These biases pertain to users and how they use media and reflect naïve, often incorrect assumptions that may prove harmful. They tend to benefit some users and disempower, exclude, and stigmatise others—especially if they include functions or features that make them difficult to operate (for example, if the user has a physical or mental disability). As noted, race, gender, class, and other biases are built into the design of algorithms (Chapter 1). There are many examples of how algorithmic-driven systems discriminate against certain groups such as the socio-economically disadvantaged, and the already marginalised and stigmatised. In Australia, a noteworthy example is the so-called 'robodebt' episode, where an automated debt assessment and recovery program used by Services Australia sent false or incorrectly calculated debt notices to people, which led to 443,000 people being wrongly issued with debt notices following the implementation of this program in 2016, causing great psychological and financial harm to many vulnerable citizens (Henriques-Gomez, 2019). In 2020, this led to class action on behalf of victims, and the then coalition government agreeing to pay at least 381,000 people $751 million and wipe all debts that were raised (Henriques-Gomez, 2021).

Even if technologies' features or functions cannot be shown to directly discriminate against or harm particular groups of users, they may be used for harmful purposes. There is abundant evidence of technologies being used in ways not envisaged by their designers, including to inflict harm and abuse. Whole communities, including ethnic and religious minorities, LGBTQI+, and people holding particular beliefs (e.g. religious, political), are subject to online vilification, stigmatisation, and marginalisation. I referred to some examples in Chapter 3 of how some groups, such as incel, may incite harm by using platforms such as Reddit and YouTube, and how during the COVID-19 pandemic extreme right groups have exploited the affordances of algorithms to recruit new members and promulgate messages of hate. On the other hand, algorithms may be used to detect fake information and harmful messages and images by, for example, employing chatbots for purposes of fact-checking. They may also be adapted and repurposed to advance programs of social change, to reduce opportunities for exploitation and abuse and to promote social inclusion and well-being in its widest sense. Through their history, digital technologies have been surrounded with hope—a hope that has both inspired programs of social and political change and been exploited by those who aim to profit from the affordances they offer (Chapter 4). The public discourse on digital technologies, however, has been dominated by narratives of constant improvement, with innovations offering faster, more efficient, seamless connections which, it is assumed, will benefit all citizens—notwithstanding technologies' many limitations and risks.

Techno-optimism and libertarianism

If one is to develop alternative models of the internet—ones that serve rather than exploit users and benefit whole communities rather than corporate interests—it is important to first reflect on the visions and related philosophies that have guided the development of the internet from its inception and that continue to be drawn on by Big Tech entrepreneurs such as Mark Zuckerberg and Elon Musk. Many of the affordances that digital media offer their users were anticipated long ago by the writers of the 1960s whose work I discussed in earlier chapters— Marshall McLuhan, Erich Fromm, and Neil Postman—and much earlier by the engineer-inventor Nikola Tesla who in 1926 described the fundamentals of the contemporary smartphone (Kennedy, 1926). His name has been given to Musk's hugely popular electric car. Tesla was a techno-optimist who saw great benefits deriving from what he envisaged to be the future virtual elimination of distance between individuals and nations which he saw as the root of 'the majority of the ills from which humanity suffers'. He wrote,

> When wireless is perfectly applied, the whole Earth will be converted into a huge brain, which in fact it is, all things being particles of a real and rhythmic whole. We shall be able to communicate with one another instantly, irrespective of distance. Not only this, but through television and telephony we shall see and hear one another as perfectly as though we were face to face, despite intervening distances of thousands of miles; and the instruments through which we will be able to do this will be amazingly

simple compared with our present telephone. A man will be able to carry one in his vest pocket.

Tesla's vision of a future wireless technology, which now seems prescient, is remarkably similar to Tim Berners-Lee's' much later prediction of a future 'single global information space' that would empower users and unite populations (Chapter 4). As noted, technological development has been underpinned by the utopian vision of connected communities and the libertarian idea that new media would empower users and democratise society—which in many respects appears to be realised in the 24/7 instant connection afforded by the digital devices that are ubiquitous today. Libertarianism is a philosophy with a long history in Western thought that is focused on the maximisation of autonomy, freedom of choice, and the minimisation of the state's violation of individual liberties. It is often espoused by Big Tech entrepreneurs and aligns with belief in the free market and the virtue of production, and the 'natural harmony of interests'. Libertarianism's 'atomistic' conception of individualism is ahistorical and denies the significance of group identity and the obligations to community and government that accompany the benefits deriving from these institutions (Boaz, 2022). It is utopian in denying the contemporary workings of politics and power and the role of commercial interests in shaping technology investments. Despite the failed promises of the internet, libertarianism continues to be espoused by Berners-Lees and, recently, Elon Musk, who in April 2022 made clear his intention to purchase Twitter—an apparent loss-making venture—with the professed claim to 'unlock' its potential as the 'digital town square where matters vital to the future of humanity are debated' (The New York Times, 2022).

Libertarianism implies no constraints on individual emotional expression which is problematic in the context of algorithm-driven media. As I noted in Chapter 1, from the early days of the internet it has been recognised that digital media transform identities and the notion of personal privacy. I drew attention to Philip Agre's (1994) concept of 'the digital individual', and Max Kilger's (1994) concept of the 'virtual self'. The 'digital individual' refers to the complex relationships between human beings and the digital representations of them (Agre, 1994: 73). As Agre argued, the distributed computer systems that were then becoming pervasive provided varying degrees of freedom in shaping how others see them. He noted that while chatting on computer bulletin boards provide individuals with much volitional scope—to control representations of themselves—computational processes based on activities such as medical care and credit card use, which are practical necessities, provide them with little control over how they represent themselves (Agre, 1994: 73). Neither Agre nor Kilger discussed the role of the 'black-boxed' algorithms, whose operations power contemporary media operations, including the programmatic advertising upon which the profits of Big Tech companies and smaller businesses rely. The algorithm-driven systems oriented to predicting people's wants and needs based on their past searches and data profiles—and then feeding them 'personalised' advertising—serve to *restrict* the scope for individuals to express themselves other than in ways aligned with the values of consumer capitalism.

The rise of the phenomenon of the social media influencer, comprising ordinary citizens and celebrities who seek to monetise their emotional labours (that is, 'sell themselves'), shows how far the 'virtual self' has evolved in the three decades since Agre and Kilger made their observations (Chapter 2). The contemporary internet epitomises the neoliberal imaginary that posits individuals as autonomous, rational decision-makers who 'freely' exercise choice in a market of seemingly endless options available to them online. This idealised conception of the internet user overlooks the many *constraints* on people's actions, thoughts, and feelings, including the operations of the digital platforms that encourage, reinforce, and discourage certain kinds of emotional experience and expression, and the global and national inequalities that profoundly shape people's opportunities and everyday lives. The profound personal and social implications of the 'virtualisation of the self' have hardly begun to be explored but likely helps explain the self-image and mental health problems experienced by many social media users, including young female users of Instagram which was revealed by Facebook/Meta's (the owner of Instagram) own research (Chapter 3). The internet may seem to offer a 'free' and democratic space for the unconstrained expression of views and feelings—the 'digital town square' described by Elon Musk—but by its design and operations is unable to deliver on this promise.

Children

The dangers posed by unconstrained expression on the internet has been of particular concern to those who advocate on behalf of children and young people. Children and young people have long been the focus of debates about the impacts of electronic/digital media from the beginnings of television (Chapter 3), and recently in relation to online gaming (Chapter 1), cyberbullying (Chapter 3) and 'addictive' media use (Chapter 5). Concerns about children's welfare have been front and centre of debates about the responsibilities of Big Tech companies (see Chapters 1, 3, 5). This includes the use of deceptive techniques for engaging or retaining young audiences. As noted in Chapter 5, children have been the focus of many digital well-being efforts, as well as the policies of governments and various authorities, including supranational bodies such as the UN. Given the history of anxieties about children's welfare in general and mental health in particular in many countries it is not surprising that Big Tech's practices have been a major focus for policy and community-based action. In May 2022, as Australians prepared for the Federal election, it was reported that mental health groups in Australia were calling on the then Australian coalition government to review 'Google's "creepy" practice of emailing children on their 13th birthday to tell them they are old enough to remove adult supervision from their Google account' as part of the coalition's election pledge (Davidson, 2022a). The coalition had campaigned on the issue of keeping Australians safe online by promising that phones and tablets would have stronger parental controls that are easy to use and activate, especially when setting up a device, and more difficult for children to bypass, by building an industry code under its Online Safety Act. The report went on to note that 'Apple and Google already featured extensive parental controls in their phone operating systems which apply to children under 13'. But 'Unlike Apple, Google actively encourages children to consider opting out of adult supervision the moment they turn 13, emailing them and their parents on their birthday to inform them they now have the option to "take charge" of their Google account, or have their parents manage their account "a little longer"' (Davidson, 2022a). Mental Health Australia, however, objected to Google's practice of emailing children, arguing that 'thirteen is too young' and that the organisation had observed that self-harm had increased significantly in the 12–18-year-old target market, which 'correlated to the increase in social media' (Davidson, 2022a).

In the above case, and other cases I discussed in previous chapters, arguments for the control of media have focused on children's vulnerability (Chapter 3). It is assumed that children's developmental stage makes them especially susceptible to the manipulations of media. The Digital Futures Commission says it is exploring the developmental requirements of children and their rights in an increasingly digitised world, paying cognisance to the UN Convention on the Rights of the Child, that place children's interests at the centre of the design of the digital world. A report outlining a research agenda published by the commission in 2020 comments that 'digital contexts are rarely designed with children in mind or, when they are, they prioritise protection over children's other rights' and that 'changing the frame is a priority' (Digital Futures Commission, 2020: 3). The report goes on to state that it addresses various stakeholders who are concerned with children and the digital environment, including the public, private, and third sectors. The aim is to undertake a 'critical examination of how children's lives are being reconfigured in a digital world, so as to reimagine the digital world in value-sensitive ways that uphold rights, and to take practical steps to meet children's needs'. Adding, 'This is in children's interests, and in everyone's' (Digital Futures Commission, 2020: 3–4).

As explained by an international children's rights consultant, Gerison Lansdown, in referring to the work of the commission, paying cognisance to children's rights means, firstly, wherever possible, taking account of the child's views regarding their own best interests and, secondly, interpreting 'best interests' within the context of the realisation of children's rights. In elaborating on article 3. para. 1 of the Convention, Lansdown explains that, while the child's 'best interests should be a primary consideration … there should be other considerations, which need to be taken into account', and that 'Adults, and states in particular, have an overriding responsibility to protect children's rights' (Digital Futures Commission, [2021a]). However, as Lansdown elaborates, 'if exercising adults' freedom of expression places children at a risk of severe harm, then the children's interests should predominate and influence the outcome. Because the loss to the adults is less than the loss to the children' (Digital Futures

Commission, 2021a). According to its website, the Digital Futures Commission focuses on three areas: 'play in a digital world, beneficial uses of education data and guidance for innovators'. The description notes that in each work stream, 'the needs and interests of children and young people will be put 'into the minds and workplans of digital innovators, business, regulators and governments' and that their work will be 'informed by the voices of children and young people, and underpinned by critical research into how children's lives are being reconfigured by innovation'. Moreover, it states that it will address designers, developers, and policymakers offering practical recommendations 'geared at reimagining the digital world in value-sensitive ways that uphold children's rights and are responsive to children's needs' (Digital Futures Commission, 2021b).

An issue often raised in debates about children's vulnerability online is individuals' exposure to certain body ideals. As noted, Instagram has come under particular scrutiny in relation to its normalisation of certain idealised portrayals of the body that allegedly harms many young female users and the promotion of radicalising, extremist information during the first year of the COVID-19 pandemic (Chapter 3). The testimony offered by whistleblower Frances Haugen, noted above, was especially damning in this respect, in that she offered an ex-insider's perspective on practices allegedly known by Facebook/Meta (Instagram's owner), notably its reluctance to change the platform's algorithm to make it safer because it would reduce the time that users spend on the site, which would impact their profits.

Scholars from different disciplines and activists can help highlight the mechanisms that account for the strong attractions of media, especially where this may cause harm. These mechanisms are utilised by advertisers and exploited by Big Tech companies and other users in their endeavours to establish 'emotional connection' with audiences, to 'attract eyeballs' (Chapter 2). This includes media designed with functions and features that exploit people's need for social acceptance and to feel part of a community and fear of failure to conform to the ideals of social norms. Designers and developers of technologies and platforms are inspired by and draw variously on psychology, philosophy, and studies of human–computer interactions. In his book *If You Should Fail*, Jo Moran discusses the factors that inspired Peter Thiel to establish PayPal. As Moran explains, Thiel was influenced by the work of the French philosopher René Girard who proposed that human beings 'are driven by "mimetic desire"'; a desire that is fundamentally social (2020: 76). This is the desire to acquire enviable assets or attributes that others possess that we do not. As Moran notes, 'Mimetic desire strengthens human bonds but also foments rivalries, as we all end up wanting the same things' (2020: 76). It is 'unconscious and pre-rational' and the desirers 'do not notice the mediator who comes between us and the coveted object' of desire. Moran continues:

> We think we want the object, but actually we want the charismatic quality we assign to the rival who also wants or already possesses that object. Mimetic desire is asking for the impossible: for us to be someone else.
>
> *(Moran, 2020: 77)*

Girard's ideas, Moran argues, led Thiel to realise 'how herd-like people are, and how much entrepreneurs could gain from not following the herd' (2020: 78). It also convinced Thiel of 'the market potential of social networks based on mimetic desire'. Moran notes that Thiel was the first investor in Facebook, buying 10 percent of the company for $500,000, making it 'one of the most lucrative angel investments ever' (2020: 78). This mimetic desire, Moran explains, accounts for the interactions on social media, which is characterised by rivalry and self-praise, which are unlike the conversations one has offline. That is, interaction online calls for a distinct kind of emotional labour and impression management (Chapters 1 and 2). Drawing on the work of Arlie Russell Hochschild (1983), I referred to the toll such labour and impression management exacts on media users, especially those who make their living online such as influencers or moderators or who depend on digital platforms (for example, Uber drivers) (Chapter 2). According to Luke Burgis, a psychologist and author of *Wanting: The Power of Mimetic Desire in Everyday Life* (2021), while mimetic rivalry 'has always existed … social media has galvanized these tendencies', especially in a context of fractured traditional media, multiple truths, the decline of traditional institutions and the formation of 'micro-communities' (Johnson, 2021). In Burgis's assessment, who elaborates on the topic in an interview, 'Social media has an homogenizing function' which is 'built into the design of the platforms'. He cites the example of profiles which 'all look exactly the same', the result of which is to create what Girard would refer to as a 'crisis of sameness'. In Burgis's view this creates a situation where 'everybody is now trying to differentiate themselves from everybody else' which fuels narcissism and exacerbates social anxiety (Johnson, 2021).

Digital wellness businesses, and mental health and professional coaching services have capitalised on this assumed mimetic desire, and related self-presentational work and anxiety. An interesting example is the Lifefaker campaign hosted by the UK-based company Sanctus, which is worth close examination since it illustrates well the aforementioned processes as well as the hyperreality of contemporary media. Sanctus has produced a website for a fictious company lifefaker.com which, at first blush, appears to be targeted at those who feel insecure about their personal online profile. The home page proclaims: 'Life isn't perfect. Your profile should be'. If one scrolls down the page, the reader will encounter short videos of young people talking about their feelings of inadequacy (for example, as 'someone who can't cook', being single while one's friends 'were getting married and having babies') and then going on to explain how their lives had turned around after purchasing lifefaker photos depicting idealised scenes or settings which presumably can be posted on social media, with one saying they 'have got my self-worth back' (Lifefaker.com, 2022). The video finishes with the statement: 'Life isn't perfect. Your profile should be. Lifefaker.com'. Further down the page appears various photo options (e.g. 'The look at my holiday and cry package', 'My sexy girlfriend/boyfriend', 'I just happen to live here', 'I can't be arty and deep') and accompanying images, under which appears two links

'Buy photos' and 'View demo'. When one clicks on the links the reader is taken to a page 'Ever felt the pressure of social media? You're not alone. 62 percent of people feel inadequate comparing their lives to others online.' Then the punchline: 'Find out more about social media's impact on mental health at Sanctus.io'. On Sanctus's website, it is explained that 'Lifefaker.com is a fictitious website' and that in creating it 'our goal was to use parody to highlight some of those unhealthy behaviours we all know exist on social media' and that 'As we become more aware of them ourselves, it can be easier to change them too' (Sanctus, 2022a). This also includes a video which describes 'The lifefaker campaign' and includes accounts by young actors explaining how they fake their 'perfect lives' on social media posts when they are unhappy, followed by other accounts of Sanctus staff and public health experts explaining how social media is used to convey fake impressions of their lives and how media can be detrimental to users' mental health and that people should reflect on their online behaviours. On its 'About us' page, it is explained that 'We created Sanctus to be a mental wellbeing space that we never had' and it goes on to say that 'What started as a blog post has turned into a brand that's trying to change the way people view mental health all over the globe' (Sanctus, 2022b). Details are provided of its 'HQ team', with a note at the bottom of the page: 'Get in touch and improve your employee wellbeing today', with dot points outlining its services ('Coaching' which 'blends personal and professional development with proactive mental wellbeing support'), along with an online submission portal for those wishing to get in touch. Another page lists the company's 'partners', explaining that 'We work with 100+ companies across the UK, supporting thousands of employees with personal & professional development and mental wellbeing' (Sanctus, 2022c).

Sanctus is a business which, like the digital well-being/wellness services described in Chapter 5, would seem to profit from personal self-image insecurities that social media arguably contribute to. On first impression, Sanctus's advertisement appears to be targeting young users of social media, but a closer examination of their website indicates that it is actually targeting the companies likely to employ them—by demonstrating that Sanctus possesses unique insights into the impacts of social media on young people's self-image and mental health and the problems this creates for businesses. While it could be argued that this clever marketing campaign is laudable and brings attention to the topic and perhaps encourages some media users and the companies who employ them to reflect on their online practices, it relies on the same deceptive practices used by Big Tech to attract its audiences. The campaign is geared not to changing the practices themselves, which would require policy and regulatory interventions to change the practices of technology companies, but rather to attracting consumers via the use of simple, easy-to-digest, entertaining messages typical of advertising campaigns. Little is known about whether these messages resonate with the intended audience. Presumably companies would need to be looking for the kind of service offered by Sanctus or assisted by others to find its webpage. Many would not know about or necessarily feel they need the services. But they are likely to be concerned about their employees' social media use if they believe it impacts their performance at work; for example, heavy use of media during work hours, or taking time off work because of mental health issues that seem related to media use. If employers search online for information about these issues, programmatic advertising will likely suggest lifefaker.

Lifefaker epitomises the hyperreality of contemporary online life in that it distorts perception of the real and the simulated which are seamlessly blended in a way that serves to disorient viewers and potentially 'suck them in'. Media scholars, semioticians, and postmodern philosophers have long pointed to the hyperreality of technologically advanced societies. The advance of AI-driven technologies in recent years, however, has taken hyperreality to a new level.

The Gruen effect?

The design of contemporary media, I suggest, can be likened to the design of a shopping mall with those going online (entering the mall) being confronted by a layout that is confusing and disorienting (which, in the case of shopping centres, is intentional), making them subject to distraction and susceptible to impulse pur-chases. The architecture of shopping centres was originally designed by Victor Gruen whose name is taken to describe the 'Gruen transfer' or 'Gruen effect', the psychological phenomenon which is a state of hyperreality where 'shoppers will be so bedazzled by the store's surroundings that they will be drawn—uncon-sciously, continually—to shop' (Hardwick, 2004: 2)—which is akin to the online environment manufactured by the attention merchants in their quest to 'attract eyeballs'. Since the early 1950s, advertisers have known that consumers are easily distracted and subject to persuasion and have employed images and associations for the object being advertised to attract attention. In Chapter 2, I referred to this history and the work of the PR consultant Edward Bernays and the obser-vations of Vance Packard, who wrote about the use of psychoanalysis and the research of the social sciences to create 'hidden' or subliminal messages in adver-tisements. The contemporary online world may seem like a shopping centre of endless opportunities for the exercise of 'free choice', but its design offers many constraints. The 'choice architects' (Thaler and Sustein, 2008) have created 'dark patterns', default options, and other nudges that aim to subtly guide users to express their agency in particular ways, sometimes via emotional expressions that are not optimal for people's well-being and may prove harmful. Yet, as I have hopefully made clear, to suggest that users have no agency would be wrong and denies the many ways individuals, working alone and/or with others concerned about the implications of digital media, may challenge their implied practices.

The ethics of digital media and AI

Given the various issues raised by digital media, especially its manipulations, some commentators demand that digital media technologies, and particularly the AI that powers them, be 'ethical' or 'responsible'. This often means the use of ethical principles to guide the design, development, adoption, and/or use of technologies. The so-called 'ethical AI movement' is broad and promoted by some government agencies, researchers, progressive think tanks, and digital activist groups who aim to incorporate 'fairness into algorithms' by undertaking research, raising awareness of the issues, either undertaking or promoting community engagement on the issues, and/or lobbying for changes of various kinds. Its supporters include Centre for AI and Digital Policy, Centre for Countering Digital Hate, Tracking Exposed, *The Social Dilemma* team from Exposure Labs, Media Done Responsibly, Distributed Artificial Intelligence Research Institute (DAIRI), Access Now, Digital Rights Watch, and Autonomy. A number of these centres or organisations involve ex-employees of Big Tech, including Timnit Gebru (DAIRI), who was allegedly hired by Google research to speak out on unethical AI but then was fired for speaking out (Harwell and Tiku, 2020), and Tristan Harris, a former Google design ethicist who appears in *The Social Dilemma* (Chapter 2). These centres or organisations focus on different issues and impacts of digital media operations, but often include the tracking of users and related infringements on privacy, and tackling the personal and social harms related to media use, including algorithm-driven processes or AI. Some writers advocate for the 'responsible' use of technologies—which raises the question responsible for what and/or to whom? Vague concepts like 'the public good' or 'the public interest' are often invoked, which assumes there is or could be agreement on what this entails. Many writers who promote ethical media or ethical AI focus on developing standards and values, advocating for users' rights, and designing an improved regulatory framework for tackling media-related harms.

Some proposals seem utopian as is the case with the young entrepreneur and former Google scientist, Alan Cowan, who in 2022 launched a research company, Hume AI and a 'companion not-for-profit' that can purportedly 'help make the whole messy business of AI more empathic and human'. According to an article reporting the initiative, Cowan claims that 'By getting trained hundreds of thousands of facial and vocal expressions from around the world, artificial intelligence on hume platform can react to how users are truly feeling and cater more closely to their emotional needs' (Zeitchik, 2022). The article notes that 'Cowan announced a set of ethical guidelines he hopes will be agreed by companies that use the platform', and claims to be concerned with 'optimising for well-being and not for engagement' (Zeitchik, 2022). As with biomedical ethics, the ethics of digital technologies is dominated by principlism, in that it explicitly or implicitly draws on the cardinal principles of autonomy, beneficence, nonmaleficence, and justice—which has been extensively critiqued (Petersen, 2011: 5–6). A major issue in adopting this principles-driven approach is that it narrows the scope for debate and action on substantive questions concerning the operations of power, commercial influence, and ownership and control of technologies—resulting in what has been called 'non-decision making' (Bachrach and Baratz (1963: 632). Some groups, such as Digital Rights Watch, however, offer proposals for more radical programs of action, such as curtailing Big Tech's data-harvesting practices and changing the designs of their algorithms.

Even if it were possible to reach broad agreement on what values, principles, or standards define ethical media or ethical AI, the question of how to translate these into meaningful strategies is complex given the different stakes in media and their future. In 2021, the Pew Research Centre reported that 'experts' doubted that 'ethical AI design will be broadly adopted as the norm within the next decade' (Pew Research Centre, 2021). The Pew report noted that 602 technology entrepreneurs, developers, business and policy leaders, and researchers were asked to respond to the question: 'By 2030, will most of the AI systems being used by organizations of all sorts employ ethical principles focused primarily on the public good?' Of these, 68 percent responded that ethical principles focusing primarily on the public good *will not* be employed by 2030, while 32 percent responded that they *will be*. Pew acknowledges that this is a non-random sample, based on the opinions of the individuals who responded and so cannot be generalised to the wider population. Perhaps of most interest from this report are the 'key themes' emerging from respondents' elaborations on why they explained their choices. The 'worries' were that 'The main developers and deployers of AI are focused on profit-seeking and social control, and there is no consensus about what ethical AI would look like'. The 'hopes' were that 'Progress is being made as AI spreads and shows its value; societies have always found ways to mitigate the problems arising from technological evolution' (Pew Research Centre, 2021). It was noted that respondents 'wrestled with the meaning of such grand concepts as beneficence, nonmaleficence, autonomy, and justice when it comes to tech systems', with some describing their own approach as comparative: 'It's not whether the AI systems alone produce questionable ethical outcomes, it's whether the AI systems are less biased than the current human systems and their known biases' (Pew Research Centre, 2021).

The role of the state and non-state actors

While there has been growing attention to 'ethical' AI or media, there has been relatively little debate about the current and future role of the state and non-state actors in shaping technologies, systems, and platforms, either through investment in particular kinds of research, the establishment of specialised institutions, the enactment of policies and programs, and/or the use of specific regulatory instruments. States are deeply invested in emotional regimes and through their actions and inactions reveal biases in their decision-making. It will be remembered that William Reddy (2001) introduced the concept of 'emotional regime' to refer to the modes of emotional expression and thought that are dominant at particular times in different societies (Chapter 1). States are not neutral arbiters in debates about what should be allowed, tolerated, discouraged, blocked, or banned in terms of emotional expressions and views. And state actors' standpoints will vary according to the time, place, and the political dispositions of authorities. I noted earlier in this chapter how national governments sometimes block platforms or their agencies police and take down material considered objectionable. This may be viewed by some as limiting free speech, but it may also serve to prevent harm to individuals or certain groups. They can also take actions against platforms that carry emotionally charged messaging or institutions that serve as carriers of such content. They could enforce expected standards governing content moderation to ensure that they are comprehensive and 'fit for purpose', and work in collaboration with regulatory agencies in other countries to ensure that criteria used for screening content are consistent and do not cause harm to the moderators themselves. But avoiding the slippery slope towards censorship and penalising small tech companies with fewer resources than Big Tech is tricky and needs careful thought via community consultation (Impakter, 2020). There is also the difficult question of how to avoid exposing content moderators to emotional harms. The platforms tend to use contractors—the exploited 'ghost workers' mostly drawn from poorer communities (Chapter 2)—in combination with AI algorithms to search posts for offensive material that is then removed. AI technologies do not (yet) have 'feelings' but human moderators do, and they often struggle against the torrent of toxic and harmful content and sometimes suffer emotionally as a result. In 2020, Facebook agreed to pay $52 million compensation to former and current moderators for the mental health issues they developed on the job (Newton, 2020). Content moderation raises many other questions, such as how to discriminate between content that is legal but objectionable, views on which may vary considerably within and between jurisdictions (Impakter, 2020).

Regulatory agencies can and already do play a role in holding Big Tech accountable for deceptive practices that manipulate users' emotions in ways that may lead them towards decisions that they would not otherwise take, some of which may prove harmful to themselves or others. This includes the regulation of dark patterns, which the Australian Competition and Consumer Authority (ACCC) announced it was 'cracking down on' in 2022 (Davidson, 2022b). The outgoing chairman of the ACCC, Rod Sims, acknowledged the potential for dark patterns to mislead people, noting:

> These are techniques where you've got false scarcity reminders, low stock warnings, false sales, countdown timers, targeted advertising using consumers' own data to exploit their individual characteristics, preselected add-ons … where you put things in your cart and you're just about to complete the transaction and all of a sudden something else is in your cart and you're paying for it.
>
> (Davidson, 2022b)

But Sims also recognises that Australian Consumer Law, 'which prohibits misleading behaviour, would not be sufficient if dark patterns were to be properly regulated'. He is cited: 'For dark patterns to be really powerful and important you've got to have data. That's the issue' (Davidson, 2022b). These comments reflect growing recognition of data politics and public concerns that underpin the 'Techlash' as well as the findings of research showing a substantial decline of trust in the tech sector between 2012 and 2021 (West, 2021).

Non-state actors such as banks and other companies may also play a role in governing their own digital platforms to encourage or discourage certain kinds of emotional expression and other conduct affecting users of their services. 'Non-state actors' is a broad category and may include non-government organisations (NGOs), academic institutions, lobby/activist groups, labour unions, social movements, and media outlets, among others. I already discussed the role played by some of these actors; namely, digital activist groups and research organisations. One set of actors that tend to be overlooked in this category is banks. As I noted in Chapter 3, in Australia in 2021, Westpac was reported to have taken action against hundreds of customers who tried to send abuse or threatening messages to victims alongside payments. Another, more recently reported case is the National Australia Bank's (NAB) efforts to block family violence perpetrators sending 'intimidating abuse in the payment descriptions on bank transfers' (Tuohy, 2022). This bank and some other banks have sought to 'block words or phrases designed to scare or control victims', and caught 'more than 6500 from 3075 customers between November 2021 and February 2022' (Tuohy, 2022). The NAB's detection system, it was reported, 'instantly recognises 1300 words and phrases—plus special characters substituted into banned words and phrases—and blocks the transaction' (Tuohy, 2022). As the different responses to emergent issues thus far make clear, regulating online harms is highly complex and calls for a multifaceted approach. Responses will be shaped by a range of factors and constantly shifting views on matters such as which platforms should be regulated and under what circumstances (the platforms themselves will change and evolve), the groups needing protection from online harms, the ability to regulate Big Tech, appropriate industry standards, and so on. While there is broad agreement between governments on some issues, notably the vulnerability of children and young people, the responses to experienced harms may differ considerably between communities, cultures, and societies (Chapter 3).

A trend that that is likely to impact Big Tech's operations in coming years is 'digital sovereignty', that is, accelerating efforts by many countries, including the United States, France, Austria, and South Africa, 'to control the digital information produced by their citizens, government agencies, and corporations' (McCabe and Satariano, 2022). The European Union, for example, has sought to guard information generation with the 27-nation bloc, and has toughened online privacy requirements and rules for AI via the General Data Protection Regulation (GDPR) which came into operation in 2018 (GDPR, 2022). In 2022, this is being strengthened by the Digital Services Act and Digital Markets Act, which restrict the uncontrolled spread of unverified, potentially harmful content (Bertuzzi, 2021; European Commission, 2022), and by the ruling of the

European Court of Justice in 2021 that the GDPR does not preclude consumer associations from bringing actions on behalf of individuals (Court of Justice of the European Union, 2021). According to a *New York Times* article, the 'digital sovereignty' trend is driven by a combination of factors, including security and privacy concerns, and economic interests and authoritarian and nationalistic impulses (McCabe and Satariano, 2022). In support of this contention, the article cites information collected by the Information Technology and Innovation Foundation (ITIF) showing that the number of policies, regulations, and laws requiring digital information to be stored in a specific country 'more than doubled to 144 from 2017 to 2021'. The ITIF, which produced this research, is a think tank founded in 2006 whose mission is 'to formulate, evaluate, and promote policy solutions that accelerate innovation and boost productivity to spur growth, opportunity and progress' (ITIF, 2022). It sees its role as 'Setting the policy agenda on technology, innovation, and global competition'. In the summary of its online report from which the above article draws, the ITIF authors bemoan 'data localization' which they see as reducing trade, slowing productivity, and increasing prices for affected industries and calls on 'Like-minded nations [to] work together to stem the tide and build and open, rules-based, and innovative digital economy' (Cory and Dascoli, 2021). This concern, unsurprisingly, is also shared by Big Tech that is invested in a global, self-regulated internet. In responding to the new data localisation rules, Amazon, Google, Apple, Microsoft, and Meta raised objections, arguing that 'the online economy was fueled by the free flow of data' and that 'If tech companies were required to store it all locally, they could not offer the same products and services around the world' (McCabe and Satarino, 2022). The article noted that Big Tech companies have signed various deals with 'local tech and telecom providers' to ensure their customers' data is managed locally. Yet, while the era of unregulated data flows seems to be coming to an end, it is far from over and contestation over the control of personal data will no doubt continue since, as mentioned, Big Tech has much at stake in the current online economy. The question of how 'data sovereignty' will affect online emotional regimes in the future, and whether it will help build trust in the companies that profit from its operations and renew hopes for the internet remains to be seen.

References

Agre, P. E. (1994) 'Understanding the digital individual', *The Information Society*, 10, 2: 73–76.

Bachrach, P. and Baratz, M. S. (1963) 'Decisions and non-decisions: an analytic framework', *The American Political Science Review*, 57, 3: 632–642.

Bertuzzi, L. (2021) 'EU Parliament's key committee adopts digital markets act', 24 November, https://www.euractiv.com/section/digital/news/eu-parliaments-key-committee-adopts-digital-markets-act/ (Accessed 4 June 2022).

Boaz, D. (2022) 'Libertarianism', *Britannica*, https://www.britannica.com/topic/libertarianism-politics (Accessed 23 May 2022).

Burgis, L. (2021) *Wanting: The Power of Mimetic Desire in Everyday Life*. St Martin's Press, New York, NY.

Cheng, A. (2021) 'Rohingya refugees sue facebook for $150 billion, alleging it helped perpetuate genocide in Myanmar', *The Washington Post*, 7 December, https://www .washingtonpost.com/world/2021/12/07/facebook-rohingya-genocide-refugees -lawsuit/?utm_campaign=wp_post_most&utm_medium=email&utm_source =newsletter&wpisrc=nl_most&carta-url=https%3A%2F%2Fs2.washingtonpost .com%2Fcar-ln-tr%2F357711d%2F61afa65e9d2fdab56bb91299%2F5e86729bade4e 21f59b210ef%2F61%2F72%2F61afa65e9d2fdab56bb91299 (Accessed 4 June 2022).

Cory, N. and Dascoli, L. (2021) 'How barriers to cross-border data flows are spreading globally, what they cost, and how to address them', *ITIF webpage*, 19 July, https://itif .org/publications/2021/07/19/how-barriers-cross-border-data-flows-are-spreading -globally-what-they-cost (Accessed 4 June 2022).

Court of Justice of the European Union (2021) 'Press release', 2 December, https://curia .europa.eu/jcms/upload/docs/application/pdf/2021-12/cp210216en.pdf (Accessed 4 June 2022).

Davidson, J. (2022a) 'Call to end "creepy" google emails', *Financial Review*, 2 May, https://www.afr.com/technology/call-to-end-to-creepy-google-emails-to-protect -kids-20220502-p5ahr1 (Accessed 5 May 2022).

Davidson, J. (2022b) 'Consumer watchdog to target "dark patterns" on the internet', *The Australian Financial Review*, 7 March, https://www.afr.com/technology/consumer -watchdog-to-target-dark-patterns-on-the-internet-20220304-p5a1u0 (Accessed 4 June 2022).

Digital Futures Commission (2020) 'Research Agenda', *Working Paper*, November, https://digitalfuturescommission.org.uk/wp-content/uploads/2021/01/DFC -Research-Agenda.pdf (Accessed 30 May 2022).

Digital Futures Commission (2021a) 'The best interests of children in the digital world', 22 February, https://digitalfuturescommission.org.uk/blog/the-best-interests-of -children-in-the-digital-world/ (Accessed 30 May 2022).

Digital Futures Commission (2021b) 'About the digital futures commission', https://dig italfuturescommission.org.uk/about/ (Accessed 30 May 2022).

Dye, J. and McGuire, A. (2021) 'Facebook news ban hits emergency services and government health departments', *The Sydney Morning Herald*, 18 February, https:// www.smh.com.au/national/facebook-news-ban-hits-emergency-services-and -government-health-departments-20210218-p573ks.html (Accessed 28 May 2022).

Edelman, G. (2022) 'Paradise at the crypto arcade: inside the Web3', *Wired*, 18 May, https://www.wired.com/story/web3-paradise-crypto-arcade/ (Accessed 27 May 2022).

European Commission (2022) 'The digital services act package', https://digital-strategy .ec.europa.eu/en/policies/digital-services-act-package (Accessed 4 June 2022).

Forbrukerrådet (2018) 'Every step you take: how deceptive design lets google track users 24/7', 27 November. https://fil.forbrukerradet.no/wp-content/uploads/2018/11/27 -11-18-every-step-you-take.pdf (Accessed 11 April 2022).

General Data Protection Regulation (2022) 'Home page', https://gdpr-info.eu/ (Accessed 4 June 2022).

Global 500 (2022) 'The annual report on the world's most valuable and strongest brands', https://brandirectory.com/rankings/global/ (Accessed 28 January 2022).

Hagey, K., Cherney, M. and Horwitz, J. (2022) 'Facebook deliberately caused havoc in Australia to influence new law, whistleblowers say', *The Wall Street Journal*, 5 May, https://

www.wsj.com/articles/facebook-deliberately-caused-havoc-in-australia-to-influence
-new-law-whistleblowers-say-11651768302?AID=11557093&PID=6415797&SID
=bi%7C6274d85b3c3f8b60515640e8%7C1653615824651ybu93zjn&subid=Business
+Insider&cjevent=fe8f5994dd5e11ec821d01980a1c0e13&tier_1=affiliate&tier_2
=moa&tier_3=Business+Insider&tier_4=3861930&tier_5=https%3A%2F%2Fwww
.wsj.com%2Farticles%2Ffacebook-deliberately-caused-havoc-in-australia-to-influence
-new-law-whistleblowers-say-11651768302 (Accessed 27 May 2022).

Hardwick, M. J. (2004) *Mall Maker: Victor Gruen, Architect of an American Dream*. University
of Pennsylvania Press, Philadelphia, PA.

Harwell, D. and Tiku, N. (2020) 'Google's star AI ethics researcher, one of a few
Black women in the field, says she was fired for a critical email', *The Washington
Post*, 3 December, https://www.washingtonpost.com/technology/2020/12/03/
timnit-gebru-google-fired/?utm_campaign=wp_post_most&utm_medium=email
&utm_source=newsletter&wpisrc=nl_most&carta-url=https%3A%2F%2Fs2
.washingtonpost.com%2Fcar-ln-tr%2F2d4afcd%2F5fca6a439d2fda0efb7e2b69%2F5
e86729bade4e21f59b210ef%2F46%2F72%2F5fca6a439d2fda0efb7e2b69 (Accessed 5
June 2022).

Henriques-Gomez, L. (2019) 'Centrelink cancels 40,000 robodebts, new figures reveal',
The Guardian, 6 February, https://www.theguardian.com/australia-news/2019/
feb/06/robodebt-faces-landmark-legal-challenge-over-crude-income-calculations
(Accessed 23 May 2022).

Henriques-Gomez, L. (2021) 'Robodebt: court approves $1.8bn settlement for victims
of government's 'shameful failure'', *The Guardian Australia*, 11 June, https://www
.theguardian.com/australia-news/2021/jun/11/robodebt-court-approves-18bn
-settlement-for-victims-of-governments-shameful-failure (Accessed 5 June 2022).

Hochschild, A. R. (1983) *The Managed Heart: The Commercialization of Human Feeling*.
University of California Press, Berkeley, CA.

Human Rights Watch (2021) 'Israel/Palestine: facebook censors discussion of rights issues',
8 October, https://www.hrw.org/news/2021/10/08/israel/palestine-facebook-censors
-discussion-rights-issues (Accessed 28 May 2022).

Impakter (2020) 'Why government involvement in content moderation could be
problematic', 26 February, https://impakter.com/why-government-involvement-in
-content-moderation-could-be-problematic/ (Accessed 4 June 2022).

Information Technology and Innovation Foundation (2022) 'About ITIF: a champion of
innovation', https://itif.org/about (Accessed 4 June 2022).

Iqbal, M. (2022) 'Zoom revenue and usage statistics (2022)', *Business of Apps*, 3 March,
https://www.businessofapps.com/data/zoom-statistics/ (Accessed 4 April 2022).

Jacobi, U. (2020) 'AI: increasing the intelligence on smartphones', *AIThority*, April 21,
https://aithority.com/guest-authors/ai-increasing-the-intelligence-on-smartphones/
(Accessed 27 June 2022).

Johnson, M. (2021) 'Why mimetic desire is key to understanding social media', *Psychology
Today*, 3 August, https://www.psychologytoday.com/au/blog/mind-brain-and-value
/202108/why-mimetic-desire-is-key-understanding-social-media (Accessed 1 June
2022).

Jones, K. (2021) 'Trustworthiness', *Ethics*, 123, 1: 61–85.

Kennedy, J. B. (1926) 'Collier's interview with Nikola Tesla', *The Library*, 26 January,
https://www.organism.earth/library/document/colliers-interview-nikola-tesla
(Accessed 17 March 2022).

Kilger, M. (1994) 'The digital individual', *The Information Society*, 10: 93–99.

Lifefaker.com (2022) 'Home page', http://lifefaker.com/ (Accessed 2 June 2022).

LTB Network (2019) 'Dominic Tarr: secure Scuttlebutt—the "localized" but distributed social network', 4 June, https://letstalkbitcoin.com/blog/post/epicenter-dominic-tarr-secure-scuttlebutt-the-localized-but-distributed-social-network (Accessed 28 May 2022).

McCabe, D. and Satariano, A. (2022) 'The era of borderless data is ending', *The New York Times*, 23 May, https://www.nytimes.com/2022/05/23/technology/data-privacy-laws.html (Accessed 4 June 2022).

Merriam-Webster (2022) 'Trust', https://www.merriam-webster.com/dictionary/trust#:~:text=1a%20%3A%20assured%20reliance%20on,credit%20bought%20furniture%20on%20trust (Accessed 4 June 2022).

Moran, J. (2020) *If You Should Fail: A Book of Solace*. Viking, New York.

Newton, C. (2020) 'Facebook will pay $52 million in settlement with moderators who developed PTSD on the job', *The Verge*, 12 May, https://www.theverge.com/2020/5/12/21255870/facebook-content-moderator-settlement-scola-ptsd-mental-health (Accessed 5 June 2022).

Petersen, A. (2011) *The Politics of Bioethics*. Routledge, New York and London.

Pew Research Centre (2021) 'Experts doubt ethical AI design will be broadly adopted as the norm within the next decade', 16 June, https://www.pewresearch.org/internet/2021/06/16/experts-doubt-ethical-ai-design-will-be-broadly-adopted-as-the-norm-within-the-next-decade/ (Accessed 2 June 2022).

Reddy, W. M. (2001) *The Navigation of Human Feeling: A Framework for the History of Emotions*. Cambridge University Press, Cambridge, MA.

Sanctus (2022a) 'Home page', https://sanctus.io/social-media-mental-health/ (Accessed 30 August 2022).

Sanctus (2022b) 'About us', https://sanctus.io/about-us/ (Accessed 30 August 2022).

Sanctus (2022c) 'Our partners', https://sanctus.io/our-partners/ (Accessed 30 August 2022).

Sun, M. and Smagalla, D. (2022) 'Cryptocurrency-based crime hit a record $14 billion in 2021', *The Wall Street Journal*, 6 January, https://www.wsj.com/articles/cryptocurrency-based-crime-hit-a-record-14-billion-in-2021-11641500073 (Accessed 31 May 2022).

Thaler, R. H. and Sunstein, C. R. (2008) *Nudge: Improving Decisions About Health, Wealth and Happiness*. Penguin Books, London.

The New York Times (2022) 'Elon Musk and Twitter reach deal for sale', 25 April, https://www.nytimes.com/live/2022/04/25/business/elon-musk-twitter (Accessed 4 May 2022).

Tuohy, W. (2022) '"The last place you expect it": Tiny money transfers used to send family violence abuse', *The Age*, 7 April, https://amp.theage.com.au/national/the-last-place-you-expect-it-tiny-money-transfers-used-to-send-family-violence-abuse-20220407-p5abka.html (Accessed 4 June 2022).

West, D. M. (2021) 'Techlast continues to batter technology sector', *Brookings*, 2 April, https://www.brookings.edu/blog/techtank/2021/04/02/techlash-continues-to-batter-technology-sector/ (Accessed 4 June 2022).

White, M. (2022) 'Web3 is going just great', web3isgoinggreat.com (Accessed 4 June 2022).

Wu, T. (2016) *The Attention Merchants: The Epic Struggle to Get Inside Our Heads*. Atlantic Books, London.

Zakrzewski, C. (2022) 'Google deceived consumers about how it profits from their location data, attorneys general allege in lawsuits', *The Washington Post*, 24 January, https://www.washingtonpost.com/technology/2022/01/24/google-location-data-ags-lawsuit/?utm_campaign=wp_post_most&utm_medium=email&utm_source

=newsletter&wpisrc=nl_most&carta-url=https%3A%2F%2Fs2.washingtonpost
.com%2Fcar-ln-tr%2F35d7f45%2F61eedd9b9d2fda14d706094a%2F5e86729bade4e
21f59b210ef%2F10%2F74%2F61eedd9b9d2fda14d706094a (Accessed 11 April 2022).

Zeitchik, S. (2022) 'Former google scientist says the computers that run our lives exploit us—and he has a way to stop them', *The Washington Post*, 17 January, https://www
.washingtonpost.com/technology/2022/01/17/artificial-intelligence-ai-empathy
-emotions/?utm_campaign=wp_post_most&utm_medium=email&utm_source
=newsletter&wpisrc=nl_most&carta-url=https%3A%2F%2Fs2.washingtonpost
.com%2Fcar-ln-tr%2F35c8709%2F61e59c9c9d2fda14d7f75943%2F5e86729bade4e
21f59b210ef%2F50%2F72%2F61e59c9c9d2fda14d7f75943 (Accessed 3 June 2022).

Zuckerman, E. (2022) 'Can Russia really disconnect from the rest of the digital world?', *Prospect*, 12 May, https://www.prospectmagazine.co.uk/world/can-russia-really
-disconnect-from-the-rest-of-the-digital-world (Accessed 27 May 2022).

INDEX

Printed in the United States
by Baker & Taylor Publisher Services